BUILDING A REVOLUTIONARY STATE

AMERICAN BEGINNINGS, 1500–1900

A Series Edited by Edward Gray, Stephen Mihm, and Mark Peterson

ALSO IN THE SERIES

Sovereign of the Market: The Money Question in Early America
by Jeffrey Sklansky

National Duties: Custom Houses and the Making of the American State
by Gautham Rao

Liberty Power: Antislavery Third Parties and the Transformation of American Politics
by Corey M. Brooks

The Making of Tocqueville's America: Law and Association in the Early United States
by Kevin Butterfield

Planters, Merchants, and Slaves: Plantation Societies in British America, 1650–1820
by Trevor Burnard

Riotous Flesh: Women, Physiology, and the Solitary Vice in Nineteenth-Century America
by April R. Haynes

Holy Nation: The Transatlantic Quaker Ministry in an Age of Revolution
by Sarah Crabtree

A Hercules in the Cradle: War, Money, and the American State, 1783–1867
by Max M. Edling

Frontier Seaport: Detroit's Transformation into an Atlantic Entrepôt
by Catherine Cangany

Beyond Redemption: Race, Violence, and the American South after the Civil War
by Carole Emberton

The Republic Afloat: Law, Honor, and Citizenship in Maritime America
by Matthew Taylor Raffety

Conceived in Doubt: Religion and Politics in the New American Nation
by Amanda Porterfield

BUILDING A REVOLUTIONARY STATE

The Legal Transformation of New York, 1776–1783

HOWARD PASHMAN

THE UNIVERSITY OF CHICAGO PRESS

CHICAGO AND LONDON

PUBLICATION OF THIS BOOK HAS BEEN AIDED BY A GRANT FROM THE BEVINGTON FUND.

The University of Chicago Press, Chicago 60637
The University of Chicago Press, Ltd., London

Published 2018
Printed in the United States of America

27 26 25 24 23 22 21 20 19 18 1 2 3 4 5

ISBN-13: 978-0-226-33435-6 (cloth)
ISBN-13: 978-0-226-54401-4 (paper)
ISBN-13: 978-0-226-54057-3 (e-book)
DOI: doi.org/10.7208/chicago/9780226540573.001.0001

An earlier version of chapter 3 was published as Howard Pashman, "The People's Property Law: A Step toward Building a New Legal Order in Revolutionary New York," *Law and History Review* 31, no. 3 (August 2013): 587–626. © American Society for Legal History, Inc. 2013. Reprinted with permission.

Library of Congress Cataloging-in-Publication Data

Names: Pashman, Howard, author.
Title: Building a revolutionary state : the legal transformation of New York, 1776–1783 / Howard Pashman.
Other titles: American beginnings, 1500–1900.
Description: Chicago ; London : The University of Chicago Press, 2018. | Series: American beginnings, 1500–1900
Identifiers: LCCN 2017044570 | ISBN 9780226334356 (cloth : alk. paper) | ISBN 9780226544014 (pbk. : alk. paper) | ISBN 9780226540573 (e-book)
Subjects: LCSH: New York (State)—History—1775–1865. | Law—New York (State)—History.
Classification: LCC F123 .P43 2018 | DDC 974.7/03—dc23
LC record available at https://lccn.loc.gov/2017044570

♾ This paper meets the requirements of ANSI/NISO Z39.48-1992 (Permanence of Paper).

For Manya

CONTENTS

ACKNOWLEDGMENTS

I was able to finish this book only with a great deal of timely and generous support. I completed much of the research with grants from Northwestern University and the William Nelson Cromwell Foundation. I also received research support from the Fort Dearborn Chapter of the Daughters of the American Revolution and the Illinois Chapter of the Society of Colonial Wars. In addition, a Mellon/American Council of Learned Societies Fellowship gave me the time and resources to complete the research and advance the manuscript. Many people also read the manuscript in its various iterations and offered helpful suggestions for improving it. Dan Hulsebosch, Dylan Penningroth, Sally Gordon, and John Brooke all helped strengthen the book by encouraging me to see the project in new ways. I would also like to thank the attendees at the Hurst Summer Institute in Legal History at the University of Wisconsin–Madison for their comments on an early version of the manuscript.

I am grateful for the time I spent as a Jerome Hall Postdoctoral Fellow in Law and Society at Maurer School of Law at Indiana University, Bloomington. The fellowship offered a wonderful intellectual environment for developing the book and, just as importantly, for enjoying the company of good colleagues. Jay Krishnan, Ethan Michelson, Ajay Mehrotra (now at the American Bar Foundation), Mike Grossberg, Jeff Stake, Ken Dau-Schmidt, Leandra Lederman, Hannah Buxbaum, Brian Broughman, Luis Fuentes-Rohwer, Mike Mattioli, Steve Sanders, and my fellow-fellow Cindy Daase all helped make my time in Bloomington so pleasant.

I would particularly like to thank Jay Krishnan, the director of the Milt and Judi Stewart Center on the Global Legal Profession at the Maurer School of Law. I completed this book as a fellow at the center, which provided critical support for the last stages of research and revision. It is no exaggeration to say that the book might have stalled without Jay and the center's continued assistance. I appreciate both that assistance and Jay's encouragement.

Long before this project existed and through to its completion, Tim and Susan Breen have been strong supporters and close friends. They have helped in every possible way, most often over excellent meals. Their friendship proves that at least two people understand what the poet meant when he wrote: "God have mercy on the sinner / Who must write with no dinner." They never allowed that to happen, and they provided much support besides, for which I thank them.

My family—particularly my parents—offered extraordinary support that kept me going at times when it seemed like this project would get the better of me. From the very beginning they encouraged me to pursue this work, and that encouragement was wonderful in spurring me to complete the book. They offered unstinting support that I hope to return with similar generosity and love.

While my family has been in my corner urging me along for much of this process, it was Manya who arrived just in time. She has been there with me through the arduous end stages, a time when, week after week and month after month, I sat down to write about the eighteenth century. She was there for me even though she had her own deadlines to meet. And, now that my story is filed, we can turn our attention from the past to the future and think about all the possibilities that lie ahead. It is with boundless love and gratitude that I dedicate this book to her, which is my small contribution to a life composed together.

Howard Pashman
Chicago, Illinois
December 2017

ABBREVIATIONS

ACHR	Albany County Hall of Records, Albany, NY
AML	Local History Section, Adriance Memorial Library, Poughkeepsie, NY
DCCO	Dutchess County Clerk's Office, Poughkeepsie, NY
NYCC	New York County Clerk, Hall of Records; also called the New York County Clerk, Archives Division, or the Surrogate's Court Building, New York
NYHS	Manuscripts Department, New-York Historical Society, New York
NYSA	New York State Archives, Albany, NY
WCARC	Westchester County Archives and Records Center, Elmsford, NY

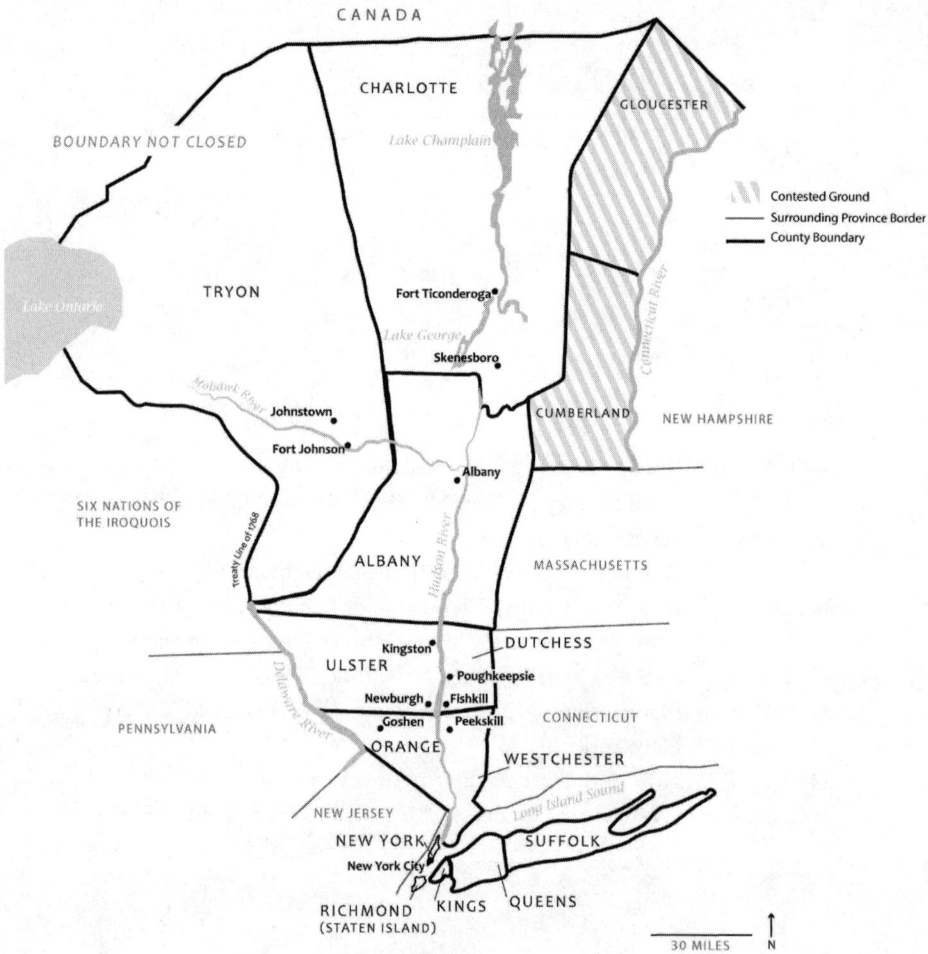

Map of New York, ca. 1775. Courtesy of University of Wisconsin–Madison Cartography Lab.

INTRODUCTION

By the time insurgents arrived at the manor house, the landlord who used to live there had already fled. He had taken much of his personal property with him, thus succeeding in keeping it out of the insurgents' hands. In that regard, he was more fortunate than others had been, many of whom had their houses ransacked by supporters of the Revolution. Nevertheless, insurgents seized and sold what they were able to find: leather chairs in a variety of colors, oak tables and desks, a box of hinges, chests of drawers, enough curtains to cover many windows, bed frames, and other household goods.[1] A few years later, insurgents returned to divide up the landlord's vast estates into hundreds of parcels and auction that property off as well.[2] The sale of real estate and movable goods stripped the landlord of his substantial property and redistributed it among many new owners.

Although this expropriation represented a significant loss for the landlord, he could hardly have been surprised that it occurred. Long before his dispossession, he had been widely despised in the neighborhood as an overbearing owner who sought to change the terms of leases and was quick to eject tenants who resisted. Such practices had become so intolerable that, a decade before his dispossession, tenants had risen up against him and other landlords in the area. Troops had to suppress the uprising. When the Revolution erupted, its ideological police force—called the Committee for Detecting and Defeating Conspiracies—interrogated the landlord because, as a Committee member put it, he had "observed an Equivocal Neutrality" that showed he was not fully enough devoted to the cause. The Committee forced an ultimatum on him and told him he must either support the Revolution or leave.[3] He chose to flee, and the insurgents arrived at his house a few months later to begin redistributing his property.

This ideological enforcement and property seizure might make one think of an émigré fleeing the French Revolution. Or perhaps the Committee for Detecting and Defeating Conspiracies calls to mind the Russian Revolution and its Commission for Combating Counterrevolution and Sabotage, the group more often called the Checka that enforced obedience to the Bolshevik faction.[4] But the story of this particular landlord did not happen in France or Russia. It took place in New York during the American Revolution. The landlord was Beverly Robinson, the son of a prominent Virginia family who moved to New York and married Susannah Philipse, the daughter of Frederick Philipse II, one of the wealthiest landlords in the province. After Frederick died in 1751, Robinson and the other Philipse heirs sought to consolidate their holdings in southern Dutchess County, today Putnam County, by trying to impose new leases on inhabitants and suing to eject them if they did not accept. This heavy-handed approach provoked a tenant uprising in 1766 that British regulars had to put down.[5]

As the dispute between Britain and the colonies escalated, Robinson tried to remain neutral. But, soon after the Committee imposed its ultimatum in February 1777, he fled to the protection of the British army, and, by November, insurgents called Commissioners of Sequestration had begun redistributing his property.[6] Such instances of confiscation and sale were common. Every state enforced some type of redistribution during the American Revolution. In New York, insurgents dispossessed thousands of people, and wealthy landlords were not their only targets. They also seized property from ordinary farmers, shopkeepers, and merchants, anyone who remained loyal to Britain.

Scholars and most Americans are not accustomed to seeing Robinson's dispossession, and countless others like it, as central to the creation of independent legal systems. A revolutionary state confiscating property from supporters of the old regime appears foreign to most Americans, something that may have been widespread in the French or the Cuban Revolutions, but not in the United States. After all, this country supposedly had a legalistic revolution, one undertaken to vindicate ancient rights and advanced through a widely shared political ideology of republicanism. Any uncertainty about the nature of new states was resolved in constitutional conventions and explained in pamphlets. By envisioning the period this way, scholars and other Americans have taken founding fathers like Thomas Jefferson at their word. In August 1777, Jefferson wrote to Benjamin Franklin and marveled at how easily Americans created new governments. He observed that they "seem to have deposited the monarchical and taken up the republican government with as much ease as would have attended their throwing off an old and putting on a new suit of clothes."[7] However, at the same moment that Jefferson wrote his letter, insurgents in New York and elsewhere were stripping Loyalists of their property and selling it to their allies. Moreover, this redistribution persisted for years after Jefferson declared the transition to new governments complete. Such ongoing revolutionary activity suggests that an independent legal order did not emerge as easily as Jefferson believed. Yet, by imagining a smooth transition, Jefferson and other Americans have exempted themselves from the confusion that has plagued other revolutions and made it so difficult for them to develop a new legal order. Because of this abiding belief that Americans never suffered intractable instability, few scholars have considered how America's revolutionary turmoil became the stable legal systems that so many take for granted today.

But the image of people clamoring around a manor house in New York, stripping a local grandee of his furniture and even his curtains, invites us to ask new questions about the nature of the American Revolution. Instead of assuming that Americans created new governments more easily than did other popular uprisings or that the period's legal changes are best understood in republican and constitutional terms, this book begins from a different perspective. It examines one state in detail—New York—to address the fundamental question of how Americans managed to transform popular upheaval into legal order. The key element in that change proved to be property redistribution. By seizing property from British sympathizers and selling it to supporters of independence, New Yorkers developed legal institutions such as courts in a way that ordinary people accepted. Moreover, New York was not alone. All states redistributed property at the same moment that they struggled to establish the authority of independent government. Examining this process in New York allows us to recapture the contingency of legal change in the revolutionary era. It also allows us to begin addressing the crucial question of how Americans transformed an insurgency into a new, stable legal order.

That change appears even more remarkable when we remember that, early in the conflict, colonial legal structures grew weak or collapsed. Committees, mobs, and other ad hoc groups emerged and took law into their own hands to enforce their own ideas of justice. But, by the end of the war, central legal systems had emerged that enjoyed popular support. Redistribution drove the change from popular uprising to stable legal systems. Confiscation had that transformative effect because it offered both material relief and revenge against Britain's supporters at a time when society demanded those actions. During the war, New Yorkers suffered internal displacement, shortages of basic goods, and high inflation. For people struggling in these conditions, property redistribution provided the subsistence they desperately needed. Moreover, it created a constituency with a stake in the revolutionary regime, people whose material security—sometimes even their survival or their political rights as freemen—depended on the regime's stability. At the same time, war stoked a desire to defeat Britain and its Loyalist allies. British occupation and Loyalist raids fed a widespread desire among New Yorkers to strike back at the army and its supporters. Property redistribution resonated with that desire and offered New Yorkers an institutional means to punish those who seemed to have caused so much suffering. Redistribution thus helped consolidate New York's legal system. It drew forward supporters and linked them to the new state while also dispossessing enemies and cutting them off from society.

To be sure, New Yorkers did not confiscate property with the explicit purpose of developing durable legal structures. No statute or legal opinion announced that confiscation would strengthen the regime's authority. Instead, New Yorkers' conscious intention was winning the war, and they believed that seizing property would help them do so. But expropriation had radical effects that the insurgents could not foresee. By analyzing redistribution, scholars studying America, as well as other societies, can see those effects and understand how insurgents built support for revolutionary legal institutions. One might assume that large-scale expropriation would have the exact opposite effect. After all, one might think that unsettling property rights and ignoring due process as New Yorkers did would only heighten revolutionary turmoil and undermine popular support. But that was not the case. In an extraordinary paradox of the revolutionary era, the forcible dispossession of British sympathizers stabilized New York's legal system and generated popular support for its authority.

Examining this central paradox of the revolutionary era is particularly timely now. Movements around the world have weakened or dismantled incumbent regimes. It is not clear how stable states will emerge from these uprisings as they struggle to direct popular energy toward creating a new legal order. In addition, the United States sends experts throughout the world to advise countries on how to develop or alter their legal systems. At such a moment, when radicals are trying to build new legal structures and Americans advise other countries on a similar task, it would do well to look back and examine America's own moment of revolutionary upheaval. It would also do well to recall that Americans rebuilt their legal systems, not in spite of harsh, partisan practices, but because of them.

To understand how New Yorkers built a revolutionary state, one must first consider the unstable environment that prevailed in New York during the war. By the middle of 1776, New York's colonial Assembly had stopped meeting, its courts had ceased convening, and its governor had fled to a British ship in New York Harbor. The British then invaded New York City in the summer of 1776 and occupied it as a base of operation for the remainder of the war, devastating the province, and throwing it into greater confusion. Though the new constitution was promulgated in April 1777, it remained a dead letter because the structures it created struggled to enforce its provisions. For instance, the Supreme Court of Judicature, New York's statewide court of general civil and criminal jurisdiction, convened under the new constitution for the first time in September 1777. However, along with the Assembly and the Senate, the Supreme Court soon fled a British raiding party and did not meet again until the following year. Other legal institutions such as county-level courts faced similar problems during the war, often struggling to conduct any legal business at all. The Revolution destroyed imperial authority before stable, independent institutions could replace the old order. New Yorkers then found themselves in a volatile society without traditional legal structures.

As royal government dissolved, a world of revolutionary law took its place. Local committees emerged at the town and county levels. These bodies called themselves the Committee of Albany, or Goshen, or New Windsor, depending on the jurisdiction they arrogated to themselves. They became the only functioning governments in much of the state as they gathered war materiel, regulated local economies, and punished Loyalists. The only institution that recalled regular government was the Provincial Convention, a rump of the colonial Assembly that had grown out of the dispute over whether to send delegates to the Second Continental Congress in 1775. The Convention sent out commissioners, including those who redistributed Loyalists' personal property, but it passed resolutions, not statutes, suggesting that its delegates recognized their limited authority. They could hardly do otherwise since the Convention lacked courts, constables, and other traditional institutions to implement its commands. As a result, it could enforce its resolutions only when, acting on their own or through local committees, New Yorkers came forward to help it do so. But nothing required this cooperation, and New Yorkers often ignored the Convention's resolutions. Nor did local committees form a coherent legal system with established procedures or a plan of how to share authority. Consequently, ad hoc committees and a feeble Convention emerged in a chaotic jurisdictional environment where the lines of proper authority were unclear.[8]

The chapters that follow address the critical question of how property redistribution helped New Yorkers overcome this upheaval and develop the authority of a revolutionary state. Focusing on redistribution, however, does not suggest that it was the only source of legal order in the revolutionary era. But analyzing expropriation and its wide-ranging effects highlights a major thread running through the period: the transformation from revolutionary instability to a society with functioning legal institutions that enjoyed popular support. The change from disorder to order is one that historians have not examined in detail and one that many people take for granted today without asking how Americans succeeded in creating legal systems when other uprisings have failed to do so. By putting redistribution at the center of the story, we can begin to understand this change and explore the complex relationship between property ownership and legal order.

Scholars generally have not thought about the revolutionary era's legal and political changes in such terms. Rather than asking how Americans transformed an insurgency into a working legal system with popular support, they have addressed other questions about the transition to independence. One group of historians has examined pamphlets, the first postindependence constitutions, and the conventions that wrote them to explain how Americans reimagined concepts of republican governance. In this view, Americans' unanimity on republican principles—their strong belief in republican ideology—animated the Revolution and made the transition from colonies to independent states easy.[9]

A second group of scholars has examined constitutional and doctrinal reform in the revolutionary era. They have analyzed constitutions, court opinions, treatises, and published lectures to see whether the war altered legal rules and constitutional arrangements. They often compare black-letter law before and after the war to see whether anything changed. That is, they ask how court systems changed after independence or how doctrines like judicial review emerged from colonial precedent. From this perspective, the war years themselves are a nonevent because they did not produce immediate reform such as abolishing the common law. Rather, legal reform did not come until the decades after independence as lawyers and jurists reimagined old ideas. Consequently, these scholars explore the decades around independence to find doctrinal and constitutional change and, not seeing any during the war, quickly move on to the early republic.[10] A third group of historians analyzes how Americans achieved a political settlement and built a civil society in the decades after independence. By working out concepts such as sovereignty and citizenship, Americans developed a political consensus that allowed them to put revolutionary turmoil behind them.[11]

While these works have advanced our understanding of legal and political change in the revolutionary era, the insights they offer have come at a cost. These three approaches—whether focused on republicanism, doctrine and constitutionalism, or political settlement—have examined change in highly abstract terms, asking how Americans reimagined notions of law and government in the decades around independence. In doing so, they have examined colonial law before the war and the growth of states and the federal government after it. But the war years themselves have gone missing as these intellectual histories have lost sight of the social realities of law and its actual application in daily life during a popular uprising. As a result, historians know a great deal about the nature of constitutional reform in the late eighteenth century and the evolution of doctrines such as seditious libel and trespass on case. But scholars know much less about how Americans encountered legal authority on the ground during a period of violent upheaval.

Building a Revolutionary State breaks with previous accounts and recasts the debate in new terms. It does so by contextualizing legal institutions and procedures in the disorder of a popular uprising. Rather than examine how doctrines or republican ideas changed over decades, this book asks how New Yorkers experienced legal authority in their daily lives during a long and painful war. Taking this approach recaptures the contingency of the American Revolution as a time when the old order collapsed and nobody knew how stable authority would emerge. Moreover, shifting our attention to law on the ground allows us to see a chaotic world of popular legal activity and to understand how a revolutionary state emerged from that turmoil. It was in these legal institutions that Americans went on to wage political battles after the war. Courts and legislatures became the arenas for disputes over debt, taxes, policies toward Native Americans, pensions for veterans, and other issues in the decades after independence. Those disputes unfolded as they did in part because during the war Americans had managed to rebuild institutions that structured later debates. Thus, by turning scholarly attention toward law on the ground during the war, this book offers fresh insights into a critical period of American state building.

To be sure, legal historians have recognized for some time that law does not reside exclusively in formal documents and high constitutional debate. Treatises, court cases, and constitutions represent only one way of understanding how a society chose to govern itself. Social norms and lived experience also constituted law and were sometimes a more significant source of a society's conception of law. Those who have looked to such norms and experiences as sources of law have called the method legal history from below. As some of the scholars who made this point most persuasively have put it, historians must interpret "legal meaning as multiple and contestable."[12] A local custom may explicitly reject a court opinion. Or people may go their own way and ignore what statutes and other formal actions of the state prescribe.

But, however historians have approached the multiple meanings of law, some of those meanings have come from a central state. That is, historians who have examined lived experiences or social context to understand law have compared those sources to state institutions. The influence of those institutions and their formal enactments could be widespread in a particular context, making up a significant part of the legal landscape. Or at a different time they could have little influence over how most people went about their daily lives. But these different possibilities, contested and multiple though they were, still compare law on the ground to law in the courtroom and administrative agency. A history from below therefore assumes that there was something above, some set of formal rules issuing from the legal infrastructure of an existing state.

As a methodological problem, however, it is not at all clear where a historian should look for law at a time when formal institutions failed and people fought over the basis of legitimate authority. The American Revolution was just such a time, and it raises difficult interpretive challenges for legal historians. By mid-1776, everyone from the king to the most vocal supporter of independence recognized that royal authority had dissolved. Royal institutions and administrators no longer governed the colonies, and nobody knew exactly what legal system would come next or how to build it. Americans found themselves in a sovereignless society, one in which the basis of legitimate authority was unclear.[13] As a result, legal historians of the period, just like the people they study, find themselves confronting a world without an established state. In such an environment, the fabric of legal order starts to come undone. There was no generally accepted legal system, no web of rules and formal documents against which one can compare other legal meanings such as local custom. The point is not that Americans experienced anarchy or that the revolutionary years were a lawless time. Instead, the interpretive challenge is cobbling together a picture of legal culture and popular understandings of law during the upheaval of an insurgency. Historians, again, just like the people they study, must find a way to rebuild legal order from the ruins of a collapsed colony.

Building a Revolutionary State represents the first time a historian has tried to overcome these problems and recover the daily experiences of law during the American Revolution. It does so by explaining the volatile process of turning a stateless society into one with a functioning legal system that enjoyed popular support. Moreover, it tells that story by bringing together a highly fragmentary set of records that historians do not usually use to understand law in the revolutionary era: records of New York's provisional governments, newspaper reports, minutes of local committees, auction books from quasi-judicial commissioners, letters, grand jury testimony, payment vouchers, and default judgments. These sources and others illuminate the revolutionary law that arose when royal government failed; they also suggest how ordinary people helped turn revolutionary law into a stable order.

Social historians have shown a similar interest in how ordinary people, rather than founding fathers and constitutional theorists, drove the Revolution forward by advancing radical changes that often went far beyond what leaders supported. In particular, these scholars have demonstrated that people once thought peripheral to the Revolution—particularly women, slaves, free blacks, and Native Americans—were in fact central to the uprising.[14] This book asks different, though complementary, questions. It explores the basis of popular support for revolutionary legal structures and considers how redistribution encouraged ordinary people to welcome state authority into their lives. Examining law on the ground in this way does not suggest that broader ideas were irrelevant in generating popular support for the new state. Rather, the goal here is reconstructing the social reality that made particular concepts meaningful at a certain time. Thus, the book offers a social history of law, one that contextualizes legal policies to suggest why rules about redistribution resonated as deeply as they did during the war.[15]

Understanding that resonance raises hard questions about the basis of popular support for revolutionary authority. In particular, it forces us to ask why Americans, many of whom had no strong commitment to independence, still came forward to support the legal institutions of revolutionary states. The war did not have to turn out that way. One might imagine a circumstance in which a general, unaligned public distrusted new governments, or perhaps such people might have grown war weary and just returned to their farms rather than continue to support the cause. If either had occurred, America might have looked like other places where pockets of insurgent authority persisted in the hills or the backcountry but failed to earn widespread popular acceptance. Indeed, there were moments during the American Revolution when this problem of popular legitimacy threatened to undermine new states. In the later years of the war, New Yorkers and other Americans lost confidence in their states' ability to address their most basic problems, such as gaining a subsistence. Committees in New

York, Massachusetts, Pennsylvania, and elsewhere flourished as people came to distrust the new states. In New York, courts sat empty as people turned their backs on state institutions in favor of local committees and other ad hoc groups. In such circumstances, those who strongly supported independence might have failed to bring others along and sustain popular trust in the revolutionary government.

Redistribution helped insurgents overcome such challenges and draw people into a network of revolutionary support. Those who had no deep allegiance to the cause still embraced it because of three crucial processes that engaged popular trust and sustained it over a long war. First, insurgent authority resonated because legal structures addressed the concrete needs of the people. Ordinary New Yorkers—those without a strong commitment to independence—invited revolutionary authority into their lives because doing so allowed them to address urgent problems in daily life: problems such as gaining a subsistence or finding a place for a refugee family to live. Moreover, such popular priorities changed over time. In the early years of the war, many New Yorkers feared for their personal safety and desperately wanted to prevent Loyalists from acting as a fifth column for the British invasion. But, as the conflict dragged on, immediate physical danger became less of a concern as New Yorkers confronted the challenges of a prolonged war: high prices, material scarcity, forced migration, and other pressing problems. As challenges arose and changed over time, the state's legal system addressed them in a way that generated trust in its ability to confront basic problems of daily life. The same process has occurred in insurgencies and guerrilla movements around the world. Insurgents have created structures that resolve critical problems that people face every day. The general, unaligned population then comes forward to work with those institutions because they address elemental needs such as providing a market for agricultural goods, offering medical care, or drilling wells.[16]

The second basis for building popular support was developing a way to punish those who had supported Britain and its occupation. Political scientists call this transitional justice, and it entails a public reckoning with those who had committed crimes in support of the old regime. By addressing these crimes, a new order establishes its moral authority and demonstrates a clear break with the old regime.[17] In the context of New York, this reckoning meant punishing Loyalists who had aided the occupying army. After seeing Britain and its Loyalist supporters wreak havoc in the area, destroying towns like Kingston and putting homeless families to flight, many in New York came to believe that Loyalists deserved to be punished. Consequently, even those who may have been indifferent to independence still came to resent the occupation and to share a desire to punish Britain's allies.[18] The exact nature of Loyalists' crimes was often unclear, sometimes being no more specific than appearing "inimical to the rights and liberties of America" and not describing any particular act. Yet this vagueness did not diminish the desire to defeat Britain and punish its allies. As the occupation continued, that desire only grew stronger and, as chapter 4 demonstrates, culminated in many towns driving out Loyalists at the end of the war. Thus, New Yorkers accepted revolutionary authority because it provided an institutional means to win the war and punish those who seemed to have caused so much hardship.

The third basis of popular trust was creating strong bonds linking New Yorkers to the new legal system over the long term. If the state had addressed only immediate needs, such as providing personal security, then public confidence might have remained highly tenuous. Its authority would have rested on little more than its ability to address the most urgent public concerns. As that ability waned, or as a new crisis arose, its legitimacy would diminish. It thus had to sustain popular confidence through the vicissitudes of a long war. As crises came and went, New Yorkers needed a bond to legal institutions that transcended immediate concerns and gave them reasons to support revolutionary authority over the long term. During the course of the war, redistribution helped create a constituency of supporters, people who had strong incentives to accept revolutionary legal structures and the authority they wielded.

Property redistribution had far-reaching effects that drove these three processes in New York and generated popular support for the legal structures of a revolutionary state. By selling confiscated Loyalist property, both real and personal, New York's feeble government convinced ordinary people to come forward and help it enforce its commands. Redistribution did so because it addressed many of New Yorkers' most urgent daily needs, such as providing necessities at a time when shelter and a subsistence were hard to come by. Moreover, expropriation offered a highly public way of reckoning with Loyalist crimes and punishing those who had helped Britain. And, finally, redistribution—particularly of real property—linked purchasers to the new state and gave them powerful reasons to support its authority. They had acquired goods and land under the new state, and a return to British rule would threaten those gains. Redistribution therefore gave purchasers strong incentive to support revolutionary government over the long term. Nobody in New York anticipated these complex effects; no one supported redistribution as a policy for drawing forward supporters and linking them to the state. Nevertheless, no other legal practice had such broad ramifications in

New York during the war. By analyzing the extraordinary consequences of redistribution, we can see how a new legal system emerged that worked for the people.

In stressing the centrality of property, this book is part of a long tradition of scholarship that has demonstrated how property holding shaped early America. Efforts to acquire and hold land and the conflicts that arose from those efforts affected nearly every aspect of early America, including migration to the frontier, spiritual seeking, economic relations, government institutions, popular understandings of rights, legal administration, political discourse, and ethnic identity.[19] Indeed, there are few processes as fundamental to early America as the ongoing efforts to get and hold property. This book explores that critical process in the context of New York to suggest how the reallocation of property, both real and personal, strengthened the authority of a revolutionary state.

There is of course another, more sinister side to this redistribution. The same processes that built up confidence in the state also intimidated opposition to it. New Yorkers who were indifferent to independence or mildly hostile could see the consequences of open opposition. As a result, redistribution did not just encourage support. It also coerced enemies into staying silent or taking some small step on behalf of the insurgent government. For instance, people might pasture confiscated livestock before it sold or help survey confiscated land, not because they supported independence, but because they feared what would happen if they did not take those small acts on behalf of the cause. Refusing to help could lead Commissioners of Sequestration to their doors next.[20] Redistribution thus both intimidated opponents of the new state and bolstered support for it.

The chapters that follow take a chronological approach to the ways in which redistribution consolidated revolutionary authority. Chapter 1 establishes the colonial context for law and property holding in New York. It also explores how the war marked a dramatic change in many colonial legal practices, particularly in New Yorkers' sudden embrace of property redistribution. Chapter 2 then analyzes how New Yorkers started to reestablish legal order in the early months of the war. As the British invaded New York City in the summer of 1776, New Yorkers desperately wanted to find Loyalists and prevent them from helping Britain overrun the province. The leading edge of that effort was the Committee for Detecting and Defeating Conspiracies. Frightened, besieged New Yorkers came forward to help the Committee jail suspected British sympathizers and send hundreds more to other provinces without any trials or opportunity to contest accusations. Many of these Loyalists remained in places such as Exeter, New Hampshire, until the spring of 1777. As odd as it might sound, these actions laid the foundation for rebuilding legal order. Jailings and removals drew supporters forward, in particular frightened New Yorkers who wanted to stop Loyalists from helping the invading army. At the same time, the Committee's aggressive enforcement punished enemies and created an environment where it was dangerous to support Britain publicly. However, the jailings and removals proved unenforceable, and, after about nine months, the Committee reversed most of its policies. Nevertheless, at that critical time during an invasion, it started to consolidate revolutionary authority by drawing in supporters and intimidating enemies.

In the spring of 1777, property redistribution helped New Yorkers continue rebuilding their legal order. Chapter 3 examines how at that time they started to redistribute the movable property of those who had fled to the British army in New York City. People such as Beverly Robinson were the targets of this dispossession. The Provincial Convention empowered Commissioners of Sequestration to seize Loyalists' personal property, auction it off, lease vacant farms, and pay anyone who helped in this redistribution. As war and occupation continued, these goods, payments, and leases offered New Yorkers critical relief. Moreover, buying goods or leasing a farm linked many people to the weak state, giving them material reasons to accept the new order and the subsistence it provided. Redistribution also punished political opponents by dispossessing them and settling new tenants in their homes.

Chapter 4 examines how the passage of a forfeiture law in October 1779 worked permanent changes that stabilized the new order over the long term. The statute made it a crime to have "adhered to the enemies of the state." The punishment was forfeiture of all property, real and personal, whether held as a present or a future interest. Between 1779 and 1783, New Yorkers enforced the forfeiture law so aggressively that adhering to the enemies of the state became the most commonly prosecuted crime. Through hundreds of convictions and property sales under the statute, they built durable bonds between ordinary people and a revolutionary state. The convictions also forced out British sympathizers and permanently severed their property connections to New York. The forfeiture act thus culminated a process of consolidation that the Committee on Conspiracies had begun years earlier: connecting supporters to the independent state while also cutting off enemies and driving them away. The appendix provides the data, methodology, and sources for the research in chapter 4. It compares the numbers of convictions for adhering to the enemies of the state against those for all other crimes and demonstrates that New Yorkers convicted more defendants for that one offense than for all other crimes combined.

These processes begun during the war continued into the nineteenth century. For instance, land that had been confiscated during the Revolution was still being sold in New York as late as 1843. Similarly, some of the Loyalists who were dispossessed and fled New York tried to return after the war. Such ongoing effects might make one wonder why this book ends when the war did in 1783. However, as the following chapters demonstrate—particularly chapter 4—the fundamental process that *Building a Revolutionary State* analyzes had concluded by 1783. During the war, New York went from being a collapsed colony without central legal institutions to a state with functioning structures that enjoyed popular support. Property redistribution drove that change by bolstering the authority of a revolutionary state at a moment of great upheaval. Moreover, wartime property redistribution was permanent. Loyalists who returned after the war or those who tried to return did not get their land or goods back.[21] Thus, while the processes begun during the war echoed long afterward, New Yorkers had managed by 1783 to develop working legal structures on a foundation of popular support. Indeed, only by reconsidering how New Yorkers and other Americans built revolutionary states can we more fully understand the polity that emerged after independence.

Insurgents in many times and places have confronted the same challenges that New Yorkers faced during the war: building a revolutionary state and generating support for the authority it wielded. Moreover, insurgents in New York, throughout America, and around the world have redistributed property during their movements. The story here thus transcends one province and highlights some of the larger processes that shaped America's experience. With this broad perspective, we can consider how the American Revolution resembles uprisings in other societies. We also recapture a foundational moment when property redistribution spoke to the needs of ordinary people.

CHAPTER ONE

Law and Property in Colonial New York

The American Revolution sparked fundamental changes in New York's legal order. Colonial New York had been a society with a wealthy and prominent elite, widespread popular distrust of local legal officers like sheriffs, and very little property forfeiture. However, the war and particularly redistribution altered these traditions. Redistribution had great symbolic significance in undermining the power of elite Loyalists. It also changed popular attitudes toward local legal officers and made property forfeiture so common that for the first time it became a central priority in the province. Of course, these were not the only legal effects of the war, but they transformed long-standing colonial practices. By exploring these three areas—the symbolic power of redistribution, attitudes toward local legal officials, and the frequency of forfeiture—we begin to understand how the Revolution marked a radical break with colonial legal and property arrangements, pushing the province in unexpected directions.

The experience of Tryon County highlights the surprising ways that the war disrupted colonial practices. The county sat along New York's western frontier, a region that had been an outlying portion of Albany County for much of the colonial period. In 1772, after thirty years of population growth, it was separated from Albany County and renamed Tryon in honor of the royal governor William Tryon who had, among other things, crushed a popular uprising in North Carolina before taking office in New York.[1] Despite this growth, the area remained thinly populated, its few settlements primarily along the Mohawk River.[2] While the river was of central geographic importance, the Johnson family dominated political and economic life. William Johnson was the patriarch, having emigrated from Ireland to New York in the 1730s. Soon after arriving, he built a home that he named Fort Johnson near present-day Amsterdam. He married a runaway German servant, and, after she died, he began a relationship with his housekeeper, Mary (Molly) Brant, the sister of the Mohawk leader Joseph Brant.[3] He turned these family connections into both diplomatic influence and lucrative trade among the Six Nations of the Iroquois. Through Indian trade and land speculation, he built up an enormous estate on which he encouraged tenant families to settle. He served as the superintendent of Indian affairs for the Northern Department and in 1755 was knighted. In 1763, he moved the family seat from Fort Johnson to Johnson Hall, a home more befitting his high status.[4]

Johnson Hall in particular captured the family's immense influence. It was a grand, two-story manor house overlooking gardens and meadows, and from it he presided over an estate that covered nearly four hundred square miles. As the superintendent of Indian affairs, he held conferences with Indian chiefs on the grounds; as a land speculator, he conducted his commercial negotiations there, meeting with neighboring landlords and potential tenants. Carved out of a dense forest, the estate embodied the Johnson family's commercial and diplomatic power on the colonial frontier.[5] Sir William died in July 1774, but not before trying to establish his legacy through the next generation. He arranged for his son, Sir John Johnson, to be knighted and for his nephew and son-in-law, Colonel Guy Johnson, to become superintendent of Indian affairs. Sir John moved into Johnson Hall, and Colonel Johnson built a home nearby at a place he named Guy Park.[6] Thus, the second generation was just coming into power when, in the summer of 1774, extralegal committees started meeting in the county to discuss the growing crisis.

When committees first met, few resembled the revolutionary groups that would soon dismantle New York's colonial government.[7] In August 1774, one such group gathered in a region north of the Mohawk River known as the Palatine District. Its members declared their "Concern and heartfull [*sic*] Sorrow" for the people of Boston, whose port Parliament had closed to punish Massachusetts for the Tea Party. Those at the meeting announced that they would support the Continental Congress, scheduled to convene the following month, as a way to resolve the crisis. Nevertheless, despite these "Allarming [*sic*] and calamitous Conditions," people in Tryon still declared their support for King George and the colonial leaders who governed in his name. The committee resolved that it would "bear true Faith and Allegiance unto him [George III], and that we Will with our Lives and Fortunes support and maintain him upon the Throne of His Ancestors." They considered it their "greatest Happiness to be governed by the Laws of Great Britain."[8]

Despite this explicit royalism, Sir John and Colonel Johnson vehemently opposed any committee or congress as direct threats to themselves. Colonel Johnson believed that outsiders, probably from New England, had secretly moved into Tryon County and were plotting with local committees to attack him at his home and take him prisoner. As a result, he fortified Guy Park and surrounded himself with armed supporters every time he left home. He even stopped unfamiliar travelers on the open road, questioning them to see whether they were the outsiders who had come to arrest him.[9] Sir John also viewed committees as dangerous groups, and he intimidated their members to prevent them from meeting. If he heard that a committee was gathering, he would lead his tenants to the meeting to break it up. In one instance, a group had gathered to put up a liberty pole. Sir John and his armed supporters rode through, knocking some people down, threatening others, and forcing everyone to flee.[10]

When Sir John was not present to abuse committee members, his close associate Alexander White did so. White was the sheriff of Tryon County, and many people told the county committee about instances in which he threatened them for supporting committees and congresses.[11] William Seeber described one incident where Sheriff White declared that he wished he had been present at a particular meeting so that he could shoot some of the people there and hang the rest. William's son Jacob overheard this threat and told White that it might not be so easy to do so. White turned on him, drew his pistol, cocked it, and said: "You d[amne]d Rebell, if you say one Word more, I'll blow your Brains out." Jacob, probably wisely, kept quiet. William Petry, a committee member, told of a time when he was in Johnstown and White stopped him to take him to jail. When Petry asked why, the sheriff refused to tell him. After spending the night in jail, Petry refused to sign a bond for his release because White still had not told him what he had done. Without any charges or process pending against Petry, the jailer let him go.[12] White had good reason to think that he could throw a committee member into the Johnstown jail whenever he wanted. After all, White's patron, Sir John, claimed to own both the jail and the courthouse in the town that bore his family's name.[13] Thus, committees in Tryon County were beleaguered groups, bullied and harassed by a powerful landlord family and the sheriff who did their bidding. Moreover, the intimidation and threats of violence succeeded in discouraging committee formation in Tryon. If they met at all, town and district committees did so as separate groups without uniting into a single committee to coordinate their actions.[14]

In April 1775, the battles at Lexington and Concord emboldened committees to confront the Johnson family and the sheriff who had been threatening them. One such change came in May, when the committee of the Palatine District wrote to the Albany committee requesting ammunition and gunpowder. As the Palatine committee explained in its letter, Sir John had begun to fortify Johnson Hall. In addition, he and Colonel Johnson had armed a group of tenants and brought them to Johnstown, where they could better protect their landlord.[15] The Palatine committee sought the ammunition to defend itself against Sir John and his militia of loyal tenants. In May, local committees joined together for the first coordinated, countywide meeting. Disregarding the opposition of the Johnsons and Sheriff White, various local groups came together in what they called the "United Committees."[16] An explosive environment was developing in the spring of 1775, one in which newly assertive committees were arming to unite against powerful opponents who had tried to intimidate them.

At that moment, a small scuffle caused this tension to erupt into open conflict. In June, one of Sheriff White's servants, Thomas Hunt, decided to walk through John Fonda's fields. Fonda was out hoeing with some other men when he saw Hunt trampling the meadows and the grounds freshly sown with peas. As Fonda explained to the county committee, he told Hunt "not to make a road through his Land to his Damage, but to use the foot-path along the fence." According to someone who was out in the fields with Fonda, Hunt replied that "he would go through that Land in Spite of said Fonda." Hunt, who was carrying a small scythe, made as though he was going to hit Fonda with it, and Fonda knocked him down with his hoe. Perhaps accustomed to hearing his master threaten people, Hunt promised to be the death of Fonda and continued to threaten him as he walked off.[17] Hunt must have reported the incident to his master because a short time later White arrested Fonda and brought him to jail.

Events quickly escalated as the seething anger at White and his patron boiled over. Fonda's friends among the county committee decided that they were not going to suffer any more abuse from the sheriff. The committee gathered about one hundred people to free Fonda. When they arrived, they exchanged gunfire with White before he managed to escape and then freed Fonda. The committee and its supporters next sought reinforcements, and about five hundred men set out to arrest White, who took refuge in Johnson Hall. However, the group that freed Fonda soon realized that Johnson Hall was so heavily fortified that they would need cannons to attack it and capture the sheriff. Not having any artillery, the Tryon committee wrote to the committee in Schenectady (Albany County) to explain what had happened and ask for cannons "with all the implements necessary." As the Tryon committee put it in the letter, since "the Sheriff gives us a great deal of Trouble Insulting us on every occasion, and bids us open Defiance, we are therefore now determined to have him."[18]

What began as a fight on a farm came to embody the mistreatment that many in Tryon had suffered from a high-handed local official and his wealthy patron. The Tryon committee, an extralegal group, reached out to other committees for help in taking this despised official who had insulted them as rebels. But, since the Schenectady committee did not have enough gunpowder to send, it forwarded the letter to the Albany committee, which rushed two of its members to Johnson Hall. The members of the Albany committee met with Sir John and convinced him to hand over White. They also extracted a promise from Sir John not to take any additional action in support of Britain.[19] The Albany committee soon sent a militia detachment that arrested White and brought him back to Albany as a prisoner.[20]

Sir John continued to stockpile weapons and, as many believed, rally support for the king among the Six Nations of the Iroquois. To prevent him from continuing this mobilization, Major General Philip Schuyler arrested him in January 1776, brought him to Fishkill, then released him on parole on the condition that he remain at home. But that restriction did not stop him, and the Albany committee continued to receive reports that he was organizing Indians and others on behalf of Britain. In May, the committee ordered the arrest of a number of people who were helping him. With a detachment of troops once again returning to Tryon, Sir John fled the family seat at Johnson Hall and led a group of supporters to Canada.[21] Much had changed in Tryon County since the Palatine committee first convened in 1774 and declared that living under British laws was its greatest happiness. Over the two years that followed, revolutionaries in western New York slowly joined together to arrest a prominent royal official and force his patron, the most powerful landlord in the area, to flee. As the war progressed, revolutionary commissioners would confiscate and sell Sir John's personal property, conducting many of the auctions at Johnson Hall.[22] Sales of his real property continued after the war as commissioners of the independent state carved up his estates and sold the lots to the highest bidders.[23]

These events allow an exploration of some of the Revolution's transformative effects. In particular, the story of Tryon County invites a look both back to colonial practices and ahead to the war's deeply unsettling consequences. As the following chapter explains, the Johnson family, with its grand estates and political prominence, highlights the influence that elite landlords had in colonial New York. Moreover, colonial New York was a place where local law enforcement officials like Sheriff White were surprisingly common. Before the Revolution, sheriffs, justices of the peace, and other officers often acted in irresponsible and even criminal ways that inspired popular contempt for officials and their authority. Indeed, that contempt was widespread enough that it hindered legal administration in the colony.

By considering this colonial background, we start to grasp the radical nature of New York's revolutionary redistribution and state building. Insurgents in Tryon and elsewhere joined together to arrest prominent Loyalist landlords, drive them from their homes, and, ultimately, dispossess them. For families such as the Johnsons, property redistribution occurred at the manor house itself, thereby announcing that the revolutionary state was aggressive enough to dispossess even its most elite enemies. Not only did property confiscation have great symbolic significance, but it also represented a major change from colonial practices in which uncompensated forfeiture very rarely occurred. And insurgents were able to implement this far-reaching redistribution because they reversed the colonial contempt for local authority and instead drew ordinary people forward to help enforce the law. Of course, these changes were not the result of a specific program to pursue legal change and state building in particular ways. No statute or other legal mechanism had the explicit goal of undermining elite landlords in a way that announced the new state's authority while also generating popular support for local law enforcement and making property forfeiture a key policy in New York for the first time. Such careful planning would have been impossible in a legal environment as unstable as New York's during the war. As the committees in Tryon suggest, insurgents dismantled royal government in New York at the start of the conflict, leaving the province without a settled government to manage the transition to independence. The destruction of royal government thus unleashed volatile revolutionary forces that transformed society in unpredictable ways.

Long before redistribution occurred in the Revolution, the patterns of property ownership had exerted a major influence on colonial New York. The Dutch initially settled the area and established commercial forts, including New Amsterdam at the southern tip of Manhattan and Fort Orange (Albany) far inland along the Hudson. The colony came to be called New Netherland, and it remained under Dutch control until 1664, when Charles II issued a patent authorizing his brother James, Duke of York, to settle the region for England. Eager to assert his claims and to weaken Dutch commercial interests, James sent a fleet to New Amsterdam that seized the colony for England in August 1664. The first two English governors put landownership at the center of their policy for the newly captured colony. Both Richard

Nicholls (governor 1664–67) and Francis Lovelace (governor 1667–74) believed that awarding large grants of land would consolidate English authority in general and their own power in particular. For example, in 1671, Lovelace granted Thomas Mayhew a tract called Tisbury that included most of the island of Martha's Vineyard and all of Nantucket. The grant also declared Mayhew "Governor or Chiefe [*sic*] Magistrate" with the authority to hold court and to determine particular matters that arose on his land.[24] Early governors made such grants to bolster the colony's government. Grantees would form a constituency of support for New York's authority, defending it as the source of their ownership rights and other privileges.[25] Thus, property ownership—particularly landownership—was vital for strengthening state authority from the earliest years of English rule.[26]

Succeeding governors continued making large grants to individuals and small groups, even though imperial officials in London opposed the policy from the 1690s on.[27] The result of such practices was that colonial New York developed a land system in which some owners possessed staggeringly large tracts. The largest was Rensselaerswyck at more than 1 million acres. Other manors also emerged, including Livingston (160,000 acres), Philipsburgh (92,000 acres), Cortlandt (86,000 acres), and many more that ran to tens of thousands of acres.[28] To be sure, the manors did not all continue intact throughout the colonial period. Proprietors gradually distributed their lands among family members and occasionally sold parcels outright.[29] Moreover, owners never exercised feudal rights such as holding courts leet and baron even though such lordly rights appeared in many manorial patents.[30]

Nevertheless, these grants set a landholding pattern that had major effects on New York down through the Revolution. One consequence was that the grantees and their heirs became wealthy landlords who, even without feudal privileges, still possessed some of the largest estates in North America. Another effect was creating a sizable population of tenants—particularly in the Hudson Valley—where the largest manors were located. Since few people owned much of the land, farmers had to settle under leases rather than possessing the land in fee. As a result, by the 1770s, at least half of the household heads in the Hudson Valley were tenants, a figure that ranked among the highest percentages on the continent and was comparable to that in the Northern Neck of Virginia.[31] Colonial New York, therefore, was a society in which wealthy landlords owned enormous estates and tenancy prevailed to a greater extent than almost anywhere on the continent.

This wealth elevated landlords socially as they translated their expansive holdings into positions of influence. For many landlords, influence began close to home as they structured their tenants' economic activity. For example, leases often required tenants to bring their crops to the landlord's mill and allowed them to go to the open market only if the landlord declined to buy. This stipulation provided landlords a right of first refusal and effectively allowed them to set prices since other mills were unlikely to offer a higher price than the estate's mill. Landlords also imposed fees when their tenants sold or devised their leases. The tenant (or the decedent's beneficiary under a will) had to pay the landlord one-quarter or one-third of the farm's value at the time of transfer; otherwise, the lease would terminate. This practice, known as the quarter-sale, could be costly on an improved farm, and it was another way that New York's landlords shaped their tenants' economic lives.[32] Moreover, prominent landholding families such as the Johnsons, Morrises, Livingstons, Beekmans, Schuylers, Van Cortlandts, and DeLanceys did not limit their control to their own estates. They also sought colonywide influence as different families competed with each other for seats on the governor's council, a judgeship on the Supreme Court of Judicature, or even lower public office such as justice of the peace for a particular county.[33] New York's landholding pattern thus encouraged the development of a wealthy elite that enjoyed political and economic influence throughout the colony.

Many landlords lived in an opulent fashion that announced this wealth and prestige. The Johnsons and others built large, multistory brick houses that they embellished with engraved firebacks and carved oak balustrades. They furnished their homes with Dutch tiles and tapestries and surrounded themselves with servants and slaves. The Philipse family, Beverly Robinson's in-laws, housed its staff in quarters that had leather straps on the door hinges so that the servants and slaves could move about without disturbing his lordship. Some landlords created fenced deer parks and formal gardens, even importing English gardeners to maintain the grounds.[34] A great proprietor occasionally invited his tenants to the house to celebrate a happy event such as a wedding. That is, he would invite them to the house but not into it. In 1758, Mary Philipse married Roger Morris. The couple's friends and relatives dined on imported china and drank from crystal glasses in richly appointed banquet rooms. Tenants celebrated the event outside and waited for the newlyweds to appear in a second-story window, where they offered a few gracious words to the people below.[35] Through their homes, deer parks, and grand entertaining, New York's landlords lived in a way that made their high status apparent to everyone around them.

In this environment, property redistribution during the Revolution acquired powerful symbolic significance. As the subsequent chapters explain, revolutionary commissioners dispossessed British sympathizers in public ways. They marched around the grounds of an estate, taking inventories of all movable property before auctioning off the clothes, cows, and carriages they found. Years later, under a separate mandate, other commissioners came with surveyors, dividing estates into lots and selling the real property. Commissioners dispossessed Sir John Johnson in precisely this way. Through waves of public confiscation, New York's revolutionary government declared that it was forceful enough to supplant a local grandee. Confiscations and sales represented public statements that a new order was emerging, one capable of dispossessing even those who had been powerful and prominent in colonial society. Consequently, New York's landholding pattern—its large estates and wealthy landlords—reminds us that simply counting the number of forfeited lots or the total value of property sold reveals little about the far-reaching effects of redistribution. While a primarily quantitative approach is helpful, it overlooks the issue of what redistribution signified to the people who saw it happen.[36] The presence of highly visible wealth meant that redistribution was not primarily a matter of revenue but rather a strong declaration of the growing authority of the revolutionary state.

The growth of that authority reveals another surprising legal change during the Revolution. Throughout the eighteenth century, New Yorkers had displayed distrust of and even contempt for local officials. Consequently, sheriffs, constables, and justices of the peace struggled to carry out basic administration such as executing warrants and writs.[37] Yet, after generations of enforcement problems, redistribution convinced ordinary people to come forward and help implement the commands of the revolutionary state. This popular support for revolutionary authority appears particularly striking when we see it against the background of the challenges—even dangers—of enforcing the law in colonial New York. In a gruesome incident from 1757, the sheriff of Albany County deputized John Van Alstyne so that he could arrest David Mariners. But, when Van Alstyne tried to carry out the arrest, Mariners stabbed him to death. John's widow Catharine then wrote to Attorney General William Kempe to plead for help in punishing Mariners.[38] While the murder of officers remained rare, violence against them was fairly common. One historian has found that 5.9 percent of all prosecutions in colonial New York were for crimes that displayed contempt for authority. Of those crimes, more than 70 percent involved attacks on law enforcement officers.[39]

Even when New Yorkers did not attack officials, threats of violence often made it impossible to enforce the law. In 1760, Jacob Van Schaack, the sheriff of Albany County, wrote to the president of the governor's council, Cadwallader Colden, to explain what happened when he tried to arrest Lieutenant George Coventry, an officer in the Royal Army. As Van Schaack noted: "[Coventry] seized a pistol, swore he would blow my Brains out, and so kept me from further prosecuting the arrest, uttering all the time the most violent oaths and other abusive language against me." Facing these threats, it is not surprising that Van Schaack concluded: "It is impossible for me to execute my office."[40] Law enforcement officials faced such problems even when they were not dealing with military officers. In 1772, the deputy sheriff of Ulster County and two others complained that they were nearly killed trying to serve a writ.[41] In another incident from 1762, Attorney General John Tabor Kempe, William's son, sent two writs to the sheriff of Albany County, Harmanus Schuyler. Schuyler tried to serve the writs and arrest the defendants for intrusion on Crown lands. But, after being assaulted in the attempt, he thought better of it and did nothing more. Kempe sent the writs again and ordered Schuyler to arrest the suspects. But the sheriff continued to refuse for fear of his safety and was eventually fined for neglect of duty. Perhaps he decided to pay with his money rather than his life, and, as a result, the defendants were never arrested.[42] Not only did violence and threats against officials suggest contempt for local authority, but such actions also thwarted legal administration.

Part of the reason for such resistance no doubt was that defendants did not want to be arrested, have process served on them, or have a judgment executed against them. But local enforcement officials also acted in irresponsible ways that inspired popular contempt, much as Sheriff White did in Tryon County on the eve of the war. For example, in an undated petition to George Clarke, probably from the time he was governor (1736–43), inhabitants of North Castle in Westchester County complained about one of the county's justices of the peace. The justice, Francis Pelham, was a man "given to Drinking" who threatened people's lives and drew up warrants that he threatened to serve on poor people unless they bought him drinks. As the complainants noted: "[Because of] these and many other Like actions wee are much oprest [*sic*]." Clarke and the governor's council responded by removing Pelham from office, but only after the petitioners had suffered under him.[43] Other justices brazenly corrupted legal proceedings. Thomas Jarvis, a justice of the peace for Suffolk County, was a tavern keeper who convened court in his tavern. Holding court in a tavern or a home was perfectly acceptable and common. But, in 1767, Jarvis allowed one party to a suit to buy drinks for the jury. The move swayed the jury—perhaps literally—and the opposing party had to appeal the action to a higher court.[44]

Other officials pursued different forms of corruption as sheriffs and their deputies collected fines but never turned them over to the court that had imposed them. Such theft happened often enough that various courts throughout the province required officials to post bond for their faithful performance in office and account for all the fines they collected.[45] However, such steps did not resolve the problem because in 1773 the legislature enacted a law that required deputy sheriffs to swear an oath. As the statute's preamble put it, these officials were "liable to corruption," and putting them under an oath would prevent such abuses.[46] Other justices of the peace made offensive comments, such as Jonathan Whitehead of Queens County declaring in 1702/3: "Religion was onely [*sic*] an Invention of cunning men to gett thaire [*sic*] living by." Whitehead also added Sabbath breaking to his offenses when on another occasion he had a packed suitcase and was preparing to travel on a Sunday. Someone told him that as "a Justice [he] ought in a particular manner to take care not to give such examples." He responded that "he thought there ought to be no difference of days and that if it should be so ordered now as to observe Thursday in a hundred years it would be as Religiously observed as the Sabbath now is."[47] The varieties of official misbehavior went further and included extortion, assault, battery, charging excessive fees, theft, and other crimes.[48] Law enforcers like justices of the peace, sheriffs, and deputy sheriffs had the unenviable task of arresting suspects and assessing fines. But misdeeds and criminality only deepened popular disdain of these officials and fostered a widespread distrust of local representatives of authority.

Popular contempt for law enforcement had significant effects on colonial administration. It impeded enforcement to such an extent that many cases—and in some regions most cases—went unresolved. In the eighteenth century prior to the Revolution, roughly 37 percent of all criminal prosecutions in New York went unresolved. In the northern counties, that number increased to 60 percent.[49] The Supreme Court of Judicature, New York's colonywide court of general civil and criminal jurisdiction, had similar trouble. By the 1750s, 51 percent of civil cases in the Supreme Court were never concluded.[50] Other colonies faced similar challenges. In Massachusetts, for instance, crimes that displayed contempt of authority constituted as much as 23 percent of all criminal prosecutions.[51] In New York, the problem became so severe that popular disdain for law enforcement, as revealed in violence, threats, and complaints against officials, hampered and sometimes completely thwarted administration. In an age without professional police forces, the justices, sheriffs, and other officials needed the active cooperation of ordinary people, and without it they struggled to implement the law.[52]

This background of unresolved cases and popular contempt for law enforcement raises the key issue of how support ultimately developed for the revolutionary state. Historians generally have not considered how or under what circumstances people came to trust central legal authority during the Revolution. But the long history of enforcement problems in colonial New York makes popular support a central question for understanding the emergence of an independent state. One could imagine a weak revolutionary state like New York failing to earn sufficient backing to implement the law. Yet, after decades in which colonial law enforcement often lacked popular support and cases went unresolved, the revolutionary state managed to implement a wide-ranging redistribution of Loyalist property. What was more, it did so at a time when institutions such as courts were feeble or completely absent. Institutional collapse made New York's provisional authority even weaker than that of its colonial antecedent, yet that authority still enforced redistribution effectively. The following chapters will analyze that extraordinary process in detail and suggest how redistribution generated support for a weak state. But it is important to note here that such support represented a sea change from colonial administration. Of course, no state ever achieves universal support, and revolutionary New York certainly had its opponents. Nevertheless, redistribution drove a major change when it encouraged ordinary people to embrace a weak state and help it carry out a sweeping confiscation policy.

Another striking characteristic of revolutionary confiscation was that it represented a radical departure from colonial practices regarding property forfeiture. The traditional English rule—one that appeared long before colonization—was that conviction for treason or felony resulted in the defendant forfeiting his real and personal property to the Crown. Forfeiture was very complicated in actual application because it involved various statutes layered on top of the real property law of the realm, which was itself a patchwork of local custom, inheritance law, and other legal fields. Despite the complexity, the Crown intended to extend the practice of felony forfeiture to colonial New York because commands to that effect appeared in royal instructions to provincial governors. However, these rules were never fully implemented in New York, and, as a result, property forfeiture for felony or treason was extremely rare in the colony. Part of the reason for this rarity was that, unlike in Britain, no Court of Exchequer existed in New York to protect royal revenues by consistently enforcing forfeiture.[53]

But, more importantly, New Yorkers in various official capacities from jurors to governors showed little desire to dispossess convicted felons and traitors. Indeed, officials often were reluctant to punish defendants at all. Throughout colonial New York, 51 percent of convicted felons sentenced to death were pardoned.[54] Not only did many convicted defendants escape with their lives, but they or their heirs also often retained their property.

An exhaustive study of criminal law in colonial New York uncovered only three instances where juries reported that the defendant possessed any lands, tenements, or chattels to forfeit. That finding of no property was a fiction, one similar to underestimating the value of stolen goods to ensure a conviction for petty larceny rather than grand larceny. Jurors reached that conclusion about property even when circumstances suggest that the defendant possessed at least a modest estate at the time of his conviction. Juries probably returned the fictitious finding for prudential reasons. They likely did not want to dispossess defendants if doing so would impoverish families and send them on to the poor rolls.[55]

Whatever the exact reasons, juries in colonial New York seldom endorsed forfeiture, preferring instead to engage in a fiction that allowed an overwhelming number of convicted felons and traitors to keep their property. Moreover, even when a felon or traitor was convicted, not pardoned, and ultimately executed, his heirs continued to enjoy the benefits of his estate. For example, Jacob Leisler led an uprising in New York in the aftermath of the Glorious Revolution. When he refused to recognize the authority of the new provincial governor, he was convicted of treason, hanged, and formally dispossessed. But Leisler's widow was never excluded from his estates, and she retained possession of them until the governor formally restored his property to her.[56] These various steps—from pardons, to juries finding no property, to heirs retaining possession of a felon's or traitor's estate—all made property forfeiture very rare in colonial New York and mitigated its effects on the few occasions when it occurred.

Forfeiture was also rare in other circumstances where officials could have enforced it. For instance, smugglers very seldom forfeited their contraband. For much of New York's colonial history, both vice-admiralty courts and the Supreme Court of Judicature exercised concurrent jurisdiction over violations of the Navigation Acts. The vice-admiralty courts sat without juries, whereas the Supreme Court was a common law court that employed juries. In the 1750s, lawyers and judges in New York started to extend authority over New York Harbor by claiming that it was not part of the high seas but rather within the province itself, thereby invoking the exclusive jurisdiction of the Supreme Court. As a result, customs officials who wanted contraband forfeited had to go to the Supreme Court and convince a jury of the smuggler's peers, many of whom may have been smugglers themselves, that a violation of the Navigation Acts had occurred and the property must be forfeited. Intimidation of informers also made it extremely difficult to bring such actions. These hurdles proved so high that customs collectors gave up trying to have contraband forfeited.[57] Consequently, in the quarter century before the Revolution, even smugglers were able to avoid having their contraband forfeited.

Perhaps the most common type of property forfeiture in colonial New York was that to the colony for public use. Today we would call this practice eminent domain, although that term did not appear in America until the 1790s.[58] Whatever one calls it, the practice involved the sovereign taking private land for uses such as building and maintaining roads, courthouses, chapels, wharves, powder magazines, jails, and many other public endeavors. Most important for our purposes here, these forfeitures usually included compensation to the former owner.[59] New York had a complicated mosaic of laws governing forfeiture for building or maintaining roads. By the start of the Revolution, some counties compensated owners only for improved or enclosed land, other counties paid compensation for all land regardless of its condition, and still others paid compensation both for the land itself and for any damages the former owner may have suffered, perhaps by having a busy road running through his property. But it is clear that, starting in 1721, the year a highway act was passed, New York paid compensation for at least some categories of land forfeited for highways.[60] New York officials also compensated owners for land taken to build wharves, forts, drains, and gutters.[61] By the 1770s, therefore, New Yorkers regularly received compensation for land they forfeited to the public. As a result, before the war, New Yorkers showed little desire to forfeit property, even under the circumstances where the law allowed that as punishment: circumstances such as convictions for treason, felony, and smuggling. And, when forfeiture occurred, other factors blunted its impact by granting pardons, finding no property to forfeit, allowing heirs to retain possession of a traitor's property, and compensating for land taken for public use.

Forfeiture during the Revolution, however, represented a far-reaching change in these practices. Whereas colonial forfeiture was very limited and usually compensated, revolutionary confiscation was the widespread, uncompensated, and permanent dispossession of political enemies. To understand why this critical change occurred—why property forfeiture became so common and aggressively enforced—we have to look to the context of a popular uprising. Analyzing the volatile and violent experiences of a society at war helps us begin to understand why this particular legal practice came to resonate as powerfully as it did.

Legal and political disorder spread quickly as the conflict with Britain intensified. After the Boston Tea Party in December 1773, Britain enacted a series of punitive statutes against Massachusetts, laws called the Coercive

Acts in Britain and the Intolerable Acts in America. These laws stationed troops in Boston, reorganized the colony's government, and made other drastic reforms. News of these changes started arriving in New York City in the spring of 1774 and spurred the city's inhabitants to action. In particular, the Boston Port Bill, which closed the port to shipping, encouraged people in New York City to begin developing a coordinated protest.[62]

Committees and factions quickly formed in response to the deepening crisis. In the weeks after news of the Port Bill arrived, the Committee of Fifty-One and the Committee of Mechanics formed in New York City. These two groups arranged the elections that picked the province's delegates to the Continental Congress in September 1774. After the Congress met, the two committees agreed in November to disband the Committee of Fifty-One in favor of the Committee of Sixty. This new committee, along with the Committee of Mechanics, began to implement congressional resolutions, particularly the Association.[63] Participation in these events outside New York City proved highly uneven. In the summer of 1774, the two committees in the city sent circular letters to every county inviting people to participate in the election of delegates to the Continental Congress. But the people who received the letters, often county-level officials, were under no obligation to respond, and some did nothing. Even if they did take action, there were no standard procedures for such an election. Some counties held a single vote to determine whether to support sending delegates to Philadelphia; others held elections in different towns, which only confused the results when some towns voted to support the Congress and others voted against it. Moreover, inhabitants of some towns decided on their own, regardless of the circular letters, to form committees that corresponded with those in New York City.[64] Thus, for a year beginning in May 1774, New York City led the colony's mobilization, with other regions following at different speeds.

As committees and the Continental Congress emerged, New York's colonial Assembly took a cautious approach. The Assembly convened in January 1775 at the same time as the Committee of Sixty, the Committee of Mechanics, and committees in some outlying counties were trying to implement the Association. A revolutionary infrastructure was starting to develop and coordinate resistance to British policies. Assembly delegates, however, chose to disregard the Continental Congress and provincial committees. Rather than acknowledge this extralegal infrastructure, the Assembly sought reconciliation by petitioning the king and sending a memorial to the House of Lords and a remonstrance to the Commons. Once the Committee of Sixty realized that the Assembly would not endorse the Continental Congress, it acted on its own. In March, it arranged elections for a

Provincial Convention whose sole purpose was choosing New York's delegates to the Second Continental Congress. Thus, the Committee of Sixty arranged elections to a Provincial Convention, which would in turn select New York's delegates to the Second Continental Congress.[65] The Provincial Convention met April 20–22, chose delegates, and adjourned.[66]

However, on April 23, the day after the Convention adjourned, news of the battles at Lexington and Concord arrived and had a dramatic effect on New York's colonial legal order. The outbreak of war made reconciliation appear impossible, accelerated mobilization, and helped expand the network of revolutionary committees. The Committee of Sixty called for elections to a provincial congress, and, for the first time, every county responded to a circular letter and sent delegates to a colonywide body.[67] On May 22, 1775, New York's first Provincial Congress met with representatives from every county present.[68] In the same month, the Committee of Sixty expanded its membership and became the Committee of One Hundred. The local committees in Tryon, Albany, Ulster, and Orange Counties grew in the months after Lexington and Concord.[69] The battles stoked anti-British sentiment and drew many people into active participation in the uprising.[70]

The battles also had consequences beyond encouraging the committee movement. The start of open war strengthened the most radical insurgents in New York and emboldened them to take aggressive, often violent action against Britain and its supporters. On April 23, the day news of the battles arrived in New York City, a spontaneous uprising occurred. One of the participants described how word of the bloodshed in Massachusetts "produced a general Insurrection of the Populace." Crowds formed across the city and marched to the docks to unload two ships that were going to resupply the British troops in Boston. Other groups continued to the armory at City Hall, where they seized muskets, bayonets, and full cartridge boxes, passing the weapons out to the crowd. After posting a guard of about one hundred newly armed men, the group continued to the powder house to remove its contents as well.[71] The uprising had been so swift that some would later wonder whether prominent officials had coordinated it. But a resident of the city assured a correspondent that unloading the ships and seizing the weapons "was not done by the Magistrates but by the people."[72] It was becoming clear to those in New York that provincial leaders—even those on committees—could not control the revolutionary movement. Some partisans were showing themselves to be more aggressive than the committees and congresses. The committees, therefore, represented the mainstream of revolutionary agitation. There was a hard core of radical insurgents who were even more forceful than the extralegal groups.

These uncompromising partisans took the law into their own hands to assault British authority wherever they found it. Indeed, they did so in direct defiance of the committees, which the most aggressive insurgents often thought were too cautious. One such example of defiance occurred in the spring of 1775. By late May, Lieutenant Governor Cadwallader Colden and Major Isaac Hamilton, the commander of the British regiment in New York City, concluded that the city had become too tense to allow British troops to remain stationed among the people. After consulting with Captain George Vandeput, they decided to move them from the barracks to Vandeput's ship, the *Asia*, which had recently arrived in the harbor.[73] The Provincial Congress feared that the sight of the troops could provoke some in the city to attack the soldiers as they boarded the ship. But it recognized that it could do little to prevent people from acting on their own to confront British authority. It could only "earnestly recommend it" to New Yorkers "not to obstruct the embarkation of the said troops, but to permit them to depart this city peaceably."[74]

Many New Yorkers, however, did not share the Congress's desire for a peaceful departure, particularly because rumors had begun circulating that the troops were going to reinforce the soldiers in Boston. On the morning of June 6, word reached a group of men in a tavern that the soldiers had begun their march. Marinus Willett, who had been active in opposing Britain, later recalled that those in the tavern were furious at the "timid disposition" of the committees that would allow the soldiers to leave "when we had it in our power to make them prisoners" and confiscate their weapons.[75] Willett and others in the tavern were not going to allow a hesitant committee or Congress to stop them from confronting the troops.

The half dozen men decided that they would confiscate the troops' weapons themselves. They split up and raced through the city, warning people that the troops were on the move and trying to find the soldiers' route to the docks. Willett found the baggage train and, hurrying to the front, halted the march. Major Hamilton rode up to see why the troops had stopped, and Willett told him that, although the Committee of One Hundred allowed the troops to depart with their personal weapons, they could not leave with the carts full of additional arms.[76] By this time, a crowd had formed, and, as Hamilton later explained, "the people harranged our Men" and encouraged them to desert. The people then began unloading the carts, carrying off trunks and packages that contained not just arms but the officers' personal effects and much of the regiment's ammunition.[77] At that moment, with Hamilton quickly becoming overwhelmed and the crowd "presing [*sic*] in on every side," prominent New Yorkers such as Gouverneur Morris and the mayor of the city, David Matthews, arrived.[78] They promised Hamilton that all the confiscated items would be returned, and Hamilton hurried his troops onto the ship. But their weapons, which later supplied a regiment of the New York militia, were never returned. The officers eventually received their personal property but, as Hamilton described it, in a "mutilated disorderly condition."[79]

Events such as these demonstrated that even extralegal committees and Congress could not keep partisan aggression in check. A group of hard-core revolutionaries defied both the British military and New York's committees to do what they thought the crisis required. Lieutenant Governor Colden, who had been active in colonial politics for more than a half century, saw clearly that not even the "assumed Power of Congresses or Committees will be sufficient to restrain the People."[80] Mobs outside these bodies acted with impunity, subject neither to royal government nor to committee control.

Some aggressive New Yorkers also splintered from a committee if they believed that it was not going far enough to punish British supporters. Isaac Sears was one such insurgent who had resigned from the Committee of Fifty-One because it had been too lenient with British sympathizers. By late November 1775, he had become convinced that New Yorkers were irresolute and that he must look elsewhere for men sufficiently committed to the cause. He traveled to New Haven, Connecticut, where he organized about eighty rangers. They marched southwest along the coast of Long Island Sound and burned a sloop at Mamaroneck that the British government had recently purchased as a supply ship. He and his men then arrested three prominent supporters of Britain: the Reverend Samuel Seabury, who had written several tracts condemning the Continental Congress; Jonathan Fowler, a judge in Westchester County; and Nathaniel Underhill, the mayor of the borough of Westchester. Sears sent them back to New Haven as prisoners. This irregular, self-appointed army continued marching south to their main target: James Rivington's pro-British printing offices in New York City. They surrounded his shop, posting guards at each entrance while they took his type and smashed his presses.[81] A cheering crowd of about fifteen hundred escorted Sears and his men out of the city and sent them on their way back to New Haven.[82] In the meantime, two of the prisoners sent to Connecticut, Underhill and Fowler, publicly apologized for signing a protest against the Continental Congress and promised never to oppose, "in the view of the people of this Continent," any congressional measures.[83]

By late 1775, no legal authority could stop a fierce partisan—one frustrated with his neighbors' caution—from gathering an armed group and punishing enemies. None of the various committees in and around New York City was aggressive enough to satisfy Sears. Neither could the crumbling colonial government prevent him from rallying a group of rangers in another province to intimidate New Yorkers, destroy their property, and enforce ideological obedience to the uprising. To suggest, as some historians have done, that the American Revolution witnessed few changes in legal doctrine or that New Yorkers simply carried over their court system from the colonial era would miss the point because no such orderly transition to independence occurred. Instead, central authority collapsed, creating an environment where aggressive partisans took matters into their own hands, intimidated opponents, and enforced their own idea of revolutionary law.

Violent insurgents continued to pose a critical challenge to the revolutionary state for years to come. New Yorkers had to find a way to contain their own uprising and to restrain its most aggressive elements. People such as those who spontaneously raided the armory, those who confronted the troops when they left their barracks, or Sears and his rangers all had shown that they would disregard revolutionary institutions if those structures seemed too timid. Committees and leaders of the uprising who claimed to represent the people had to convince the most violent insurgents to stop taking matters into their own hands and instead accept revolutionary authority. As the subsequent chapters demonstrate, New York's harsh and vindictive legal policies—particularly expropriation—ultimately resolved this challenge by convincing such insurgents that they did not need to punish British supporters on their own. They could trust the revolutionary state to do it for them. But, in the early years of the conflict, that process had not yet begun, and revolutionary committees were unable to contain the most belligerent partisans among them.

The outbreak of war in Lexington and Concord not only emboldened violent partisans; it also put what remained of New York's colonial government on the defensive. The colonial Assembly adjourned on April 3, 1775, and was scheduled to reconvene the next month. Although nobody knew it at the time, it would never meet again. When news of the battles arrived, Lieutenant Governor Colden decided to prorogue it until June for fear of what it might do if it convened when anti-British sentiment ran so high.[84] However, popular anger only grew over 1775 as committees expanded and violent insurgents became more active. As a result, Colden and Governor William Tryon prorogued the Assembly nine times between May and December. Tryon and the governor's council even retreated to ships in New York Harbor because the province had grown so hostile to British authority. From aboard ship, the governor called for new elections, which happened in January 1776.[85] But if Tryon thought it unwise to convene the Assembly in

1775, it was even more dangerous to do so early the next year. By January, soldiers from the Continental army under General Charles Lee had arrived in New York City to begin preparing the city's defenses against an expected British invasion. The newly elected Assembly never convened. The governor prorogued it twice in 1776, but doing so was only a formal recognition of what was already clear to everyone in the province: royal government was crumbling in New York.[86]

As colonial government collapsed, New Yorkers struggled to establish new legal institutions to replace the old order. The provincial committees and congresses proved to be disorganized and often feeble structures that did not form a coherent legal system. Indeed, the Provincial Congress regularly failed to gather a quorum. For instance, the second Provincial Congress sat from December 1775 to May 1776, but it convened for only six weeks over those five months. During the rest of the session, the delegates appointed twelve men to sit as the Committee of Safety, with a quorum being just seven delegates.[87] But the Committee of Safety could not even gather that many, and it too often failed to muster a quorum, although it occasionally convened anyway. The Provincial Congress, the only colonywide body coordinating revolutionary mobilization throughout the province, could not even bring together seven delegates.[88]

That small group, moreover, had no enforcement mechanisms such as courts or justices of the peace. It relied primarily on local committees to implement its resolutions, and those committees had emerged unevenly throughout the province. Some regions had many committees at both the town and the county levels, while others had few such groups, thereby creating an environment with highly variable levels of enforcement.[89] Congress occasionally appointed its own commissioners and subcommittees to go out into the field to enforce specific policies such as jailing British sympathizers and redistributing their property. But such commissioners required the active assistance of ordinary people. Indeed, New Yorkers redistributed so much property precisely because so many people came forward to help a weak central authority implement that policy. But, without help from local committees and individuals, the Congress and its commissioners would have achieved very little. At that chaotic time in 1775 and 1776, it is little wonder that aggressive partisans acted with impunity. The revolutionary infrastructure was far too weak and disorganized to form a coherent legal system or even one capable of coordinating revolutionary action.

By the spring of 1776, no settled legal system existed in New York.[90] The colonial Assembly had not met for almost a year, and it was so clearly at an end that after March the governor no longer bothered to continue proroguing it. Perhaps he knew that, even if it convened, neither he nor his Council could work effectively with it since they had fled to British ships. Colonial courts throughout the province met for the last time in April and May, and George Washington arrived in New York City to take over command of the troops preparing the city's defenses.[91]

This volatile time not only left New Yorkers without a settled legal system; it also raises problems of terminology for the modern researcher. Insofar as New York had any institutional presence, it was no longer a colony because royal structures had crumbled. But it also lacked the coherence and established authority that the word *state* implies. The following chapters, therefore, refer to New York as a *province* or a *revolutionary state* and call its institutions a *revolutionary regime*. Doing so stresses the provisional nature and loose connections among the various committees and the Provincial Congress that emerged in the chaos of a popular uprising. But, whatever one calls New York and its committees and congresses, the critical underlying problem remained the same. Royal government had failed, while revolutionary institutions remained weak, disorganized, and often ignored by many aggressive insurgents. New Yorkers would have to rebuild their legal system and do so in such a way that ordinary people would accept the feeble authority of a revolutionary regime.

The conditions in Tryon County by the middle of 1776 highlight the challenges that New Yorkers as a whole were facing. Committees there had slowly come together and grown bolder before ultimately attacking the county's most prominent defenders of royal government. As an instance of revolutionary mobilization, they had succeeded. Extralegal groups had united to arrest the royal sheriff and force one of the most powerful landlords in the colony to flee. But the uprising had only dismantled the old order. The people of Tryon County and New York more generally still had to develop a new legal system. Now that colonial government was at an end, now that the landlord had fled the great house, how would New Yorkers develop a new order in its place?

CHAPTER TWO

Confronting Disorder

New York's revolutionary legal system took root in the violence and disorder of military invasion. By the middle of 1776, the colonial government had collapsed, leaving a province without traditional legal structures such as courts. The British invasion in July turned this unstable environment into a terrifying place: the provisional government was on the run; battles raged between British and Continental forces; sick and wounded troops needed care; and thousands of refugees fled in every direction, often with little more than the clothes on their backs. War had come to New York in all its ugliness and destruction.

This chapter analyzes how, as the British occupation began, New Yorkers came to trust a weak provisional government. The leading edge of that process was an ideological police force called the Committee for Detecting and Defeating Conspiracies. Created by the Provincial Convention, the Committee tracked down hundreds of suspected British sympathizers and, without trials, jailed them in New York or sent them to other provinces. At a time without courts, a legislature, a governor, or a constitution, the Committee represented one of the few ways in which New Yorkers encountered central legal authority. Moreover, without those structures, the feeble Provincial Convention struggled to meet basic public needs such as providing personal safety. To overcome this weakness and make good on its claims to authority, the Convention and its Committee on Conspiracies needed the active assistance of ordinary people. The Committee generated that support for revolutionary authority because its actions resonated powerfully with a frightened population facing military invasion. Many New Yorkers came forward to help the Committee by reporting suspicious activity or delivering up prisoners whom the Committee then dispatched to New Hampshire, Pennsylvania, and Massachusetts. Through this harsh enforcement, the Committee developed a sense of mutuality—of common purpose—between New Yorkers and the people who claimed to govern them. At the same time, its jailings and removals intimidated potential enemies and drove them underground, where it proved difficult to organize a counterrevolution. In this paradoxical way, the Committee started to consolidate the new order: it drew in supporters while intimidating enemies and making it very dangerous to oppose the uprising openly.

It might appear odd to claim that an insurgent Committee that dispensed with trials and ignored other traditional procedures would form the basis of New York's independent legal system. After all, historians often point to constitutional conventions—either those of the states or that of the federal government—as America's foundational legal moments. But the upheaval of the British invasion marked a critical new beginning for New Yorkers. It created the social conditions in which ordinary people embraced the aggressive, partisan institutions of a revolutionary regime. In particular, the invasion terrified New Yorkers and made them eager to suppress Loyalism. Even if someone was not a strong supporter of independence, he might still welcome the Committee as a way to contain the chaos that threatened to overwhelm the province. In that volatile time, New Yorkers reached out to the Committee in a way that laid the foundation for a new legal order.

The breakdown of New York's colonial government ushered in a period of tremendous instability. By mid-1776, even before the British invaded, New York's legislature had stopped meeting, its courts had ceased convening, and its governor had fled to a British ship in New York Harbor.[1] Local committees then emerged in a legal environment without clear jurisdictional lines.[2] The only institution that recalled colonywide government was the Provincial Congress, which changed its name to the Provincial Convention when it adopted the Declaration of Independence in July 1776.[3]

At the same time that formal legal structures collapsed and revolutionary institutions emerged, an imminent British invasion threatened the province. In June 1776, George Washington was positioning defenses in New York City in advance of the attack that everybody knew was coming. In a letter to John Hancock, the president of the Continental Congress, Washington explained that he had received reports that British troops had already embarked from Halifax, Nova Scotia, for New York City:[4] "[This intelligence] added to a thousand incidental circumstances . . . leaves not a doubt upon my mind but that troops are hourly expected at the Hook [i.e., Sandy Hook]."

To make matters worse, a secret network of British sympathizers was operating in advance of the assault. Washington could not learn exactly how these people moved, or how they shared intelligence on the strength and deployment of Continental troops. He found this shadowy network "more easy to perceive than describe."[5] Nevertheless, he anticipated a British attack aided by a nebulous group of local supporters. Moreover, New York's colonial legal system had failed, leaving the province without settled institutions to confront such challenges.

In that environment, discovering Loyalist schemes grew urgent because they would prepare the ground for a British attack. Even a few indiscreet words were cause for concern since they suggested that the speaker knew some secret information about the invasion. For instance, in June, a Continental army officer was on a ferry from New York City to Paulus Hook in New Jersey. Another passenger on the ferry, Samuel Witten, said that he believed the British would land troops on Long Island and destroy New York City by bombardment. The comments alarmed the officer, who took Witten into custody and sent him to Washington for interrogation.[6] Witten claimed that he had been "in liquor, and spoke something too free." And, in any event, he had only expressed his opinion about how the British would invade and knew nothing of the actual plans.[7] A sense of fearful anticipation prevailed, one in which even offhanded comments by an inebriated ferry passenger deserved Washington's attention.

At that tense moment on the eve of an invasion, New Yorkers demanded that the provisional government act against British sympathizers. In June, the local committee in Salem (Westchester County) wrote to the Provincial Congress because its members faced so many Loyalists they were unsure how to proceed against them. The Loyalists were numerous and "determined not to comply with nor adopt the doings of the [Provincial] Congress." The Salem committee tried to force Loyalists to put up bonds for their good behavior. But it had been unable to enforce the terms of the bonds. Suspects just left town, sometimes taking their property with them, which made it impossible to satisfy the bonds by seizing suspects' goods. The committee struggled to confront all these British sympathizers, which, it declared, "has been our whole business ever since we have been formed as a Committee."[8] Containing Loyalists' influence had become a popular priority, and the committee reached out to the provisional government for help in addressing that problem.

The suppression of Loyalists gained particular urgency because many New Yorkers believed that pro-British plots threatened their lives. In June, committees for the towns of New Windsor and Newburgh (Ulster County) had become so concerned about Loyalists that they held a joint meeting to consider the problem and write to the Provincial Congress for assistance. Two militia officers also attended the meeting to give their advice on "the alarming situation" they found themselves in. After discussing their circumstances, they concluded: "[Our enemies] are secretly arming and preparing to surprise [us] and take our lives." They asked the Provincial Congress for gunpowder and ammunition so that they could defend themselves against their Loyalist neighbors.[9] Many New Yorkers believed that Loyalists were joining together into an armed force that would wreak havoc in the province. That danger heightened popular concern about Loyalist schemes because failing to act might cost New Yorkers their lives.

Events the following month in Dutchess County, just across the Hudson River from New Windsor and Newburgh, confirmed the fears about Loyalist plots. In July, Egbert Benson, the chairman of the Dutchess County committee and later attorney general of New York, reported to the Provincial Convention that "a dangerous insurrection" had just occurred in the county. Small groups of Tories had stolen weapons before uniting in such force that supporters of independence had barely managed to defeat their plans. They disarmed some enemies, but the rest were still "skulking in woods," menacing the entire county. Benson and the committee found themselves nearly overwhelmed: "[The] number of delinquents in this affair is so great that we are at a loss how to proceed."[10] New Yorkers felt themselves surrounded by Loyalists who might descend on them from the woods at any moment.

Some New Yorkers did not bother to write to the Provincial Congress to ask for help in confronting Loyalists. Riots in New York City in June demonstrated how some people just took the law into their own hands to punish British sympathizers. Mobs hunted down suspected Loyalists, stripped them, and rode them on rails. If the victims fell off, the mobs would kick and drag them down the street until they were bloodied and covered in grime. At night another mob led a group of Tories on a candlelit procession, pushing their heads into the flames to burn their faces.[11] One participant exulted that these "Grand Toory [*sic*] Rides" had intimidated enemies and that, after days of violence, "there is hardly a toory face to be seen this morning."[12] Aggressive New Yorkers assaulted the Loyalists whom they thought were plotting against them. Rather than write to the Provincial Congress to demand assistance, these partisans attacked their enemies in the street.

The Provincial Congress struggled to convince these violent insurgents to stop taking matters into their own hands. It realized that it could not compel obedience to its authority; the province lacked courts, constables, and other officials who might have punished rioters in more peaceful times.

Instead, Congress promised to confront Loyalists in the hope that such pledges would persuade New Yorkers to stop rioting. It resolved: "[In order] to urge the warm friends of liberty to decency and good order, this Congress assures the public that effectual measures shall be taken to secure the enemies of American liberty."[13] But it had little time to make good on that promise before British ships appeared off the coast two weeks later. Nevertheless, the resolution suggested a counterintuitive but critical point: by taking vigorous action against Loyalists, Congress might actually promote stability or, as the resolution called it, "decency and good order." A promise to root out political enemies might appear today as a sign of disorder or as evidence of the erosion of law. But in fact such assurances suggest how the revolutionary regime ultimately restrained popular violence and brought aggressive partisans under its authority. By confronting Loyalists, it demonstrated to New Yorkers that they need not take it on themselves to punish enemies. Instead, they came to realize that revolutionary institutions would do it for them. Partisan enforcement thus proved to be a stabilizing influence by persuading "the warm friends of liberty" to stop assaulting Loyalists in the street and instead allow the provisional government to deal with British sympathizers.

As British troops landed in early July, the invasion turned the suppression of Loyalists into a paramount concern for New Yorkers and their fledgling government. The British chased George Washington and the Continental army through Long Island, Manhattan, Harlem Heights, and Westchester and then south into New Jersey. These running battles caused tremendous physical destruction, particularly in the southern part of the province. Both armies sent out foraging parties that commandeered livestock and grain, ripped fences out of the ground for firewood, and took from inhabitants whatever else the soldiers thought they needed. The invasion also affected areas beyond the actual fighting as New Yorkers had to care for sick and wounded troops. Moreover, militia units were often deployed far from home, leaving many towns without local defenses.[14]

At the same time, refugees fled in all directions. They had been leaving New York City for months before the British attacked, leaving it largely depopulated. Although the exact number of refugees is impossible to determine, most estimates put it at about twenty thousand people fleeing in advance of the invasion.[15] There was also a reverse migration of colonists pouring into the city to seek the protection of the British army. The migration toward the British only increased in September 1776, once the British had driven out Washington, captured New York City, and secured the harbor.[16] After fleeing New York City for Kingston, a printer described late

1776 and early 1777 as "a sea of tyrannic violence and rapine."[17] New Yorkers were suffering the devastation, forced migration, and terror of military invasion. Even before this disorder erupted, many New Yorkers had feared that Loyalist plots threatened their lives, and some had reached out to the provisional government for help. But now Loyalists could organize under the protection of British arms and take advantage of the chaos of war to launch counterrevolutionary attacks throughout the province.

During this upheaval, the Provincial Convention sought some way to stop Loyalists from aiding Britain. The delegates to the Convention, like other New Yorkers, ran for their lives. They retreated north, and, on September 21, the day a fire burned one-fourth of the homes in New York City, the members found "themselves reduced to the great laws of self-preservation." Britain and its Loyalist allies were plotting to destroy the province, and previous attempts had failed "to detect and suppress such iniquitous practices and conspiracies" that threatened independence. To that end, the Convention created the Committee for Detecting and Defeating Conspiracies—or, to call it by its full name, the committee for "enquiring into, detecting and defeating all conspiracies which may be formed in this State, against the liberties of America."[18] The Convention appointed John Jay, William Duer, Charles DeWitt, Zephaniah Platt, Leonard Gansevoort, and Nathaniel Sackett as the Committee. Individual members, however, mattered little in how the Committee operated. Over the following nine months, the Convention added and removed members; it reorganized the Committee as a Commission. But those changes did not alter how it implemented its expansive powers. The resolution authorized the Committee to arrest suspects, seize their papers, and generally "do every act and thing whatsoever, which may be necessary" to defeat conspiracies against American independence. To carry out this broad emergency power, the Committee could call out the militia in any town or county and raise up to 220 of its own troops.[19]

The Convention also envisioned the Committee on Conspiracies as presiding over local committees. The September 21 resolutions ordered those local groups to send to the Committee on Conspiracies "all such information as they shall receive, relating to any machinations and conspiracies against this State."[20] It is worth noting what the Committee did not have to do. It had no procedural restrictions such as grand or petty juries; it did not have to obtain warrants or writs before acting; it did not have to meet any minimum evidentiary standard for proving conspiracy. Its expansive authority, supported by armed force, represented the regime's frantic effort to prevent disorder from overwhelming society.[21]

In the confusion that followed the invasion, the Committee had broad effects that nobody anticipated. For months, New Yorkers had been trying to thwart Loyalist plots, and some had reached out to the Provincial Convention for help doing so. Others had ignored the Convention and assaulted British sympathizers in the street. But, after the invasion, those Loyalist plots gained the support of British arms, and all the worst popular fears of violence and devastation were coming to pass. The Committee thus emerged in a society that wanted an ideological police force to find British sympathizers before they organized on behalf of the invading army. Its partisan mission resonated with a frightened public, and New Yorkers came forward to help enforce its commands. In this way, it generated popular support for revolutionary authority. It began to strengthen the provisional government by drawing in supporters and convincing them that they could rely on the regime to confront Loyalists.

Soon after its creation, the Committee signaled to New Yorkers that it would take aggressive action against British sympathizers. On October 17, it met in Fishkill, about seventy miles north of Manhattan on the east bank of the Hudson River. It declared that "persons of known probity and attachment to the American cause" had named "the most disaffected persons" in Dutchess County.[22] From those anonymous informants, it had discovered "divers [*sic*] treasonable conspiracies" to enlist men in the king's army.[23] It also learned that the former royal governor William Tryon had aided the plots. The involvement of a powerful patron made "it absolutely necessary and expedient" that the "notoriously disaffected persons" be moved to another province where they could not communicate with other Loyalists or the British army. To that end, the Committee ordered 112 residents of Dutchess County deported to Exeter, New Hampshire.[24] It conducted no trials, and its only source of evidence was the anonymous denunciations.

New Yorkers welcomed the large-scale removal of suspects as a crucial step against Britain and its supporters. Although the October 17 order was not the first time during the war that New Yorkers removed dissidents, it was the largest single removal, and the Committee acknowledged how desperate New Yorkers had become.[25] It declared that the province "is now actually invaded by a powerful Army, now in possession of its capital" and moving north into Westchester County.[26] Moreover, the province lacked regular courts to try prisoners for their offenses. Such circumstances left the Committee no choice but to remove Loyalists until "such times as proper courts shall be instituted in this State for the due trial and punishment" of those imprisoned.[27] These justifications suggest that the Committee believed that New Yorkers—particularly the Convention and local committees—might reject such a drastic move. It feared that some might object to a policy that separated families, dispensed with trials, and detained prisoners abroad. But a society under military occupation whose legal system had collapsed had no other choice. Thus, insurgents on the Committee knew that removing suspects was an aggressive policy. Yet they believed that New Yorkers would accept these deportations as the only way to prevent Loyalists from organizing themselves into regiments or otherwise helping the occupying army.

The Committee's sense of its own authority proved prescient. Just as anticipated, New Yorkers accepted its sweeping actions as people came forward to ask for the regime's assistance in stopping Loyalist conspiracies. On October 21, less than a week after the Committee removed Loyalists from Dutchess, the Albany County committee wrote to the Provincial Convention to plead for help. The committee warned: "Every district in this county is crowded with disaffected persons, the woods are full of them." The enemies had become more brazen. Not only were they breaking into houses at night, but they were also robbing people of guns, blankets, and other provisions, often in broad daylight on the open road. People in Albany County were convinced that the Tories committing these crimes were only waiting for the militia to be called away before they would "fall upon the remainder of us." The committee begged for some assistance in "this serious and alarming situation." And, as if to underline just how urgent the threat was, the committee would soon send "about fifty prisoners" to the Convention in Fishkill "to be left to your direction."[28] Although the committee in Albany did not know what to do with the prisoners, the regime did. The Committee on Conspiracies received the suspects and immediately deported them to Exeter on October 29.[29] Frightened, besieged New Yorkers, such as those in Albany County, were starting to realize that they could trust the regime and its Committee to address the problem of Loyalists.[30]

The Committee's vigorous enforcement resonated with New Yorkers. Even before the British attack on the province, local committees searched for ways to defeat Loyalist plots. Once the invasion spread disorder and violence, that desire only grew, and New Yorkers leaped at the chance to remove dangerous suspects. They rushed forward to turn their prisoners over to the Committee, which then moved the suspects to other provinces. Between October 11 and November 8, the Committee removed at least 252 people: 219 to Exeter and 33 to Pennsylvania.[31] New Yorkers brought prisoners to the Committee from Dutchess, Westchester, Albany, Orange, Ulster, and Suffolk Counties, all over those parts of the province not occupied by the British. The militia sent New Yorkers who had been captured fighting in Loyalist units.[32] County-level committees sent prisoners for such vague offenses as being "highly disaffected to the American cause."[33] The Westchester committee sent prisoners from the jail in White Plains to the Committee on Conspiracies, never bothering to explain the prisoners' offenses.[34] The Committee removed all these suspects without conducting any trials or further investigations. New Yorkers were eager to confront potential subversives, and they came forward to help the Committee deport Loyalists.

The Committee's aggressive anti-Loyalist policies helped build popular support for revolutionary authority. Indeed, New Yorkers embraced the Committee so quickly that, before long, they were reporting private conversations showing the speaker to be a Loyalist. In December 1776, Peter Noxon from Dutchess County appeared before the Committee to report a conversation that had happened in his kitchen. Noxon explained that John Maloyd had stopped by for a drink. He probably stayed for more than one because "he got a little in Liquor" and raised a toast "to Capt. Kane and his company."[35] It was a dangerous toast to make because at that moment John Kane was in jail, having been imprisoned for receiving a certificate of safe passage from British officers, known as a protection.[36] Maloyd quickly realized the gravity of his mistake. When Mrs. Noxon "said what is John Kane raising a Company," Maloyd "seemed to be a little embarras'd and said he meant a Kane in some other Country [i.e., county]." But it was too late. Maloyd had already revealed himself, as Noxon put it, "to be disaffected to the American Cause."[37] In a similar case from February 1777, Gilbert Bedell reported to the Committee that he had recently been with Thomas Carman when Carman "exclaimed against the Cause of America and damned the Congresses and Committees and drank a Health to King George."[38] Many were frightened that people such as Maloyd and Carman might assist the British army. New Yorkers reached out to revolutionary authority and invited it into their lives, even into their kitchens, to help protect them from dissidents.

The fear of Loyalist plots proved so great that New Yorkers were always on guard, monitoring conversations for hints that someone held subversive views. When they found such a person, they brought him to the Committee. In March 1777, James Campbell and a Lieutenant Lawrence appeared before the Commission on Conspiracies, one month after the Convention renamed the Committee as a Commission.[39] They reported that a group had been drinking toasts to George Washington and the success of American arms when James Goslin raised his own toast. Goslin had already come to the Committee's attention the previous fall as someone who might be disaffected, which could have made his drinking companions wary of him even before he spoke.[40] But any uncertainty vanished when he declared that he hoped Americans would never run short of powder and ball. If they did, he assured everyone, they would get "their Bellies full of it shortly." Campbell reported that Goslin also made "many other Traitorous Expressions against the American States, & spoke very disrespectfully of the Legislative Authority of this State." The Commission arrested him and put him in jail.[41]

Individuals such as Campbell and Noxon were not the only New Yorkers who came forward to denounce enemies of the cause. Local groups also rounded up suspects and hauled them before the Committee on Conspiracies. In December 1776, William Harper brought six prisoners from the local committee in Tryon County. He explained that the Tryon committee had examined them and found them "so notoriously disaffected that they ought in his Opinion to be prevented from going at large." Two of the prisoners, Henry Hough and George Ramsey, were "in particular dangerous, and desperate fellows." The Committee ordered all six men jailed in Poughkeepsie, one of the few places that had space to accommodate more prisoners.[42] Denunciations and jailings signaled to New Yorkers that they had an ally in their fight against British sympathizers. As they brought suspects before the Committee, they saw that revolutionary institutions worked for them and that central authority would address their urgent desire to suppress Loyalism.

New Yorkers also denounced enemies to settle old scores, ones that may have had little to do with a suspect's political beliefs. The case of John Kane suggests how this process occurred. This was the same Kane to whom John Maloyd raised a toast, leading to Maloyd's denunciation and imprisonment. But, long before the war, Kane had been a tenant of Beverly Robinson's, one of New York's largest landowners whose holdings were primarily in southern Dutchess County. As far back as the mid-1760s, Kane enjoyed a privileged status as a loan agent to other tenants on behalf of Robinson and lenders from New York City. Such a close association made Kane extraordinarily unpopular when Robinson and other landlords in the area tried to exert greater control over their property. The landlords' ejectment suits and efforts to modify the terms of leases caused a tenant uprising in 1766 that British regulars had to put down.[43]

Kane remained in the area over the following decade. When war broke out, he found himself harassed by various revolutionary committees. When a neighbor denounced him in December 1776, he admitted to the Committee on Conspiracies that he and the accuser "have been upon very bad Terms for a long Time."[44] The Committee interrogated and jailed him before other insurgents confiscated his personal property.[45] Later in the war, the legislature attainted and banished him.[46] Kane very likely was a British sympathizer, and he admitted to the Committee that he had received a protection from a

British officer.[47] But his Loyalism was probably not the only reason his neighbors denounced him. His close association with an overbearing landlord and his job as an agent of creditors made him a likely target for his neighbors' revenge. Consequently, New Yorkers might have denounced someone not only to thwart pro-British plots but also to settle a private vendetta that had begun long before the war.[48]

Nevertheless, the possibility that some denunciations arose from personal animosity should not obscure the broader context in which the Committee operated. The invasion, pro-British insurrections such as the one Egbert Benson described in Dutchess County, and groups hiding in the woods and stealing provisions were all menacing enough to cause real fear. At that time, New Yorkers reached out to the revolutionary regime and demanded that it find Loyalists to prevent them from threatening inhabitants. Every denunciation implied a call for action. The New Yorkers who reported conversations to the Committee and the local groups that sent prisoners to it implicitly called on revolutionary authority to intervene against those who might help the occupying army.[49] Therefore, a frightened public was making insistent demands on the provisional government. When the Committee responded—when it jailed and removed suspects who might help Britain overrun the province—it answered those demands and announced that revolutionary authority shared popular priorities.

The sense of common purpose proved crucial in connecting ordinary people to a revolutionary regime. New Yorkers from around the province reached out to the regime for help in preserving legal order and providing security against subversives, functions traditionally performed by state institutions such as courts. The Committee, in turn, met those popular demands when it removed and jailed Loyalists. By demanding that the Committee fulfill public responsibilities, New Yorkers treated it as an arm of the central state, and, by responding, it behaved like one. By providing basic state functions such as protection from enemies, the Committee started to generate popular acceptance of revolutionary authority.

Scholars have examined a similar process in other revolutionary societies where insurgent institutions gained popular acceptance. Insurgents in many different contexts have created shadow governments that, as one political scientist described them, "engage in statelike activities" such as organizing policing, administering justice, and performing other state functions. By meeting these basic needs, they lead the general, unaligned population to accept revolutionary authority, not because of any ideological affinity, but because that authority addressed important considerations in daily life.[50] Creating institutions that take the place of the state and resolve popular concerns has been a crucial step in establishing insurgent legal institutions. No insurgency succeeds exclusively on violence and intimidation.[51] By meeting elemental public needs, insurgents have persuaded others—many indifferent to the broader goals of the uprising—to accept revolutionary institutions and bring them to bear on the problems of daily life.[52]

The Committee on Conspiracies drove this expansion of insurgent authority in New York. In addition, popular engagement with the Committee was a mutually reinforcing process. New Yorkers invited revolutionary authority into their lives by denouncing suspects, and, when the Committee acted, that authority expanded and gained in public acceptance. At a time without courts, a legislature, or a constitution, the Committee had begun, albeit in a limited way, to behave like a state when it offered security against internal enemies and maintenance of legal order. New Yorkers—even unaligned ones—could thus welcome revolutionary authority to address problems of basic order and preserve themselves from destruction. Consequently, the Committee drew people toward revolutionary authority and convinced them that they could rely on the regime to address urgent public needs.

This process persisted into the spring of 1777 as New Yorkers continued monitoring one another's political views and bringing suspects before the Committee. In April 1777, John Maxfield appeared before the Commission on Conspiracies to describe what had happened a week earlier.[53] He and William Wilsey had been at a neighbor's house. He may have already suspected Wilsey of Loyalism because, when they started talking, he "pretended to be on the same side of the Question respecting the present Troubles," doing so "in hopes by that means to make some discovery." Wilsey fell into the trap and asked Maxfield "if he might depend upon him," and Maxfield assured him that he could. Wilsey admitted that he had personally delivered his son and provisions to one Henry Ostrom knowing that they were going "to the Enemy." He confided that he also intended to go himself. Maxfield denounced Wilsey to the Commission, which moved him from one jail to another for two months before he took an oath of allegiance and was released.[54]

Rather than goading Loyalists into revealing their views, other New Yorkers confronted enemies directly if something about them appeared suspicious. In January 1777, a militia officer encountered a man and a woman heading toward a mountain where Loyalists often hid. When the officer stopped them, he saw that the man "had on two under Waistcoats, one Waistcoat and Coat, & an over Coat, and in a Bundle a pair of Trowsers, and Clean Shirt." His presence in an area with many Loyalists and his layers of clothes all suggested that he was going to hide in the woods and change his appearance to avoid detection. When the officer questioned the two people, they "greatly prevaricated," so he arrested them and reported the incident to the Committee.[55] New Yorkers were working through the legal institutions of a provisional government. As they did so, they supported a weak provisional government and brought it to bear on matters of great public concern.

The Committee, however, did not only generate public support among panicked New Yorkers. Its actions also intimidated opponents. Its harsh anti-Loyalist measures frightened many British sympathizers into hiding their views rather than risk being reported as a disaffected person. The jailings and deportations did not eliminate Loyalism as a political view; such actions did not stop people from wanting Britain to prevail or convert them into strong supporters of independence. But the Committee's aggressive policies started to develop a legal environment that was extraordinarily hostile to Loyalism. That hostility grew over the duration of the war and culminated in the permanent dispossession and banishment of Loyalists. The Committee's actions—assisted by denunciations from New Yorkers—initiated that process by discouraging open opposition to the revolutionary regime. As a result, the Committee began to consolidate the new order, not only by drawing in supporters, but also by intimidating potential enemies and driving them underground.

These effects of revolutionary enforcement are often difficult to discern today. After all, one is searching for an inclination to silence, a desire among Loyalists not to reveal their beliefs. But in fact that reluctance did appear in New Yorkers' dissimulation and doublespeak. If two people—particularly strangers—fell into conversation, they would dance around Loyalism, hint at it with double entendres, and make vague references as they tried to find out where the other person stood. This dissembling reveals the consequences of anti-Loyalist policies and suggests how they frightened opponents into trying to keep their views to themselves. Those opponents did not all keep quiet. As discussed above, people such as Carmen and Maloyd felt emboldened to announce their views to anyone who would listen, often after raising a sociable glass or two. But many others were not as audacious in their support for Britain. With an aggressive, anti-Loyalist Committee deporting suspects and potential informants at taverns or even in a neighbor's kitchen, many British sympathizers learned to be cautious about what they said.

The fear of being denounced forced many Loyalists to hide their real beliefs rather than risk detection. Oliver Bailey reported one such incident to the Committee when a suspected Loyalist attempted to mask his true intentions. In January 1777, John Dusenbury of Westchester County had arrived at Bailey's house at 1:00 in the morning. He had a group of men with him who wanted to come in to warm themselves. They said that they were in the militia and that they were being deployed to the south. But Bailey was immediately suspicious because he had heard that Dusenbury "had been sent as a Tory to one of the Forts" along the Hudson River. He invited them in and became even more suspicious when Dusenbury asked for directions to two people's houses, "both of whom this deponent understood were Tories." Perhaps trying to gauge where Bailey stood, Dusenbury hinted that the group "wanted to go secure" and that, if Bailey "wou'd not expose them, they wou'd be friends to him hereafter." Dusenbury never indicated from what they wanted to be secure or to whom Bailey might expose them. But, at a time when hundreds of suspected Loyalists were in jail and removed to other provinces, he did not have to make his meaning explicit. Bailey had already concluded "from the whole of their Conversation and Conduct" that the entire group was "going to Join the Enemy." He gave them the directions they wanted, but, "the better to pass himself upon them as a friend," he told them that the road "led by the houses of three or four Whigs."[56] The two men were hiding their real purposes from one another—Dusenbury wanted directions to particular homes without saying why he was going there, and Bailey pretended to be a Loyalist.

Although Dusenbury never declared that he wanted to find his way to other Loyalists, even his oblique references revealed too much. After about an hour, he and the group left in the direction Bailey had sent them. As soon as they were out of sight, Bailey grabbed his gun and alerted local militiamen. They arrested part of the group before seeking reinforcements at a tavern where soldiers from New England were lodging. The party then went on to arrest the remainder of Dusenbury's men and turn the whole group over to the Committee, which jailed them in Fishkill.[57] By jailing such suspects, the Committee helped create an atmosphere where Loyalists like Dusenbury had to travel by night and speak in roundabout ways to avoid detection. The constant threat of denunciation—of being exposed, as Dusenbury put it—frightened Loyalists into trying to disguise their intentions from people who might turn them over to the Committee.[58]

Loyalists had to move from one safe house to another to escape the Committee's attention. But they occasionally misjudged their surroundings and, thinking they had found a like-minded person, spoke openly about their Loyalism. In July 1777, George Freligh of Dutchess County denounced two men who had mistakenly thought that he was the Loyalist contact who was to shelter them. Freligh testified before the Commission on Conspiracies that he had been at his mill when two strangers approached him and asked whether they could pasture their horses on his land. He agreed and began talking with one of the men, William Showers. He learned that they had just come from the north and asked Showers for news about British general John Burgoyne's march from Canada. Before answering, Showers asked "wether [*sic*] or not he [Freligh] was a True friend to the Old Father the King." Perhaps sensing a trap, Freligh dissembled and said only that "it was to [*sic*] hard a Question to answer in those Difficult Days." Showers, however, did not hesitate to declare that "he was True for the King as Ever Before" and that he would ask a few questions if Freligh "would be True to him." When Freligh assured him that he "Need not be Concerned," Showers admitted that he needed help getting his travel companion, Francis Hogal, "to the Regulars."[59]

Although he did not know it at the time, Showers had just made a terrible mistake. As a newspaper later reported, he had confused two people named George Freligh. He thought that he was talking to "a staunch Tory," but he was actually speaking with a Whig of the same name.[60] Bemused at Showers's poor judgment, Freligh agreed to help but warned him that he "must be very Crafty, Else he wo'd be Taken up." Freligh carried the ruse so far that he invited the two men to eat with him. Over the meal, and during a long discussion afterward, Hogal admitted that "he had been with Burgoyne & was now going to Bring intelegance [*sic*]" to the British in New York City. When he had heard enough, Freligh detained the two men and brought them before the Commission on Conspiracies, which confined them in the Poughkeepsie jail.[61] People such as Freligh and Bailey lied to Loyalists to lead them into making incriminating statements. Loyalists found themselves in an environment where it was dangerous to support Britain openly and a misstep could lead to jail or removal to another province. The Committee thus started to silence opponents and drive them underground where it was difficult to organize against the revolutionary regime.

Loyalists in that underground network faced tremendous challenges in trying to join together for their cause. The experiences of Enoch Crosby, a spy who worked on behalf of the provisional government, reveals how they went to great lengths to avoid being caught and hauled before the Committee. In the fall of 1776, Crosby came to the attention of the Committee on Conspiracies when the local committee in Westchester County recommended him as an able spy.[62] In his pension application after the war, Crosby described how over the next nine months, the Committee sent him on missions in Albany, Ulster, and Dutchess Counties to uncover Loyalist plots. His infiltration of Loyalist networks reveals the secrecy with which they had to operate. At a time when a spy such as Crosby infiltrated Loyalist groups, neighbors monitored one another's political views, farmers reported suspicious visitors, and the Committee jailed dissidents, Loyalists had little room to maneuver. They could not openly join together to advance their plans. Instead, they had to gather in remote places where it proved extraordinarily difficult to organize against independence.

Examining just one mission suggests how the fear of being discovered pushed Loyalists underground. In the fall of 1776, the Committee sent Crosby from Fishkill across the Hudson and into Ulster County, on the west side of the river. He traveled about ten miles inland to "a neighborhood of Loyalists" where the Committee had heard rumors that "a company was there raising for the British army." The Committee scheduled a rendezvous with Crosby back in Fishkill to report what he had found. Supplied with a fake pass, Crosby ingratiated himself with a group of people who planned to escape to the British and receive arms as a Loyalist unit. He spent a week hiding in a cave with the Loyalists, pretending to have joined their plan, before they decided to make their run south to British-occupied New York City. However, the Loyalists decided to begin moving before Crosby's scheduled rendezvous, forcing him to find a way to alert the Committee that the plan was afoot. He suggested to the Loyalists that they separate the night before their departure so that, if they got caught, they would not all be taken. The group agreed, and, once alone, Crosby tried to find a way of passing the intelligence to the Committee.[63]

Crosby did not have enough time to travel ten miles to the Hudson River and cross east to Fishkill. And he did not know anyone in that part of Ulster County to carry the message to. His only choice was finding a stranger he knew simply as Mr. Purdy. All he "knew of him was that the Tories called him a wicked rebel & said that he ought to die." He assumed that, if the conspirators hated this Purdy, then he must be someone he could trust. Mr. Purdy turned out to be Captain Silas Purdy, an officer in the Ulster County militia. Crosby told him everything—where the Loyalists were hiding, when they were leaving, what their route would be, where they would stop on the way—and Purdy promised to pass all the intelligence to the Committee. Crosby returned to the group in time to leave with them the following evening. In the middle of the first night, the Loyalists stopped at a safe house and hid in the barn. But, as day broke, they found themselves surrounded "by American troops" who arrested everyone, including Crosby to maintain his cover. The troops marched the Loyalists to Fishkill and confined them in a church that served as the jail. Crosby found that "near two hundred prisoners" were already there.[64] After he had spent just one day in jail, the

Committee summoned Crosby and told him to leave because it was not safe for him to remain among the other prisoners. They suggested that he lay low for a while, which he did by working as a cobbler on a nearby farm until John Jay arrived a few weeks later to send him on his next mission.[65]

Crosby's experiences suggest how the Committee began to stabilize the revolutionary order. It and its network of informants—from spies, to farmers, to militiamen—started to push Loyalists to the edges of public life, thereby limiting the field in which they could operate. Afraid of being discovered, they retreated to the woods, where they gathered in caves and moved by night from one safe house to another. And, as Crosby's successful mission makes clear, even those precautions did not always protect British sympathizers from being arrested. Thus, New Yorkers began to stabilize the new order by driving enemies underground, where they organized only with great difficulty and at the risk of being jailed or removed to another province.

Such aggressive enforcement started to develop popular trust in revolutionary authority. Suffering the fear and violence of an invasion, New Yorkers came forward to help the Committee jail Loyalists and remove them to other provinces. This punishment signaled to New Yorkers that they could rely on the regime to confront those who might help Britain overrun the province. At the same time, the Committee's harsh policies frightened many Loyalists and drove them underground, where they struggled to organize a counterrevolution. The Committee bolstered New York's legal order by drawing in supporters—linking them to the regime in a sense of common purpose—and making it very dangerous to support Britain publicly.

This process continued throughout the war as insurgents drew in supporters and drove off enemies. Nevertheless, although that broader process continued, the Committee's policies did not last. The Committee and the Provincial Convention came to realize that large-scale jailings and removals were unsustainable. The provisional government proved too feeble to keep large numbers of people imprisoned in New York or detained indefinitely abroad. Moreover, the prisoners sent to other provinces did not patiently abide by their detention. They insisted on their innocence and looked for ways to return to New York. The regime's weakness and the agitation of prisoners made it impossible to continue such actions. Therefore, although the Committee started a process of rebuilding legal order that continued through the war, its jailings and removals proved short-lived.

Problems with these policies began to appear by the winter of 1776–77. In December 1776, Mesech Weare, the president of the Council of New Hampshire, wrote a draft letter to the Committee. In it he explained that "great uneasiness prevails" among the prisoners as they insisted on their innocence and complained about "being sent here without an examination at home." He acknowledged that "the confusion and unavoidable hurry" of the previous months may have caused some innocent people to be arrested inadvertently. But he believed that the time had come for "an impartial inquiry" into the accusations that would allow innocent prisoners to go free. He also suggested that the prisoners themselves were not the only ones complaining about mistreatment. The people of New Hampshire found it unfair that New Yorkers sent suspects "who appear poor and naked" to endure a long New England winter. This treatment, along with the denial of any chance to contest the accusations, "has had considerable influence among the people in these parts in their [the prisoners'] behalf."[66] Indefinite detention without any inquiry bred resentment among the prisoners themselves. Moreover, the manner in which New Yorkers treated these suspects—sending them to another jurisdiction with little more than the clothes on their backs to await trial at some later, unspecified date—encouraged sympathy for the same people they wanted to isolate as dangerous subversives.

Other prisoners echoed this frustration at being sent abroad without due process. In January 1777, seven suspects held in Springfield, Massachusetts, petitioned New York's Provincial Convention, praying "that they may be sent for and Tried" rather than remain abroad any longer. The Convention referred the matter to the Committee on Conspiracies, which rejected all the petitions. The Committee resolved that the prisoners in Springfield "and all others in the like predicament" must wait until "proper Courts of Judicature shall be Established in this State for the Trial of offences." Only then will they "receive a fair & impartial Trial for the several misdemeanors with which they respectively stand charg'd." Meanwhile, the Committee ordered that "no greater Liberty be allow'd them than what humanity may require."[67] It refused to bring suspected Loyalists back to New York because, without a legal system, they might act with impunity.

Promises of a trial and humane treatment, however, did little to assuage prisoners' anger. In February 1777, the New Hampshire Committee of Safety reminded the Committee on Conspiracies that it had sent two previous letters about the prisoners and received no response. During that time, the prisoners had continued to complain "of the hardship of being sent from their homes without trial, and make solemn Protestation of their innocence." The letter insisted that, if the Committee on Conspiracies wanted the suspects to remain in New Hampshire, it "send some particular charge of their crimes" to stop them from claiming that they had done nothing wrong.[68] The suspects had grown insistent and made it impossible for the Committee to keep them in New England indefinitely.

These restive prisoners ultimately forced New Yorkers to change their policies toward Loyalists and reverse many of the Committee's actions. During the winter and early spring of 1777, many of those sent abroad did not simply demand a trial. Instead, they asked the states holding them for permission to return to New York, and prisoners soon began coming home. In January 1777, the local committee in Albany County acknowledged that many people sent abroad "for their evil practices against our present and Justifiable measures have by false Insinuations and Mal practices [*sic*]" received permission to leave their confinement. Their return was entirely unwelcome since it would "again Strenghten [*sic*] the Hands of opposition." The Albany committee resolved that any prisoner who returned without first receiving permission from New York's Convention or from the Albany committee should be jailed.[69] As they came home, the prisoners defeated the Committee's efforts and forced New Yorkers to find other ways of addressing Loyalist plots.

The Committee realized that returning prisoners represented a grave threat to the regime's authority. In the opening months of the war, the regime had started to establish trust with New Yorkers by confronting enemy sympathizers. New Yorkers had come forward to help the Committee and the Provincial Convention enforce aggressive, anti-Loyalist policies. But the returning prisoners threatened to destroy that sense of common purpose and make the regime appear unworthy of popular support. The Committee acknowledged this danger when it wrote to the Convention on March 4, 1777. Many prisoners "have left the places they were sent to, and are either gone off to the enemy, lurking privately about the country, or appear openly in contempt of the authority of the State." The Committee also received petitions every day asking to return "to submit to a legal trial, or become subjects to the State." While it had not acted, "excepting in a few instances and upon special circumstances," the members requested "some general plan" for confronting the threat of Loyalist infiltration.[70] The suspects who returned had reinforced the Loyalists hiding in the woods. Moreover, everyone who came back represented an open rebuke to the regime and its weak institutions. By returning without permission, the prisoners flouted revolutionary authority and made it appear contemptible.

However, despite the danger of losing popular trust, the Convention managed to alter these policies before revolutionary authority eroded even further. It developed a series of ad hoc solutions to the problems Loyalists posed. As New Yorkers saw it, the challenge was that they lacked the institutional capacity to maintain their policies. They never developed any great sympathy for the Loyalists they jailed and sent abroad. They did not change course because they decided they had been unjust in their treatment of British sympathizers. They still believed, and would continue to believe throughout the war, that they could never enjoy stable legal order if they failed to address the threat Loyalists posed. But, by the spring of 1777, they realized that their first response was institutionally infeasible; they did not have enough jails and guards to keep large numbers of prisoners where they put them. Thus, the same people who jailed and deported Loyalists in the fall of 1776 began to cast about for new solutions.

The Convention's first response was to bring back some suspects before they all returned on their own. On March 7, just three days after the Committee's letter requesting a plan, the Convention passed an "act of grace" that empowered the Committee to send for disaffected people held in other states. As New Yorkers understood it, the term *disaffected people* referred to those who had expressed pro-British views, such as John Maloyd and William Wilsey. Once the prisoners returned, the Committee would administer an oath swearing that they "will bear true faith and allegiance to the State of New-York." Suspects had a week to decide whether they wanted to take the oath. If they did, the Committee would release them. If they refused, it would order them "to repair, with their families, apparel and household furniture, to the city of New-York, or some other place in the possession of the enemy." If they disobeyed that command, it must jail them or otherwise treat them "as the open enemies of the State." The act applied only to those held on a suspicion of disaffection and exempted those "who are charged" with enlisting men for the British, accepting a commission from them, supplying them with provisions, passing intelligence, or taking up arms against the United States.[71] Those suspects would remain in other provinces while the Convention sent militia detachments to retrieve the disaffected persons. Just five months after deporting suspects en masse, the regime started to recall them from abroad.

However, the first returning prisoners reminded the Committee why it had sent the suspects away in the first place. Many of those returning were in fact Loyalists, and they treated the act of grace as a chance to come home and oppose independence. One such enemy sympathizer, John Halsted, appeared before the Committee and refused to take the oath. As the act of grace required, the Committee gave him time to reconsider before he would face any punishment. But he did not spend the following week searching his soul to locate his true loyalties. Instead, as the Committee learned, he "publickly Declar'd his Attachment to the King of Great Britain & openly avowed his purpose of taking up Arms against his Country & fighting thro' Blood."[72] The Committee ordered him to jail, but he was only the first of many returning prisoners who wanted to rejoin the fight against independence. Two days the Committee dealt with Halsted, five more prisoners returned and "Declar'd their Determination not to take the Oath of Allegiance." The Committee lost patience with these recusants. It pointed out that, according to the preamble of the act of grace, the exiles had petitioned the Convention for permission to return. Yet, once back in New York, they "most Contumaciously Refus'd" to obey the Convention, preferring instead to take advantage of New Yorkers' grace in letting them come home. In the face of such duplicity, the Committee abolished the grace period. Any suspects who refused the oath when it was offered would "be immediately Committed to Jail."[73] Feeble, but still surrounded by enemies, the regime was struggling to address the problem of Loyalists in a way that it could actually enforce.

As the regime groped for a solution, imprisonment soon proved unenforceable as well. Throughout late winter and early spring 1777, the Committee's actions had filled many jails, and there was little room for people such as Halsted. Meeting in Fishkill, the Committee ordered a militia detachment to the town to guard the jail. It also tried to move some of the prisoners from Fishkill, noting: "Our Guard here is very weak and the number of persons confined in the Guard House great." To make matters worse, smallpox started to spread in April, forcing the Committee to leave for Poughkeepsie to protect "the security of our guards and prisoners."[74] The regime seemed to be running out of options. New Yorkers desperately wanted to stop Loyalist plots. But the regime could not send disaffected people abroad because they would return and rejoin Loyalist ranks; nor could it put more suspects in overcrowded and diseased jails. New Yorkers faced the same urgent need for protection from Loyalists as they had for months, but the possibilities for resolving that problem were disappearing.

For all the enforcement problems that the "act of grace" caused, it still applied only to some Loyalist prisoners. It covered only disaffected people and exempted prisoners accused of particular acts of Loyalism. Thus, after having failed to implement a policy toward disaffected people, the Convention turned its attention to these other exempted prisoners. In addressing these suspects, it relied on the only adjudicative process that had survived the colony's collapse: courts-martial.[75] On April 1, it acknowledged that it had already passed resolutions "for the Trial of Treasons, and other offenses against this State" but that it had been unable to enforce any of those earlier resolutions. It now believed that military courts would help punish four of the most egregious Loyalist crimes. The resolution specified that anyone captured outside enemy lines while supplying the British, enlisting soldiers for them, spying, or passing intelligence would be subject to "a General Court Martial of the Continental Army, or of the Militia of this State." If the court-martial found a defendant guilty, it could impose any penalty, including death. The resolution noted, however: "The sentence shall not be executed until approved by this Convention, or a future Legislature of this State." The resolution would be in effect only until July 1, by which time the Convention believed that a new government would exist to try the suspects in civilian court.[76] That expectation, like so many others that anticipated legal stability to be just a few months away, proved premature. But in April the Convention did not foresee the troubles that awaited in the summer. Instead, in the wake of previous failures, it once again shifted course and tried a new approach by sending particular Loyalist crimes to military courts.

By granting a limited jurisdiction to the military and reviewing all sentences, the Convention tried to approximate the full trials that the regime still could not conduct. The first court-martial under the new resolution took place in Peekskill and resulted in a death sentence against Simon Mabee for spying. On April 16, just over two weeks after empowering the military to hear cases, the Convention confirmed the sentence and ordered Mabee to be executed.[77] Other cases soon followed as militia officers convened courts-martial in Albany, Fort Montgomery, and other places.[78] A judge advocate presided over the proceedings, while a panel of officers—usually eleven or twelve—sat as "members of the court." The court read the charges against the defendants, allowed them to enter a plea and testify on their own behalf, examined evidence (such as proceedings from local committees), and heard witness testimony. It then sent its decision up to the Convention, which reviewed the record before deciding whether to confirm the sentence.[79] In one instance, the Convention reviewed three death sentences imposed for enlisting men in the British army and other offenses. It confirmed the first two sentences but pardoned the third man, Job Babcock, for "being a person of weak mind." The members of the Convention offered clemency because they thought "it their duty in some cases, by extending mercy to mitigate the rigor of justice."[80] In other cases, the Convention reduced death sentences to fines or imprisonment.[81] Through these trials and mandatory appeals, courts-martial introduced some formal due process into an otherwise chaotic, extrajudicial effort to punish Loyalists.

But military courts represented only part of a much broader and much less successful attempt to address the problem of Loyalism. Those courts had only a limited jurisdiction, while the Committee and the Convention continued struggling to manage the suspects who came back to New York.[82]

Some returned without permission, and others did so under the pretense of the "act of grace" only to refuse to take the oath of allegiance. Many of the returning suspects joined the underground network of Loyalists. The Committee's policies had proved unenforceable, and the coda to its work came in June 1777 when the Council of Safety ordered it to bring back all the prisoners still held in New England.[83] The revolutionary government then restructured the Committee in February 1778. Instead of a single Committee, boards would sit in every county to prevent conspiracies.[84] Although the new boards met intermittently during the war, they were never as influential as the single Committee had been in late 1776 and early 1777, nor did the several boards ever enjoy the popular resonance that the Committee did over that time.[85] In particular, by the middle of 1777, New Yorkers faced increasing inflation and scarcity of basic goods, neither of which problems the Committee was in any position to resolve. Popular concerns thus grew beyond stopping Loyalist plots and, as a result, the Committee never again spoke to those concerns as fully as it had in the early months of the war.

Even though the Committee never regained its prominence, it had laid the foundation for rebuilding legal order. At a critical time, it started to draw supporters forward—those who wanted to stop Loyalists from helping the occupying army—and punish enemies. In doing so, it signaled to New Yorkers—many of whom had been taking the law into their own hands—that they could trust the regime to confront Loyalists. But, if that process was going to continue, if the consolidation was going to persist even after the Committee reversed its policies, then the provisional government had to find new ways of generating popular support.

A letter from the Albany County committee captures the predicament New Yorkers found themselves in by the spring of 1777. In April, the committee wrote to the Convention to explain that inhabitants in the county had recently uncovered yet another Loyalist plot. The culprits were starting to look familiar because many of them "have long since been considered as enemies to our cause, and as such have been treated." But that treatment had failed to stop them from pursuing "their hellish schemes." The Albany committee was unsure what to do: "Experience has taught us that banishing disaffected persons out of this State, to a neighbouring one, answers no good end; keeping them among us we are apprehensive will prove our ruin. Lenity [i.e., leniency], instead of having its due weight, is construed by those people in a different sense; they insinuate we are afraid to pursue more spirited measures." The Albany committee found itself in an impossible situation: "Our jails are full—if banished, they [Loyalists] are returned—punishment we can not [*sic*] inflict—among us they ought not to be."[86]

The committee's letter reminds historians that building a stable, independent state was not as simple as writing a new constitution. It was a highly contingent process, one in which New Yorkers did not always know how to overcome their urgent and constantly changing wartime challenges. Moreover, no one could be sure that the weak provisional government would find solutions that it could actually enforce. As the Albany letter suggests, the spring of 1777 was one such moment when the Convention reversed its policies and New Yorkers found themselves at an impasse. To break through, the Convention would have to find a new basis for addressing popular concerns and do so as Britain invaded the province for the second time in as many years.

CHAPTER THREE

A Bonanza of Tory Goods

New York's revolutionary government could easily have crumbled in the early years of the war. The Committee for Detecting and Defeating Conspiracies had made some gains in extending revolutionary authority. But, by the middle of 1777, as the British invaded the province for the second time in as many years, New Yorkers found themselves at a precarious moment. Devastation, forced migration, and growing material hardship plagued the province, while formal institutions such as courts still had not reconvened. Some New Yorkers, as they had done since the beginning of the war, did not wait for the provisional government to act and instead just took the law into their own hands to address these urgent problems. In such circumstances, New Yorkers might have failed to establish stable institutions. The turmoil of war and occupation—the extralegal action of mobs and committees—might have overwhelmed the feeble state. Indeed, many contemporaries made that point when they predicted that states like New York would collapse under their own confusion. But that did not happen, raising the question of how, rather than becoming mired in the disorder of their own uprising, New Yorkers managed to continue developing the authority of a revolutionary state.

New Yorkers overcame that challenge in surprising ways. Redistributing movable property generated popular support for the regime at a time when it desperately needed New Yorkers' active assistance to enforce its commands. One might assume that unsettling property rights could only weaken a legal system. But, in the context of war and occupation, property redistribution had counterintuitive effects. It was precisely the partisan attack on property that resonated with popular concerns and drew New Yorkers toward a revolutionary state.

We can see the paradoxical process of revolutionary state building in the experience of Bartholomew Crannell. In the early 1740s, Crannell moved from New York City to Poughkeepsie and soon developed the social connections and wealth that made him one of the most prominent people in town. He married Sarah Van Kleeck, one of six children in a locally influential family.[1] Bartholomew and Sarah had five daughters, three of whom were married before the war began. One daughter, Gertrude, married the Reverend John Beardsley, the rector of Christ's Church in Poughkeepsie, which was affiliated with the Church of England and was where Bartholomew was a vestryman.[2] Catherine, another daughter, married Gilbert Livingston, who belonged to one of the most influential families in the province, albeit a minor branch that did not inherit the family's vast estates.[3] A third daughter, Elizabeth, married Peter Tappen, a medical doctor in an area with few such professionals. He came from a family in nearby Kingston that traced its lineage to early Dutch settlers in Fort Orange (Albany).[4]

In addition to these family ties to prominent people, Crannell enjoyed high standing as one of the largest landowners in town. He owned almost two hundred acres in Poughkeepsie and the surrounding countryside, nearly all of it improved with houses, barns, mills, and outbuildings.[5] His holdings provided him with an income in rents, milling, and other enterprises that he supplemented by carrying on a successful law practice with Henry Livingston, Gilbert's father.[6] Regardless of the sources of his income, it was large enough on the whole to allow his family to live very well. His application to the Loyalist Claims Commission, an administrative body that the British government created to compensate Loyalists after the war, suggests the prosperity that he and his family enjoyed. It included affidavits attesting to his ample property, both real and personal. One deponent remembered in particular that his "House was well furnished, he had Waggons, Sleigh and a plentiful Stock of every kind."[7] Crannell went even further and itemized all the personal property that once filled his house and surrounding grounds. He had everything from pewter dishes to a wagon with spring seats, presumably to smooth the ride along rough country roads, spare millstones to "elegant Paintings with Frames," flax to a "Pleasure Sled."[8] Thus, by the 1770s, his property in land and personal goods, his profession, and his connections to the local church and prominent families all established him firmly as a local grandee.

However, in just a few years, the Revolution destroyed all the prosperity and status it had taken Crannell decades to cultivate. From the beginning of the conflict with Britain, he opposed all efforts at colonial mobilization.[9] As he recalled after the war, his Loyalism invited death threats and other harassments, forcing him to flee Poughkeepsie. He left his family and escaped to Orange County, where he thought he would bide his time until passions cooled. Perhaps his reputation preceded him because he was arrested in Goshen by a revolutionary committee. He was released and returned home only to flee again, this time arriving on Long Island in December 1776 and eventually making his way to the British army in New York City.[10]

Bartholomew's wife, Sarah, remained at home after he fled to New York City. She thus had the misfortune in May 1777 of watching insurgents seize all their movable property and auction it off.[11] Perhaps she sensed that her family would be a likely target for her neighbors' revenge because she tried to hide property before insurgents got hold of it. As Crannell's application for compensation explained, she tried to hide some of the family's goods "by lodging them with persons she thought she could trust."[12] The effort failed. In an undated document headed "Memorandum of Tory Goods," a revolutionary commissioner noted where property belonging to various Loyalists had been hidden. He had learned about livestock "put away belonging to Mr. Crannell" that he would then track down.[13] However, most of the Crannells' property was not far to seek because it remained in their home, one of the finest in town, for everyone to see. Thus, when revolutionary commissioners arrived, they inventoried all the feather beds, blankets, clocks, and paintings and even the pleasure sled, which the commissioners called a "Pleasure Slay."[14] They then sold the property to the highest bidder and kept the proceeds for the revolutionary government.

Expropriation such as this could be a personal matter as it involved acquaintances and relatives on both sides of the confiscation. For instance, it is unclear which commissioner confiscated and sold Crannell's property. But one of the commissioners who seized Loyalist property in Dutchess County was Henry Livingston Jr., the son of Crannell's law partner, Henry Sr., and brother of Gilbert, who was married to Crannell's daughter Catherine. It is therefore possible that the commissioner dispossessed a family that had been close to his own for decades. Moreover, such family connections did not deter insurgents from aggressively enforcing these partisan rules. On December 5, 1777, the Council of Safety directed two commissioners to remove the Reverend Beardsley from Poughkeepsie as a notorious Loyalist and send him and his family behind the lines into New York City.[15] One of the two commissioners was Peter Tappen, Beardsley's brother-in-law. Tappen and his fellow commissioner Andrew Billings then wrote to Henry Jr. to advise him that he should take possession of Beardsley's property because they intended to implement the resolution "with all posable [*sic*] dispatch." And, to make the point even clearer, they added in a postscript that they hoped to carry out the expulsion the next day. Although the letter is undated, Livingston marked it received on December 12, suggesting that they enforced the resolution just days after its passage.[16] What was more, they did so against Tappen's brother-in-law. Once Beardsley arrived in New York City, he became the chaplain to Beverly Robinson's regiment of Loyal Americans.[17]

Dispossessed and destitute, Sarah joined Bartholomew in New York City. As Bartholomew recalled after the war, Sarah and their two unmarried daughters fled with little more than "their Cloathes [*sic*] and necessary Bedding."[18] However, their flight did not end the assault on their property. With a powerful Loyalist gone and his goods redistributed, insurgents continued making his property serve their cause. By late 1777, George Clinton, the independent state's newly elected governor, moved with his family into Crannell's house and remained there for the rest of the war.[19] He likely ended up there through Peter Tappen, who was both Crannell's son-in-law (he was married to Crannell's daughter Elizabeth) and Clinton's brother-in-law (Clinton was married to Peter's sister Cornelia).[20] After driving an enemy away and redistributing his goods, the revolutionary state was now emerging on confiscated property. Indeed, so intertwined was this seized property with the new state that Crannell and the Loyalist Claims Commissioners referred to his former home as "the Government House" because Governor Clinton took up residency there.[21] Crannell never saw his home again, and at the end of the war he went into exile along with thousands of Loyalists from throughout America. He settled in Nova Scotia, where he subsisted on a clerk's salary that he found to be "of very little Profit."[22] Looking back from exile, he wrote to his son-in-law Gilbert that the "Idea of former property or possession appears now to me like a dream."[23] After suffering such hardships, it is little wonder that he could barely recall the comfort he once enjoyed in Poughkeepsie.

Though the dispossession of Loyalists like Crannell was a harsh practice that divided families and punished dissidents, it proved vital to consolidating the new order. Redistribution generated popular support and created strong bonds between the people who bought property and the revolutionary state that delivered it into their hands. Moreover, and perhaps more cruelly for people like Crannell, exiled Loyalists could do little more than look back at their former homes and despair. What they could not do, however, was meddle with the revolutionary state. Redistribution thus developed popular support while also weakening enemies and making it very difficult for them to undermine the new regime. Those effects highlight a key paradox of revolutionary state building: the same aggressive property redistribution that dispossessed Loyalists and drove them away also strengthened the new order at a crucial time. Perhaps it was this apparent contradiction that lent an air of unreality to Loyalists' suffering and made it hard for exiles like Crannell to grasp all that they had lost. But in fact the volatile context of war made such paradoxes possible that a partisan assault on property actually stabilized a chaotic legal environment and bolstered revolutionary authority.

For much of 1777, New York remained a society without traditional legal institutions. The few early signs of regular government did not develop into stable structures such as courts or a legislature. The Provincial Convention promulgated a new constitution in April, but that document did not by itself produce a working legal system. New Yorkers, however, faced serious problems that would not wait for a legal system to emerge. An urgent concern for the regime and for New Yorkers more generally was how to address the internal migration of people whom the British had forced from their homes. Thousands of New Yorkers had fled the British and endured great hardship to avoid living near an occupying army.[24] In 1776, many escaped across Long Island Sound to Connecticut, where they arrived destitute and terrified. In October, Jonathan Sloss Hobart, a delegate to the Convention, reported what he found in Fairfield. He explained to the Committee of Safety that "the indigent from the island" had arrived in such numbers that people in Connecticut would soon be unable to care for them. Moreover, these refugees required a basic subsistence because they did not bring "the means of support with them."[25] The Convention brought this long internal migration to an end in June 1777 when it moved the refugees from Connecticut to Dutchess County, New York, where they joined others who had fled New York City.[26]

However, bringing them back into New York did not resolve the challenge of providing them with a subsistence. New Yorkers still had to find them food and shelter, and many counties such as Orange, Ulster, and Dutchess were in no position to do so. During 1776 and 1777, the running battles between the British and the Continental armies had already strained the resources of the region. In April 1777, the Ulster County Committee wrote to the Convention to ask for reimbursement for those who had cared for sick and wounded Continental troops. The letter explained that the people of Ulster County were "in low circumstances" and struggling to look after the troops, most of whom "were lousy and in wretched" condition.[27] Refugees from New York City and Long Island arrived in a place that could not afford to support them.

The context of war and occupation also raised the question of what to do with Loyalist property. Some Loyalists fled to Long Island or New York

City and simply left their movable property behind. As a result, there were livestock, hay, grain, and other goods on farms that Loyalists once occupied.[28] Others hid their property or put it up in barns and storehouses before fleeing to the British, presumably in the belief that they would one day return to collect it.[29] But, in either case, their flight left valuable goods scattered about the province. Local committees, militia officers, and others then found it and wrote to the Provincial Convention for guidance on what to do.

In late 1776 and early 1777, the Convention responded to the issue of abandoned Loyalist property with limited, ad hoc solutions. When it received a report of goods being found, it directed particular people to seize specific property from certain named Loyalists. For instance, in November 1776, the Committee of Safety received a report about the movable estate found on the farm of Thomas Barclay, who had "gone over to the enemy."[30] The Committee directed William Duer, one of its members, to appoint people "to take all the hay, forage, and grain on the said farm." It then named three people to appraise the seized goods, sell the livestock, and deposit the proceeds with the state treasurer.[31] More important than the specific procedures employed in these seizures and sales is the fact that the Convention addressed each report individually as it arose. But, by the spring of 1777, there was too much property in too many places to continue addressing the problem piecemeal. Moreover, Loyalists were leaving their property behind at a time when material conditions were deteriorating and many people needed such goods to survive. Redistribution thus appeared to its supporters as a way to direct Loyalist property toward refugees and others who needed a basic subsistence.

In March 1777, under the strain of an ongoing war, New Yorkers began their first systematic effort to redistribute enemy property. The Convention empowered officials called Commissioners of Sequestration to operate in every county outside British control. The Commissioners' duties were straightforward. They were to confiscate all the personal property of those who had fled to the British, advertise the seizure in the newspaper, then auction everything off. They would turn the proceeds of the sales, and any money they found in the houses, over to the state's treasurer. It is worth pointing out what the Commissioners did not have to do. They did not have to conduct investigations; they did not have to empanel grand or petty juries; nor did they have to obtain any warrants or writs. The only restriction on the confiscations and sales related to the families left behind. The Commissioners had to leave the families' clothes, some of their furniture, and three months' worth of provisions.[32] Their powers grew throughout 1777 as the Convention added additional responsibilities, such as renting out, on one-year leases, farms left unoccupied. The rent, just like the proceeds from the auctions, went to the Convention.[33]

The resolution that empowered the Commissioners highlights the context in which redistribution emerged as a policy. In the preamble, the Convention acknowledged; "Diverse ill disposed persons . . . have joined our cruel and inveterate foes and the effects of such persons . . . are liable to waste or maybe employed for wicked purposes within this State . . . or consist of goods & merchandise useful to the well affected inhabitants of the same."[34] It declared that many New Yorkers had gone to support an occupying army, leaving their possessions behind. Rather than risk those goods falling into Loyalist or British hands, and rather than letting them go to waste by letting cows starve or wheat rot in the fields, New Yorkers—the good ones at least—could benefit. In one move, New Yorkers would systematize their efforts to find Loyalist goods and help political allies needing assistance.

Nobody anticipated that redistribution would have far-reaching effects or that in the later years of the war it would become a central focus of the revolutionary legal system. But, as they so often did, war and occupation shaped legal policy in unexpected ways. In June 1777, British general John Burgoyne invaded New York from Canada, spreading fear and violence as his army moved south. By July, he had taken Fort Ticonderoga at the southern end of Lake Champlain. In August, he captured Fort Edward on the Hudson River a short distance north of Albany. As he advanced from the north, a British raiding party moved up the Hudson from New York City and in early October drove American troops from forts in the Highlands, near the current site of West Point. The raiding party continued up the river, occasionally landing troops to burn storehouses, homes, and barns and arrest supporters of independence before destroying the town of Kingston and returning to New York City. This violence intensified New Yorkers' misery and came very close to bringing the entire Hudson River valley under British control. However, that did not occur, primarily because General Sir William Howe decided to invade Philadelphia rather than move his army north to meet Burgoyne's force in Albany. Without Howe's support, Burgoyne's progress slowed, and ultimately he was defeated at the battle of Saratoga.[35] Nevertheless, despite Burgoyne's defeat, suffering two invasions in as many years drove more refugees from their homes and deepened New Yorkers' hardships.

To make matters worse, severe inflation began to take hold in the summer of 1777, making it hard to procure basic goods. Inflation became such a concern that some thought it could destroy the state and undermine the entire Revolution. In July 1777, the printer John Holt decried how inflation forced New Yorkers to pay as much as ten times as usual "for the necessaries of life." Such inflation would weaken the state and "be extremely dangerous to our common rights and liberties."[36] Consequently, a second British invasion worsened material conditions just as revolutionary commissioners started redistributing goods.

The disruptions of war also made it impossible to turn the new constitution into working legal institutions. The Supreme Court of Judicature reconvened briefly under that constitution in September 1777 before fleeing the British raiding party that sailed up the Hudson. It did not meet again until the following year.[37] The legislature faced similar problems when it sat briefly in Kingston in September 1777. Just a few weeks later, the same British raid also scattered legislators. County-level Courts of Common Pleas and General Sessions of the Peace started to reconvene at different times throughout 1778, leaving many parts of New York to go more than two years without regular court meetings. Even when courts finally met after Burgoyne's defeat, they had very short dockets and often failed to gather all the people needed to conduct business.[38] Thus, New Yorkers confronted inflation, material hardship, and forced migration without a settled legal order for addressing such crises.

Supporters of independence realized that they had to relieve wartime suffering even in the absence of courts and other traditional structures. Indeed, they sensed that the legitimacy of their legal authority depended on it. In October 1777, Jonathan Sloss Hobart reminded the Convention that it had promised to provide salt and that New Yorkers expected it to do so. As he explained, "the honour of government" depended on delivering such vital provisions.[39] The following month, New York's Council of Safety prohibited the exportation of any flour or grain because the delegates believed that the state had "the indispensable duty" to provide its citizens with the basic articles of life.[40] Providing material relief had become a crucial responsibility of government, and supporters of independence realized that New Yorkers would never accept a state that allowed them to suffer and starve. In those straitened circumstances, New Yorkers needed a subsistence, and the Commissioners were in a position to provide it.

Many New Yorkers suffering the ravages of war did not wait for the Commissioners to redistribute property. When Loyalists fled to the British, neighbors often took personal property left behind. Some Loyalists tried to avoid this looting by distributing their goods to friends and family. As we have seen, Sarah Crannell did exactly that when she tried, unsuccessfully, to hide property with people she thought she could trust. But, between the

Loyalists who tried to hide their property and the neighbors who wanted to take it, the Commissioners struggled in the initial task of locating the property to confiscate. And, even when they could find it, few people willingly gave it up. They had to overcome the hostility of those who did not welcome the intrusion of central legal institutions. As the Committee on Conspiracies had already started to do, the Commissioners convinced New Yorkers to stop taking matters into their own hands and instead work with the legal institutions of a revolutionary regime.

The Convention soon expanded the Commissioners' power to help them overcome this problem. On March 21, 1777, just a couple of weeks after empowering the Commissioners, it acknowledged that the initial grant of authority "may, in some instances, be found incompetent." Now, when someone refused to turn over personal property, the Commissioners could ask local committees or militia officers "for such aid as may be judged necessary."[41] The resolution added a coercive power that the Commissioners were eager to employ. In May, the Commissioners for Dutchess County—Theodorus Van Wyck, Henry Livingston Jr., and Isaac Sheldon—took the opportunity to warn those who might be hiding enemy property.[42] They announced in the newspaper that people might "fraudulently, or inadvertantly [*sic*]," buy goods "from the friends of those who have gone over to our enemies." The Commissioners wanted "to give public notice" that "the personal property of all such disaffected persons will be considered liable to sequestration, let it be found in whosesoever [*sic*] hands it may."[43] Aggressive Commissioners, supported by the power to call out the militia, declared their intention of carrying revolutionary authority to people disinclined to accept it.

The Commissioners employed everything from bribery to intimidation to overcome initial distrust. Their first step was linking up with a like-minded revolutionary who knew the political landscape of a town. An inventory of goods prepared by Benjamin Birdsall for the Dutchess County Commissioners suggests how insurgents and their supporters brought central legal institutions to people who had been ignoring them.[44] Birdsall was not a Commissioner himself. But, in December 1778, he prepared an inventory that appears with the Dutchess Commissioners' papers. The document resembles a road map, one that could lead the Commissioners through convoluted attempts to hide Loyalist property. It offered an "Account of Confiscated Goods" that used to belong to "Mr. French."[45] Birdsall explained that Zebulon Seaman and John Conckling had found various goods, including joiner's tools, "in a heap of Straw" near "the Barn Mr. French ust to owyn [*sic*]." When Seaman and Conckling brought the items into the house,

Richard Marks and Robert Giffords were surprised because they had hidden the tools after finding them in French's cellar. Marks and Giffords had found all the axes, trowels, augurs, chisels, and boring bits "in the Conceald [*sic*] place" behind a wooden partition. Giffords told Birdsall that he knew to look in the partition because John Commins had suggested doing so. And Commins had received his information from Bryant. Thus, French, or someone else, had hidden the tools behind a wall in the basement, Bryant found this fact out and told Commins, Commins mentioned it to Marks and Giffords, who broke open the wall and hid the tools behind the barn, and then Seaman and Conckling "axsidently [*sic*] found the articles" there.[46]

Birdsall unraveled this twisted chain of possession only when the parties told him about it. Marks and Giffords hid the goods because when "they first found them they thought they had as good a Rite [*sic*] to them as any body [*sic*]." But, they claimed, they thought twice about it and decided to explain everything to Birdsall, who in turn reported it to the Commissioners.[47] More likely, however, Giffords and Marks realized that they would have a hard time keeping the goods for themselves after Seaman and Conckling found them. But, whatever their motives, all these machinations occurred out of the sight of the revolutionary regime. New Yorkers were willing to take Loyalist property and hide it without any regard for the regime or its Commissioners.[48] The Commissioners relied on allies such as Birdsall to guide them through this tangle of local considerations.

Not everyone volunteered, as Marks and Giffords had done, to give up the Loyalist goods. In instances where they did not, the Commissioners would try to negotiate with those who had taken the property. An account from the Middle District of Albany County suggests how this bargaining happened. In September 1777, the Commissioners—Flores Bancker, Myndert Rossboom, and George White—had found enemy property scattered about in different people's possession. Those people had taken everything from horses, to desks, to bushels of rye. Initially, they refused to allow the goods "to be Accounted for or delivered up." But the Commissioners were persistent, and, after "Different Applications," they "obtained settlements" from those who had taken the goods. They listed the amount each person agreed to pay to keep the items he already had in his possession.[49]

The settlements that Commissioners extracted, however, were not the product of free and open bargaining. Those who refused to cooperate might find a militia detachment at their doors. The procedure often began with a denunciation, as it did in August 1778, when someone named Storms informed the Commissioners for Dutchess County of "Tory goods that are

Kept Conceald [*sic*]" and which of his neighbors was hiding them.[50] The Commissioners ordered a captain in the militia, Bernardus Swartwout, to arrest those named in the denunciation along with others who had aroused suspicion. Swartwout then reported that he had gathered the suspects together for the Commissioners' "own examination and further Pleasure."[51] In addition to detaining suspects, the Commissioners might also order the militia to seize enemy property from the person who had it in his possession. In August 1779, the Dutchess Commissioners ordered Captain William Pierce to go to Edmund Ferris's farm in Pawling's Precinct. Ferris had two cows that belonged to someone who "has joined the Enemies of the State of New York." The Commissioners ordered Pierce "to take as many of your Company of Militia, as you may think proper" to seize the cows.[52]

It is unclear when a Commissioner might stop bargaining and call in the militia. But this coercion represented part of the legal authority of the revolutionary regime.[53] Someone who refused to turn over goods or whom a neighbor had denounced could find himself confronting soldiers who wanted to arrest him or seize his livestock. Thus, Commissioners relied on bargaining, information from allies, and intimidation to overcome public wariness and bring revolutionary legal authority to the people.

Bribery proved far more common in enforcing redistribution than any of those techniques. When a Commissioner seized property and auctioned it off, he needed help with a thousand little tasks, from creating an inventory of goods to pasturing livestock. And, to make sure that they received that help, Commissioners paid for it under the heading "Contingent Expenses" or "Incidental Charges." They paid people who came forward to help them, collected vouchers from these assistants, then submitted the vouchers to the Convention for reimbursement. In addition, the treasurer and the Commissioners each maintained accounts of the balance of payments. These routine administrative records reveal a vast network of hired support, one in which Commissioners paid New Yorkers—essentially bribing them—to come forward and help insurgents dispossess their enemies.

For New Yorkers suffering during the war, and even for those who had been taking property for themselves, direct payments represented a powerful incentive to support the regime's fledgling legal institutions. When a Commissioner arrived in town, he hired people to perform a wide variety of tasks, some lasting a short time, and others employing people for months. A voucher from September 1779 suggests a brief employment for Alexander Lamb. Lamb gave the voucher to acknowledge that Van Wyck, one of the Commissioners for Dutchess County, had paid him just over three pounds "for Carying [*sic*] off the property" of someone "gone to the Enemy."[54] Similarly, James Hunt, one of the Commissioners for Westchester County, gave a voucher to John Haines. In September 1777, the Commissioners paid Haines for the time he spent "in Search of the Stock the property of the State and wriding [*sic*] express to Set up Advertisements" of upcoming auctions.[55] The regime was paying people to fulfill the tasks that its legal institutions were too weak to perform on their own.

Commissioners paid New Yorkers to help with every conceivable aspect of confiscation and sale. George Palmer's accounts—from the Northern District of Albany County—suggest the range of these responsibilities. In May 1777, Palmer began gathering the goods from two confiscated estates. To do so, he had to hire a small army of assistants, beginning with seven people to gather the goods and pasture livestock. He also paid someone to spend four days taking an inventory of all the property before beginning the enormous undertaking of carrying the goods to one location for sale. Palmer then hired seventeen people to spend days carting the goods and moving the livestock.[56]

The procession must have stretched far out along the roads as it drove confiscated cows, sheep, and horses alongside wagons full of everything from waistcoats to iron kettles. Moreover, Commissioners such as Palmer did not wait for a particular auction to hire assistants. They kept some people employed for weeks searching for enemy property. Palmer paid three people for five weeks "Collecting Tory goods." He paid others for five days, a week, or nine days spent at the same task.[57] He would then have to pay others to pasture the livestock, drive the animals to auction, and carry out all the other steps in redistributing property. New Yorkers had begun to accept the legal institutions of a revolutionary regime when those institutions paid for the assistance.

Palmer's itemized lists represent part of a much larger revolutionary world of payments. Other Commissioners accounted for their contingent expenses without specifying the person hired or the services performed. For instance, the state's account with Elihu Marvin and Isaac Nicholls, Commissioners for Orange County, reveals that they had disbursed money as they went about their work. The state then accounted for the debt it owed the Commissioners.[58] Similarly, the Commissioners from the Middle District of Albany County accounted for their disbursements, only occasionally noting that the payments went to someone "for Pasturage" or a similar service.[59] In some instances, Commissioners paid suffering families who had not performed any service but required relief. Peter Dygart, one of the Commissioners for Tryon County, on the western frontier of New York, accounted for the money and grain he had given to "distress'd families."

He paid out specie, Continental currency, flour, and grain to people struggling to survive the war.[60] To be sure, the revolutionary government ran behind on its accounts, and people often had to wait to receive payment in full. Nevertheless, Commissioners traveled around New York, distributing money to an impoverished population that had few other means of support. All these direct payments to a suffering society helped persuade New Yorkers to accept the regime's authority.

Auctions also helped provide the material relief that New Yorkers needed. After the Commissioners and their paid assistants gathered all the property, they were under great pressure to sell quickly. Commissioners hurried because they could not always find sufficient pasture for the livestock, nor could they locate secure places to store the goods, away from greedy neighbors and British raids. A December 1777 letter from Hugh Rea to Isaac Sheldon, one of the Dutchess County Commissioners, suggests why they needed to hold auctions quickly. Rea, a farmer from Northeast Precinct in Dutchess, informed Sheldon that he had taken "the Inventory of the personal Estates of those that has [*sic*] Obsconded to the Enemy."[61] But he warned that "forage is scarce for Cattle" and "some of the Goods may be lost Notwithstanding all the Care that Can be Taken." He explained that he "would therefore be Glad you proceed To the sale of them as soon as you Can."[62] The difficulties of storing goods multiplied when Commissioners oversaw confiscations in several towns at once. Thus, New Yorkers required basic necessities, and the Commissioners were in a hurry to sell them the goods they needed.

The Commissioners offered that subsistence through a bonanza of confiscated property. Auctions took place in those parts of the state outside British control, particularly in the early years of the war. The most detailed auction books come from the Northern and Middle Districts of Albany County. From 1777 to 1779, the lists record 429 individual sales to 205 different purchasers, suggesting a sizable market in a part of the state where traveling to auctions was difficult much of the year. The median price of these goods was £2.11.0.[63] However, sale prices remain only a rough guide to the actual cost because purchasers went years without paying. Commissioners from Dutchess and Westchester Counties compiled lists of bad debts in which they recorded the names of people who purchased goods on credit but went years without satisfying the debt. Given the lack of circulating currency, Commissioners had little choice but to sell on credit. These generous terms meant that New Yorkers enjoyed frying pans, sorrel mares, desks, oats, and cartwheels for as long as five years without paying anything.[64]

The auction lists from around the state reveal an enormous selection of goods. The Commissioners got their hands on everything: bushels of wheat, corn, rye, and barley; millstones; wheat still growing in the ground; blankets; joiners' tools; an anvil; a pair of tongs; sleighs; tackling for the sleighs; a yoke of oxen; ten sheep; a sow; a sow with pigs; five looms; a piece of polished tin; a pair of stockings; axes; three sloops; windows and doors stripped out of houses; even just a single stick of ash wood. They also offered more elegant items: table linens; feather beds; costume jewelry; mahogany desks; silver plate; mirrors; bolts of finished cloth; even a jacket for £20, which was more than the going rate for an ox.[65] All of these goods went out to a needy society that had few other means of support.

The Commissioners themselves found these auctions as beneficial as other New Yorkers did. In fact, they exercised a right of first refusal, selecting the property they wanted before putting the rest up for sale. In December 1777, the Dutchess County Commissioner Van Wyck told his fellow Commissioner, Livingston, about some property that he had set aside for himself. He mentioned that among the confiscated goods on a particular farm were "4 fatt hoggs" that he had already picked out. Van Wyck asked Livingston not to sell those animals, for which he promised to pay "the Market price."[66] But nobody knew what that price could be since, like other New Yorkers, the Commissioners bought most of their goods on credit. They seldom paid at the time of sale and were not in any hurry to do so afterward either.[67] Moreover, they purchased goods at auctions that they themselves were overseeing. For instance, the Orange County Commissioners John Coe and Gilbert Cooper bought property at sales that they had organized.[68] These practices led to the curious circumstance whereby a Commissioner bought goods from himself, on credit, then became responsible for collecting the debt from himself. While this arrangement did not violate any of the Convention's resolutions, it was a self-serving one that Commissioners used to enrich themselves. In having this opportunity for private gain, however, they were no different from other New Yorkers. All allies of the revolutionary regime—anyone who accepted its legal institutions and their authority—benefited from confiscation when they bought goods or worked for a Commissioner. All could see that allegiance had its rewards.

Other auction lists hint at a much larger redistribution network. For instance, the lists from the Middle District of Albany County summarize sales numbered twenty through twenty-six, suggesting that at least nineteen additional auctions took place for which records no longer exist.[69] The sale books from Ulster County once filled four volumes, before they all burned in a 1911 fire at the capitol building in Albany.[70] Relying on documents that later burned in that fire, one editor compiled a list of 1,365 people whose personal estates were confiscated and sold during the Revolution.[71] Taking the sale period to be the six years beginning in April 1777, the Commissioners confiscated the property of 227.5 people every year. That frequency meant that they expropriated 4.375 people every week for six years.

The auctions, therefore, were ubiquitous events in revolutionary New York. Even when the regime was feeble—too weak to convene courts—it sent out Commissioners who rounded up property and sold it. Not only did these sales represent one of the few ways that New Yorkers regularly came into contact with central authority, but the auctions also bolstered that authority. At a time when the regime had an indispensable duty to provide basic goods, it did so by redistributing property.

Leasing real property such as farms—the Commissioners' other key responsibility—also helped extend the regime's legal authority. On May 13, 1777, the Convention empowered the Commissioners to lease, on one-year terms, farms that belonged to Loyalists who had fled to the British. The resolutions specified two requirements for the lessees. First, the Commissioners had to lease the farms "to persons friendly to the cause of America." Second, they should give priority to those "who have been driven from their habitations by the enemy."[72] These resolutions placed the regime, through the Commissioners, at the top of a patronage network that distributed material relief to allies. Supporters of the cause and those who suffered at the hands of an occupying army would have a roof over their heads in winter or a few acres to feed their families. Others would find themselves left to the vicissitudes of war. By rewarding allies with a subsistence, Commissioners offered a powerful motive for New Yorkers to accept the regime's authority and to count themselves among the friends of the cause.

The Commissioners quickly embraced their new duties. In June 1777, the Commissioners for Dutchess County took out a newspaper advertisement to announce their new leasing power. In a notice resembling the commercial advertisements that filled newspapers before the war, they quoted the resolutions and then declared that they were "ready at all times to attend persons applying for farms as before particularized."[73] They were open for business, and New Yorkers—suffering material shortages and internal displacement—leaped at the chance to gain a farm.

Hopeful lessees came forward on behalf of themselves, their friends, and their families, all eager to win some of the patronage that the regime had to offer. In December 1777, Theodorus Van Wyck, one of the Dutchess Commissioners, wrote to a fellow Commissioner, Henry Livingston Jr., explaining that Daniel Pelton had asked for a certain farm "in favour of himself, his mother's and sister's families." He suggested that, if Livingston had not already promised the farm to someone else, then he was "willing he [Pelton] should have" it.[74] Other applicants arrived with a letter of introduction to persuade Commissioners to lease a farm to them. In the same month, Hugh Rea wrote to the Dutchess Commissioner Isaac Sheldon asking him to sell confiscated property quickly. But Rea made sure to have John Schemerhorn deliver the letter since Schemerhorn "wants to hire John Peter Rows [*sic*] place of you and I would be Glade [*sic*] you would Assist him in Getting of it by Speaking to the rest of the Commissioners for him."[75] Whether they requested a farm on their own behalf or through a letter of introduction, New Yorkers welcomed the Commissioners and the subsistence they provided.

Most New Yorkers who applied for a farm, however, knew that merely asking for one was rarely enough to secure a lease. They had to establish their political bona fides for the Commissioners, and, as the Convention's resolutions made clear, they could do so in one of two ways. They could demonstrate either that they were friends of the cause or that, as refugees, they had suffered at the hands of a common enemy. These requirements encouraged New Yorkers to announce their support for the regime as they tried to persuade Commissioners to offer a lease. In October 1778, Herman Hoffman wrote to Van Wyck and Livingston to suggest that Mr. Fisher receive the dilapidated farm of Jacob Poucher, who "is now with the Enemy at New York." Hoffman wanted to "Take the Liberty of Recommending him [Fisher] to you as a good friend to the Good Cause of America."[76] New Yorkers such as Fisher and Hoffman understood the connection between allegiance and material relief. If someone hoped to receive a farm, he needed to demonstrate that he welcomed the regime and its authority.

With the possibility of a subsistence at stake, New Yorkers disputed with one another over whose devotion to the cause was purest, whose support for the Revolution was most clearly demonstrated. One such disagreement arose in March 1778 when the local town committee of Rhinebeck wrote to the Commissioners of Dutchess County. Peter Heermans, the chairman of the committee, objected to the Commissioners' decision to lease a farm to John Vradenburgh. He protested that another tenant who was more deserving, Harmon Knickerbacker, already lived on the property. Vradenburgh did not deserve the farm because he "only pretends to be" neutral when in fact he "is not a friend to the Cause of America." Moreover, he already had "a good House which he Occupys [*sic*] and does not want the other place, Unless it be to make gains by." On the other hand, Knickerbacker "is Warmly Attach'd to our Common Cause which he has prov'd by his voluntary Service in the Army with the Militia as Lieut[enant]." And, if he did not receive that farm, he would have "no Other place for himself and family." Because Knickerbacker was a strong supporter of the cause and he needed the farm, "it is the Sense of this Committee that he ought of Right to have the preference."[77] In this context, where allegiance could bring tangible benefits, New Yorkers were eager to declare just how fully they supported the Revolution. The Commissioners' leasing power thus rewarded strong support and created an environment in which New Yorkers welcomed the regime's authority.

Some New Yorkers needed no incentive to embrace revolutionary legal institutions. They were in such desperate circumstances that a subsistence from the Commissioners represented the only chance for survival. In January 1779, during a long winter, Van Wyck decided to lease a farm to John Campbell. Campbell then wrote to Livingston to ask whether he agreed with the decision. He described how dire prospects had become for his family, all of whom were refugees. He pleaded with Livingston because his two brothers-in-law "have Twelve Children the Oldest not Eleven years old and to my knoledg [*sic*] one of those Famelies [*sic*] have been Six weeks this winter without Bread." Campbell's own family was not faring much better: "When the small remains is gone I brought out of New York [City] this must be my situation unless you relieve me."[78] The Commissioners placed all three refugee families on the farm.[79] For many New Yorkers trying to survive the war, the regime's legal institutions provided the only stable subsistence. These people welcomed the Commissioners because their power to grant leases kept starvation at bay.

The promise of material relief proved such a strong attraction that the Commissioners struggled to accommodate everyone who applied for a lease. To meet all the requests, they shuffled tenants around, moving them from one house to another, or dividing the yield from a farm among different tenants.[80] The Commissioners also leased outbuildings on the same farm to different tenants, especially if many people had asked for a specific building such as a brew house.[81] So many applicants came forward—some desperately in need of shelter—that the Commissioners hurried to settle everyone on farms. In their hurry, however, they did not inquire into whether anyone had competing claims to the property they leased. As a result, New Yorkers—usually Loyalists' family members—came forward to object, often threatening to turn out the lessees. In one instance in February 1779, Van Wyck wrote to Livingston to let him know that he had leased a house and two acres to a refugee named Richard Willis. The property used to belong to John Haviland, who "was now with the Enemy." But John Haviland's father, Isaac, "has warn'd Mr. Willis out" and threatened to appeal to Egbert Benson, the attorney general. Van Wyck, however, was not concerned about the lease because Haviland had fled and Willis, who had preference to the land as a refugee, had taken possession.[82]

Although neither the applicants nor the Commissioners worried about uncertain leaseholds, the people who claimed a prior interest in the land started to complain about new tenants being put in possession. In 1779, the objections to leases reached the legislature, which began very slowly to review them. In the following month, it empaneled a joint committee of inquiry of the Senate and the Assembly to investigate the Commissioners' conduct because, according to the law that created the committee, some people "may have sustained damage" as a result of the Commissioners' work.[83] However, neither the joint committee nor the objections to leases slowed the Commissioners down.[84] The only effect of such complaints was that some Commissioners began to demand indemnifications from lessees and then continued renting property as eagerly as they had done before objections arose.[85]

While detailed evidence comes primarily from Dutchess County, the records suggest a much broader system of property leasing. For instance, Commissioners from Albany and Westchester Counties leased farms and collected rent; or at least they tried to collect it, as new tenants often fell into arrears.[86] These records suggest a network of revolutionary patronage that distributed farm leases to allies. Commissioners in war-torn regions like Westchester could hold out the possibility of a subsistence to friends of the cause. In a suffering society, that chance for material security offered a strong reason for New Yorkers to accept the regime's authority.

This largesse—from confiscated goods, to direct payments, to farm leases—contributed to the general welfare at a time of scarcity. As the honor of government depended on providing basic necessities, the regime would appear illegitimate—it would appear to have shirked an indispensable duty—if it allowed New Yorkers to suffer while the British rampaged through their territory. Moreover, through sales, payments, and leases, insurgents coaxed their reluctant neighbors to support the cause or at least to acquiesce in the regime's authority. Hesitant New Yorkers gained a material stake in the survival of the state. When the state succeeded, they succeeded, or at least they survived, which gave them good reason to accept the authority of revolutionary legal institutions. Property confiscation thus strengthened a new legal order because it provided material relief to a desperate society.

The bonds that connected New Yorkers to revolutionary legal institutions ran deeper than immediate relief. By redistributing property, insurgents also made countless New Yorkers complicit in the Revolution.[87] Many people participated in despoiling subjects of the Crown when they assisted a Commissioner, bought goods from him, or signed one of his leases. If any guilt ever attached to the uprising—if Americans were ever held to account for raising arms against the king—many New Yorkers would be culpable. The regime's largesse, therefore, represented more than a winter's subsistence. It linked New Yorkers to the revolutionary project by giving them a vested interest in maintaining insurgent government. If the regime developed stable, independent institutions, many New Yorkers' position would be secure, and they could keep all the goods they had acquired. But, if the regime failed and New Yorkers returned to British rule, they would have to explain how they ended up with all their neighbors' property. They would also, at the very least, have to return all of those cows and clothes or compensate the former owners. Expropriation thus not only allowed the regime to support New Yorkers; it also gave New Yorkers good reason to support the regime.

In addition to providing a subsistence, property confiscation offered a weapon of revenge, one that spoke to New Yorkers' desire to intimidate and punish enemies. As they had done since the invasion, New Yorkers embraced the regime's legal institutions because doing so helped them punish Britain and its supporters. In a society under military occupation, revenge remained an urgent priority as every day seemed to bring more news of British and Loyalist attacks. In November 1777, a newspaper described how "a number of Tory Villians [*sic*]" had robbed Jacob Baldwin and his family, who lived outside Fishkill. The armed thieves surrounded the house before stealing food and clothing, "leaving the family almost naked."[88] Such crimes had become common. Westchester County was particularly vulnerable because "Tory thieves," as a newspaper described them, could strike homes and then carry the goods and livestock across the lines into British-occupied New York City.[89]

Other New Yorkers suffered physical abuse and homelessness at the hands of the British. During their raid up the Hudson in October 1777, a newspaper reported, the British "wickedly destroyed" buildings along the way, including the stores of John Holt, printer to the state. They also burned Holt's "dwelling house, barn, &c. not even leaving a hovel to shelter" his family.[90] During the same raid, they landed at Kingston, where the legislature had convened for the first time under the new constitution. They chased away the new government and burned the town to the ground. A witness described how the fire spread quickly, reducing the town's "elegant and convenient dwellings . . . to a heap of rubbish." The attack dispersed more desperate refugees. Whole families were now "obliged to take up with such huts as they [could] find to defend them against the cold blasts of approaching winter."[91]

Not every assault was as stunning as one that obliterated a town. The train of daily abuses also included less spectacular events. In December 1777, a newspaper reported: "[The] enemy have lately burned three or four houses below Tarry-Town [in Westchester], abusing and wounding some of the inhabitants, particularly an aged person, who suffered much from their inhuman hands. They carried off three or four prisoners."[92] Facing robberies, assaults, and burned towns, New Yorkers came to believe that they were all suffering at the hands of a cruel enemy.

Moreover, that experience of occupation convinced them that their injuries demanded vengeance. In May 1777, the local committee in Amenia, in Dutchess County, wrote to the Convention to warn that a terrified population would soon take revenge against Britain's supporters. People in the area were in such "fear of being murdered, burnt or destroyed in the night, that they seem determined to rise in a body, and kill all the Tories they can find in the county." The committee asked for some way to "settle the minds of the people in quiet" and avoid a gruesome bloodletting.[93] New Yorkers could not bear the British raids and Loyalist plotting for very long before they took revenge on those they blamed for their suffering.

The Continental army officer General Horatio Gates understood how such grievances turned revenge into an urgent priority of the war. On October 20, just a few days after accepting Burgoyne's formal surrender at Saratoga, he sent a letter to Major General John Vaughan, the British officer commanding the raiding party that sailed up the Hudson. He berated Vaughan for reducing "the fine village of Kingston to Ashes, and most of the wretched inhabitants to ruin." He explained that, if Vaughan had hoped to frighten New Yorkers into abandoning the cause, such wanton destruction would have the exact opposite effect. Vaughan's "unexempled [*sic*] cruelty" would establish independence "upon the broad basis of the general resentment of the people." Gates recognized that this resentment would soon resolve itself into retribution. When that moment arrives, he warned Vaughan, "it may not be in the power of any thing [*sic*] human to save you from the just revenge of an injured people."[94]

As they saw an occupying army burn towns and turn families out of their homes, New Yorkers came to share a desire to strike back at those responsible for such calamities. No constitutional theory could provide that wellspring of common experience. No abstraction such as separation of powers resonated as deeply as the desire to seek revenge against Britain and its supporters. The war made vengeance, along with material relief, central to revolutionary authority.

The desire to strike back at Loyalists proved so strong that New Yorkers sought reprisals on their own. In May 1777, a militia officer in New York reported to the Convention what happened when his men heard about the British attack on Danbury, Connecticut, near the New York border, the previous month. The men "were so exasperated" by stories of how the British treated "the friends to liberty" that the soldiers were disobeying orders. Instead of marching south as commanded, they were marching east to Danbury to "take vengeance on the disaffected persons in that quarter."[95] Mobs even attacked supporters of independence who seemed too soft on Loyalists. In 1778, a mob decided that the local committee in Cambridge, New York, was not doing enough against enemy sympathizers. As a witness reported, the group waited until the committee was meeting and then dragged its members from the building before forcing them to run a gauntlet and whipping them for not punishing Tories severely enough.[96] Rioters of earlier years had not gone away, and this core of insurgents punished anyone who they thought lacked a strong commitment to the cause.

Revolutionary officials struggled to build legal institutions that would resonate with such violent partisans. On the one hand, if the regime went too far toward bloody retribution, it could provoke a counterrevolution. The Convention regularly received reports of British machinations and bands of Loyalists roaming the woods, shooting out the windows of militia officers and stealing their weapons.[97] Coming down too hard on disaffected people could embolden such attacks and lead to a response organized under the protection of British arms. But, on the other hand, if officials did not go far enough, they could find themselves being run through a gauntlet. Those officials had to make the state aggressive enough to convince violent revolutionaries to stop taking matters into their own hands but not so aggressive that they drove people to the British. The Commissioners of Sequestration accomplished that delicate task by redistributing property. Expropriation allowed the state to co-opt the hard core of insurgents, making popular violence unnecessary. Insurgents never anticipated that confiscation would have this effect; no stated policy assigned that responsibility to the Commissioners. But expropriation announced that New Yorkers did not have to launch partisan assaults. They could trust the regime to do it for them.

The Commissioners communicated their aggressive partisanship by starving the families of those who fled to the British. In August 1777, American major general Israel Putnam wrote from Peekskill to the Council of Safety. He complained that the Commissioners for Westchester County had been selling all the goods belonging to those who fled to the British. They had left abandoned families destitute, including some with many children to care for. Putnam objected to "starving the innocent families" who had begun to ask him for relief. The Council in turn asked the Commissioners whether they had not "in some instances rather drawn the cord too strait [*sic*]" by leaving families without even a little pasture or hay.[98]

The Commissioners, for their part, remained unapologetic. They responded that they had not heard of any such instances. If any had occurred, however, they noted: "We are justifiable, as we conceive, having acted in strict conformity to the resolutions." They were required to leave the families with three months' worth of provisions, clothes, and furniture. Since more than three months had passed since the March resolutions, any families "in a suffering condition" must have run out of the allotted provisions and thus cannot "be charged to their [i.e., the Commissioners'] account."[99] Commissioners' rigorous enforcement, with all its ugly consequences, made the regime acceptable to those willing to commit violence on behalf of independence. Each family that sought Putnam's charity testified to the insurgents' hard line on Tories. Violent New Yorkers, such as those who marched to Danbury to seek revenge, could look to the Commissioners' poor treatment of families and see that they had an ally in the regime's legal institutions.

Every confiscation—even those that did not leave families destitute—signaled the regime's willingness to confront Loyalists. Property seizure was a highly visible act, one performed in front of an entire community. When the Commissioners expropriated a known Loyalist, his aggressive neighbors—those who might have taken the law into their own hands—could see the regime punish enemies on their behalf. The inventory of goods confiscated from Bartholomew Crannell suggests how this process occurred. After Crannell had fled to New York City, the Commissioners seized his personal property in May 1777. With Crannell's wife, Sarah, still in possession, they carefully went through the home, recording all the goods exactly where the Commissioners found them. The front room, where the Crannells entertained guests, recalled the prosperity they once enjoyed. There Commissioners found a china case, a couple of "large looking Glasses," and a set of mahogany furniture, complete with a dozen chairs. Upstairs, away from where guests would have been, they found items of more mundane use, including a writing desk, a small table, and "4 Common Chairs." Below stairs they discovered an enormous variety of goods, from wooden pails to desks, from fishing nets to forks. Outside the house, they found items that ranged from the commonplace to the extravagant. They noted livestock such as calves, oxen, hogs, colts, and horned cattle, barrels of flour, and a chaise. Soon after compiling the inventory and taking possession of all the goods, they held an auction.[100]

The image of Commissioners going up and down the stairs, passing around the grounds, methodically looking into every room, reminds us that such actions were public displays of the new legal order. Anyone who might take the law into his own hands or who might doubt the fledgling state's willingness to confront its enemies could look out his window and see Commissioners picking apart the estate of a prominent Loyalist. Or perhaps he saw hired helpers leading a train of confiscated goods to auction. In either case, people who wanted retribution against Loyalists did not need to pursue it on their own. They could see that the Commissioners provided it through the legal institutions of the revolutionary regime.

New Yorkers also embraced revolutionary legal institutions because doing so allowed them to take revenge against personal enemies. As chapter 2 explained, the experience of John Kane suggests how revolutionary enforcement could serve private ends. For a decade before the war, Kane had been a loan agent on behalf of Beverly Robinson.[101] His close association with Robinson made him extraordinarily unpopular among other tenants. When war erupted, his neighbors denounced him to the Committee for Detecting and Defeating Conspiracies, with one accuser declaring him to be "an Artful Subtle Man."[102] After the Committee on Conspiracies questioned him and then jailed him, the Commissioners of Sequestration confiscated his personal property, thereby continuing the partisan enforcement that the Committee had begun.[103] Kane almost certainly was a British sympathizer. But his work as Robinson's loan agent made it likely that his neighbors singled him out for retribution. In this way, expropriation allowed New Yorkers to conscript the Commissioners onto one side of a feud. People denounced an unpopular neighbor, one despised for years, and the Commissioners would help them settle old scores.

At a time when New Yorkers were looking to punish enemies, property confiscation resonated with that desire for retribution. But dispossession did not affect only the individual victim of this revenge. Publicly dispossessing a known Loyalist—especially a powerful one—intimidated hesitant New Yorkers, those whom supporters of independence called *equivocal characters*. The confiscation and sale of Sir John Johnson's property suggests how these equivocal characters could see expropriation as a warning and accept the regime's legal authority rather than face the consequences of opposition. As explained in chapter 1, the entire Johnson family, Tryon County sheriff Alexander White, and their militia of supporters tried to intimidate local committees to prevent them from meeting. Sir John even fortified the family seat at Johnson Hall, making it a stronghold for Loyalist interests and royal government more generally. However, he ultimately fled to Canada in the spring of 1776, leaving Johnson Hall and its lavish furnishings behind.

After withstanding the Johnsons' abuse, insurgents were eager to dispossess what had been one of the most powerful families in the province. Commissioners of Sequestration began collecting enemy property in the area as fast as they could, and they held the first sales on May 1, 1777, just seven weeks after the Convention empowered them. The sales went on for months, many taking place at Johnson Hall, and by December the Commissioners had sold over three thousand items. Sir John's personal property, including his harpsichord, went to the highest bidder.[104] A short time earlier, loyal tenants and other dependents had rallied to Johnson Hall, the seat of the family's dynastic power, to protect their landlord. But now Commissioners and their hired assistants ransacked the house and redistributed the family's wealth. It was a striking and highly public reversal that warned equivocal characters about the danger of opposition. Such a scene, repeated over months of auctions, intimidated hesitant New Yorkers by putting the cost of dissent on full display. Similarly, Crannell's public dispossession declared that the revolutionary government was aggressive enough to strip bare one of the finest homes in town and turn it into Governor Clinton's residence. These events made it clear that, if the regime's legal institutions could dispossess someone as exalted as Sir John or as locally prominent as Crannell, then they could do it to anyone.

Enoch Crosby, who was one of the most active spies in the service of New York's independent government, described how such confiscations intimidated people who might have supported Britain. Crosby took assumed names and spent weeks hiding in the woods with suspected Loyalists. If he determined that suspects were plotting to form a regiment or escape behind British lines, then he secretly alerted the Committee on Conspiracies or the local militia, which then arrested the Loyalists.[105] But the Committee and the militia were not the only weapons at his disposal. Dispossession also proved to be a powerful way of coercing allegiance from hesitant New Yorkers. In his pension application after the war, Crosby recalled "that the confiscation of the personal property of the Tories & the leasing of their lands had a great tendency to discourage them from joining the British Army."[106] Fear of dispossession intimidated many New Yorkers into accepting the regime. Expropriation frightened these equivocal characters away from the British and convinced them to acquiesce in the regime's authority.

For a hesitant New Yorker, the confiscations offered a bleak choice. When he looked to the center of town or to a neighbor's house, he saw what happened to those who rejected the revolutionary legal order. He would see the Commissioners marching around the grounds making lists, a group of paid helpers carting everything to auction, and other neighbors picking out a spoon or a blanket to buy. With this example before him, he could keep quiet and receive some material relief from the auctions. Or he could reject the uprising and risk the sort of dispossession he saw all around him. The vision could be a frightening one, a warning to those who would oppose the Revolution. Confiscations, repeated thousands of times, signaled to equivocal New Yorkers that they could accept the confiscated property and the regime that delivered it into their hands. Otherwise, Commissioners might soon be at their door. And, as Crosby made clear, confiscations succeeded in forcing many New Yorkers to choose acquiescence over opposition.

At the same time, expropriation co-opted aggressive New Yorkers, those who wanted to take their revenge in blood. For such people, rather than being a warning or a source of unease, the auctions signaled the state's willingness to pursue a partisan campaign against Loyalists. This partisanship convinced violent New Yorkers to stop taking the law into their own hands. Instead of seeking punishment on their own, such partisans could denounce a neighbor and then just watch a Commissioner and his payroll of helpers swarm all over the property, fixing it so that the family would never want to return to a looted farm. Commissioners thus announced to aggressive New Yorkers that the law worked for them.

Although the process was often ugly and vindictive, property redistribution helped insurgents strengthen the authority of a revolutionary government. New Yorkers needed material relief, and they were seething with resentment at the occupying army. In that context, redistribution drew people toward the new order with the promise of relief and linked their subsistence to the regime's authority. As they came forward to buy a neighbor's property or to help a Commissioner, they became active participants in the revolutionary cause. They joined other New Yorkers—the aggressive partisans seeking revenge—and together they helped revolutionary Commissioners enforce the law. The process resembled the stripping of the monasteries in Reformation England. In that instance, many who did not share the Reformation's broad theological goals still helped plunder monastic property. As they did so, they joined their more active, evangelical neighbors in a common enterprise that advanced radical change.[107]

When New Yorkers dispossessed Loyalists, they too came to the assistance of a revolutionary regime and helped it enforce a sweeping confiscation policy. Property redistribution therefore had a twofold effect. On one hand, it offered a suffering, vengeful people powerful reasons to support the regime's legal institutions. By doing so, New Yorkers gained a subsistence and a chance to strike back at those they blamed for their hardship. On the other hand, confiscation punished political enemies and left them little reason to return to a ransacked farm where refugees had been resettled. Expropriation drew in supporters on one side, who then impoverished and intimidated political opponents on the other, thus strengthening the authority of a revolutionary order.

Insurgents extended the regime's authority in a way that suffering, vengeful people accepted. And they did so without formal legal structures. But, beginning in 1778, after two years of absence, those institutions started to emerge as the legislature and courts began convening more regularly. Revolutionaries would have to continue building popular support for a weak legal system as war dragged on and inflation spiraled ever higher.

CHAPTER FOUR

The Enemies of the State

After New York's provisional government survived two British invasions, the wartime economy nearly destroyed the feeble state. Beginning in late 1778, inflation grew rapidly, and the value of Continental currency plummeted. New Yorkers came to believe that redistributing Loyalists' real property would stabilize economic conditions and punish the enemies whom they blamed for this hardship. Commissioners of Sequestration had already expropriated movable goods, but they only leased Loyalists' land. New Yorkers wanted to sell real property and permanently dispossess political enemies. Nevertheless, despite public demands for further confiscation, the state did not immediately expropriate land, and that failure severely damaged its authority. Throughout the summer and fall of 1779, New Yorkers re-created local committees, most of which had become defunct, to address the problems their feeble state was failing to resolve. These rejuvenated committees enforced price controls, limited merchants' profits, and even considered ways of confiscating land on their own. New Yorkers were turning their backs on state institutions. This popular distrust eroded state authority, and many New Yorkers became convinced that institutions such as courts could not resolve their most basic needs.

The passage of a forfeiture law, however, represented a transformative moment in New York's revolutionary history. In October 1779, the legislature finally enacted a statute that attainted fifty-nine Loyalists for having "adhered to the enemies of the state." Those defendants were dispossessed of all property—real and personal, present and future interests—and banished. The law also created a court procedure through which New Yorkers went on to convict hundreds of additional defendants of the same crime. This punitive statute rejuvenated the state's legal system and restored popular support for the authority it wielded. Committees died away soon after its passage as New Yorkers convicted enemies, redistributed their property, and drove them away forever.

Over the later years of the war, implementing the forfeiture law became a central legal policy in the state. As this chapter demonstrates, New Yorkers convicted more defendants for adhering to the enemies of the state than they did for any other crime. This aggressive enforcement proved crucial in bolstering New York's government. Even those New Yorkers who may not have shared a firm commitment to independence still resented the harm that the occupation caused. Consequently, the statute generated support for the revolutionary state: it dispossessed Loyalists and drove them from the province in a way that resonated with a deep popular desire to strike back at Britain. Moreover, the statute linked purchasers to the state, many of whom became freeholders for the first time, and gave them strong reasons to support revolutionary authority. Thus, the forfeiture law drew in new landowners and people seeking to defeat Britain who then cut off political enemies.

Historians—particularly those who examine Loyalists—tend to overlook these effects of dispossession and exile. Some scholars have described the injustices that Loyalists suffered in New York and elsewhere.[1] Other historians have examined how Loyalist refugees in America and exiles overseas struggled to build new lives and find meaningful ways of participating in the British Empire.[2] However, such studies do not suggest how this treatment of Loyalists, severe though it was, strengthened the bonds of those who remained in New York. The point is not to ignore Loyalists' distress but rather to consider the domestic consequences of expropriation and exile. By doing so, one starts to see the forfeiture law's paradoxical effects and to understand how a harsh, partisan statute proved crucial in strengthening a weak state.

It would be hard to overstate the depth of anti-Loyalist sentiment that existed in the later years of the war. An anonymous newspaper column from May 1783 suggests the intensity of the desire to punish Loyalists and drive them from the province. The author called on readers to swear "never to be at peace with those fiends the refugees, whose thefts, murders, and treasons, have filled the cup of woe." Rather than overlook those crimes in the spirit of peace, the people must "shew [*sic*] the world that we prefer war, with all its direful calamities, to giving those fell destroyers of the human species a residence among us." Even though news of the Treaty of Paris had arrived and New Yorkers knew the war was formally over, the newspaper declaration ended with a chilling conclusion: "We have crimsoned the earth with our blood to purchase peace, [we] therefore are determined to enjoy harmony uninterrupted with the contaminating breath of a tory."[3]

Preventing refugee Loyalists from returning home had become a central priority for New Yorkers, one that shaped their notion of legal order. Indeed, they believed that they could vindicate their wartime suffering and preserve harmony in the new state only if they lived in a society without Tories.

The forfeiture law spoke to the desire to take revenge on Loyalists and drive them out. This chapter reconstructs the entire prosecutorial record under that critical statute, from grand jury testimony to final judgment. Eager to punish Loyalists, New Yorkers came forward to seize enemy property and sever the legal bonds that once connected former owners to the state. The overwhelming majority of those forced into exile never returned. Thus, the forfeiture law did not only offer material incentives for allegiance by creating a constituency of new landowners. It also generated popular support for the revolutionary government by offering an effective way to gain retribution against Loyalists. By 1783, the committee system had ceased, and New Yorkers accepted the legal authority of formal state structures, two changes that had seemed impossible only a few years before.

Beginning in late 1778, the wartime economy became one of New Yorkers' most urgent concerns. In particular, price inflation and currency collapse made it increasingly difficult for New Yorkers to acquire basic necessities. Teunis Tappen, one of the people hired by the state to supply prisoners with bread, submitted a bill to the state that reveals how quickly the price of a commodity such as flour rose. From July 1779 through January 1780, the price of flour tripled, from £20 to £60 per unit.[4] At the same time, the bottom fell out of the currency. The value of Continental currency dropped from 16.31 to 1 pound sterling in July 1779 to 31.1 to 1 pound sterling in January 1780 and to 40 to 1 pound sterling in March 1780.[5] New Yorkers were finding themselves in an impossible situation. The disruption of war and occupation drove up prices, but, at the same time, it became increasingly difficult to pay for goods with worthless Continental currency.

As they had been doing for years, New Yorkers looked for ways to punish the British sympathizers whom they blamed for this hardship. In August 1778, state senator Ebenezer Russell wrote to Governor George Clinton to remind him how strong this popular desire to punish Loyalists remained. Russell had heard that some leaders supported a law that would pardon all Loyalists, regardless of what they had done, if they simply took an oath of allegiance to New York. He warned Clinton: "I am Sure it [a general pardon] will Cause a Grate Deel of Deficulty and Disatisfaction [*sic*]." New Yorkers wanted to punish Loyalists who had taken up arms against the independent state, plundered goods and livestock, and generally "have Don their best Indeavors to In Slave our Country by assisting our Enimy against us [*sic*]." He believed that, by striking back at the "unhuman villins [*sic*]" who had helped the British, the state's leaders would do justice for those killed and other victims who had lost all their possessions or been chased from their homes. "[If, however,] those that hold the Rains of Government will not aspouse their [the victims'] Cause, I fear they will bring a more heavy Judgment upon the Land and cause the Generation yet unborn to Lement the misconduct of the forefathers In Not Revenging the Blood of those Noble marters [*sic*]."[6] The suffering of the war's victims demanded a forceful response against Loyalists, and anything less would cause tremendous popular anger.

New Yorkers soon came to believe that property confiscation would provide this response while also resolving their economic troubles. The Commissioners of Sequestration had already redistributed the personal property of many Loyalists. But they only leased Loyalist farms.[7] By the end of 1778, however, New Yorkers were starting to demand that the state confiscate real property and transfer title to new owners rather than merely settle tenants on the farms under one-year leases.

In October of that year, a group of Dutchess County residents petitioned the legislature to pass a confiscation law to relieve economic distress and strike back at Loyalists. The petition came from "Freeholders and Others," suggesting that it represented the views not just of property owners but also of tenants and perhaps refugees from New York City who had resettled in Dutchess. The petitioners saw many problems, all of which recommended confiscation as a solution. They feared "the alarming Depreciation of our paper money" as well as the enormous public debt incurred in fighting the war. Referring to themselves in the third person, they found it unfair that, after suffering "severely, many of them in their own proper persons and effects," they would have to bear the financial costs of war as well. They were carrying all the burdens of war. First, they faced the violence and destruction of military occupation; then they bore the financial cost of defending themselves against such depredations. Forcing them to repay the war's debts would be, they noted, "as intolerable for us and our children to bear, as it will be cruel to exact it of us." Under such circumstances, the cost of the war should fall on "those unnatural Enemies . . . by whose wicked practices the War, with all its horrors, Calamities and consequent charges, was brought upon us."[8] As the petitioners saw it, Loyalists who caused the war should bear its economic costs, rather than the New Yorkers who had been trying to defend their homes from an invading army.

Expropriating Loyalists, therefore, was not just an economic policy but also a matter of justice, of an injured people punishing offenders for their crimes. The petitioners believed that Loyalists deserved to lose their property. Echoing Russell's letter to Clinton, the Dutchess inhabitants announced that failing to punish Loyalists would be another injustice against a people who had already suffered too many of them. Referring to Loyalists, the petitioners declared: "Lenity to such atrocious offenders, we conceive, to be cruelty to the State in General and to mankind, unwarrantable either by the Laws of God or Man." The most fair and effective solution was "a Law for the confiscation and sale of the Real and personal property of the Enemies of this State."[9] Allowing Loyalists to escape punishment would not only leave New Yorkers with unbearable debts but also add another cruelty to their suffering. Thus, the petitioners demanded expropriation as a way of resolving two of their pressing concerns: defeating Loyalists while also relieving the economic burdens of war.

The petitioners announced that their support for the new legal order depended on whether the revolutionary state redistributed property. In an ominous conclusion, they warned that failing to confiscate Loyalists' property would "in all probability produce Tumults and insurrections, and tend to a Domestic Tyranny and confusion as much to be dreaded as the evils brought upon us by our connections with Great Britain."[10] This not-too-veiled threat of popular revolt demonstrated, in stark terms, how property redistribution was becoming crucial in convincing New Yorkers to accept the new legal order. If the legislature enacted a comprehensive forfeiture law, then the petitioners would welcome its economic relief and the chance to defeat Britain and its supporters. But, if the legislature failed to do so, then many New Yorkers would reject the revolutionary legal order and an insurrection might ensue. To be sure, Dutchess residents were particularly aggressive in calling for redistribution, and not all New Yorkers shared their belligerence.[11] Nevertheless, all New Yorkers had suffered years of violence, occupation, and economic hardship that was only getting worse. New Yorkers generally, not just those in Dutchess, were coming to believe that the state had an obligation to relieve their distress by redistributing Loyalist land.

As economic troubles deepened, New Yorkers from around the state began calling on the legislature to expropriate Loyalists. Petitions started arriving in January 1779, as soon as the legislature reconvened for the second sitting of its second session. On January 29, just two days after reconvening, the legislature received a petition from 173 inhabitants of Philip's Manor in Westchester County. Referring to themselves in the third person, the petitioners reminded the legislature that they had "exerted themselves to the utmost of their abilities, in the Cause in which we are engaged." Through their support "they have suffered great Losses, and been greatly distressed by the Ravages of the Enemy." The war had left them destitute, which situation they believed entitled them to compensation in the form of confiscated land. They wanted the right of first refusal in purchasing "the improved Farms of such Persons as have taken a Part with their Enemies."[12] Confiscated land would relieve the distress of allies who had suffered in support of the cause. Just a few days later, another petition arrived showing similar support for confiscation. Sixty-six inhabitants of Skenesboro, in Charlotte County, northeast of Albany, asked to buy the entire township of Skenesboro. They believed that, because the landlord Philip Skene supported Britain, all his property "has forfeited to the People of this State." They suggested that the legislature should then facilitate the transfer of his land.[13] Property redistribution had gained widespread popular support as a way of punishing political enemies and helping allies who were struggling to survive.[14]

Events in neighboring states intensified New Yorkers' desire for redistribution at home. In 1779, New England and mid-Atlantic states, like New York, suffered high inflation and currency collapse; many tried to develop price controls and other policies to resolve those problems.[15] Moreover, the people in those states—particularly Massachusetts and Pennsylvania—both of which had experienced British occupation, wanted revenge against Loyalists as much as New Yorkers did. New Yorkers' economic troubles and their war weariness were challenges that they shared with their neighbors. Unlike New York, however, those other states began confiscating Loyalists' real property in the spring of 1779. On April 12, Pennsylvania's Supreme Executive Council proclaimed thirty-seven people to be traitors, thereby forfeiting all their property to the state.[16] At the end of the month, Massachusetts passed two confiscation laws on the same day. One dispossessed twenty-nine former colonial officials such as Governors Francis Bernard and Thomas Hutchinson. The other created a court procedure for confiscating the property of anyone who sought British protection or who had "adhered to the said King of Great Britain."[17] Confronting challenges similar to those in New York, states such as Massachusetts and Pennsylvania developed price controls and confiscated Loyalist property.

With this example before them, New Yorkers challenged the legal authority of their own government for failing to take similar actions. Early in 1779, New York's legislature had passed a confiscation bill. But powerful opponents in the legislature such as Robert R. Livingston had managed its passage in a way that the statute was vetoed by the Council of Revision and did not become law.[18] These legislators continued to oppose confiscation throughout 1779 even as popular demands for seizing real property became more urgent. In May, a correspondent calling himself "Country Man" wrote to a New York newspaper and captured the growing frustration with the government. Writing just a few weeks after Pennsylvania and Massachusetts passed confiscation bills, he demanded to know why "similar proceedings have not taken place here." New York's failure to enact a confiscation law "is a matter of the highest regret to great numbers," with the result that the "public are impatient to know through whose means that most necessary and important bill was obstructed and put off." Redistributing Loyalist property had become a core concern for New Yorkers, and their leaders' failure to address that problem had eroded public confidence in the state's legal authority. As "Country Man" explained, "surely no one can have the least pretension" to popular support if he opposed confiscation.[19] New Yorkers petitioned for redistribution for months, and they had grown angry with their government's failure to pass such a law. Expropriation in neighboring states only sharpened this frustration and caused New Yorkers to become dissatisfied with a state that seemed incapable of resolving popular concerns.

New York's young government soon lost public support when it failed to redistribute land. Through the summer and fall of 1779, New Yorkers took matters into their own hands to deal with the urgent problems that their state was not addressing. They re-created local committees, many of which had become defunct by that time, to gain relief from economic hardship and punish Loyalists. In August, "W.D. in Orange County" lamented in a newspaper that his fellow New Yorkers were suffering "a complication of new invented villainies and abuses, to which the confusion incident to war adds a sanction of impunity." Formal legal institutions were little help because those wartime conditions created "evils the law cannot reach." New Yorkers thus had no choice but to re-create the committees that had first emerged at the start of the war. W.D. reminded his readers how effective those groups had been and that, "as soon as the authority of your Committees ended, knavery shewed [*sic*] its head." But W.D. believed that "the old and true friends of our country" were finally roused to action. Committees had already reemerged in places such as Philadelphia and Boston, and New Yorkers should follow their example. W.D. urged his readers: "Let no time be lost then, my countrymen, in forming your committees."[20] The war created urgent problems that, as New Yorkers had come to believe, were beyond the reach of formal legal structures. They therefore returned to a committee system, rather than those structures, to address the problems of high prices and Loyalism.

New Yorkers quickly revived committees all over the state. In July, Rombout Precinct established a committee to fix prices.[21] Elsewhere in Dutchess County, Poughkeepsie created a committee of "Freeholders and Inhabitants . . . to correspond with the other Precincts of this County, in order to devise ways and means for appreciating the currency" and resolving other economic problems.[22] In August, the Albany committee announced that it was setting prices on all commodities, limiting merchants' profits, and implementing a system of permits for moving goods within the county. The committee appointed a subcommittee to enforce these rules and seize any goods traded in violation of the new regulations.[23] Some did not stop at price controls. Just a few weeks after its creation, the Poughkeepsie committee called for the immediate confiscation and sale of Loyalist estates.[24] Frustrated at their government's failures, New Yorkers were rejecting its authority in favor of local committees that they believed would resolve their problems.

As committees spread, the authority of the young state's legal institutions receded to a low ebb. Courts in particular became feeble institutions as New Yorkers started to withdraw their tentative support. In 1778–79, county-level courts throughout the state struggled and often failed to conduct legal business. In Westchester County, the General Sessions of the Peace, a criminal and administrative court, convened for only two days in its November 1778 term. In that short time, it never empaneled a jury, grand or petty, and many constables failed to appear before the court adjourned until May 1779.[25] The General Sessions of the Peace for Albany County did not even try to empanel a grand jury for two consecutive terms of court, October 1778 and January 1779. As a result, it went a full year, from June 1778 until June 1779, without indicting a single person for any offense.[26] Civil courts had similar trouble. The Dutchess County Court of Common Pleas convened for twelve days in 1779. However, on nine of those twelve days, it met and adjourned without conducting any legal business at all.[27] The rejuvenation of committees degraded formal legal structures. As New Yorkers rushed to revive committees, they left many courts empty and conducting no legal business.

Not every court became as weak as the county-level courts. The Supreme Court of Judicature, New York's provincewide court of general civil and criminal jurisdiction, enjoyed some limited success in prosecuting crimes. Its minutes for 1779 suggest a preponderance of prosecutions for different types of theft—burglary, robbery, petty larceny—with other prosecutions for violent crime such as assault and battery.[28] In a speech to the legislature on August 24, Governor Clinton claimed that, owing to these prosecutions, robberies and other breaches of the peace had "become less frequent."[29] But that vague comparison suggested that the Supreme Court had succeeded only in making robberies less frequent than they had been in the earlier, most chaotic years of the war. Moreover, that limited success was limited still further as the court struggled to gather the jurors and constables who often failed to appear in court. The lists of these delinquents, as they were called, sometimes ran to forty names, demonstrating how difficult it was for the court to bring together all the personnel that it needed. For instance, the Supreme Court did not convene its October 1779 session until November. But, even after the postponement, no witnesses, jurors, or constables appeared for days, making it very difficult to move through the calendar.[30]

At the same time, therefore, that people in places such as Albany and Dutchess Counties were reviving committees, the courts there limped along, prosecuting few defendants, and resolving even fewer civil disputes. County courts sometimes failed to do anything at all except meet and immediately adjourn. The ongoing war contributed to this weakness by making it difficult to gather all the officials necessary to hear cases.[31] But the rejuvenation of committees accelerated the decline of the state's legal authority. Committees offered an alternative legal infrastructure for a people frustrated with their young government. When the state failed to redistribute property in a way that would punish Loyalists and relieve economic trouble, New Yorkers began addressing those problems outside of formal channels.[32] Thus, war and popular anger at the state helped weaken the legal authority of the courts and push those institutions to the margins of public life.

Governor Clinton sensed that, just like the courts, the legislature had lost the support of ordinary New Yorkers. On August 24, in the middle of the resurgence of committee activity, he opened the third legislative session with a speech to the Assembly and Senate. It was the same speech in which he praised the modest reduction in robberies. But he also touched on other challenges facing the state. He reminded the legislators that many of the enlistments in the militia would expire soon and that they should consider ways of filling those vacancies. He promised a war-weary public that, after suffering Loyalist and Indian raids, "a just vengeance will be taken on their [New Yorkers'] savage enemy." He also told the legislature that it must take "immediate and decisive steps" to end the festering problem in Vermont, a region he called "the north-eastern counties of this State." But his confidence in the state's authority faltered when he discussed New York's dire economic condition, especially inflation and currency depreciation. He acknowledged that those issues were "of the first importance." He was also fully aware of popular pressure to resolve such problems and of "the sense that your [the legislators'] constituents loudly express, of the necessity of applying some suitable remedy to this growing evil." However, rather than just instructing the legislature to add the issue to its agenda as he had with the other points, he thought it necessary to reassure his audience that the public would accept the legislature's economic regulations. He offered the legislators "the strongest assurances of their [the constituents'] acquiescence, in any plan, which their constitutional representatives" chose to enact.[33]

Governor Clinton spoke like someone who thought his audience needed to be convinced that the public would obey laws enacted by the legislature. This portion of his speech was the only part where he mentioned strong popular opinion on an issue. It was also the only time he tried to reassure the legislature that New Yorkers would accept its solution to an urgent public concern. He took pains to reassure legislators precisely because he knew that many New Yorkers had lost confidence in the state's legal authority. His promise of popular acquiescence betrayed his doubts about the strength of that authority. Instead of following the formal enactments of what the governor called New Yorkers' "constitutional representatives," the people might just continue working through committees with little regard for what the legislature did. They no longer trusted the state's formal legal institutions to resolve critical economic problems, and, as a result, the governor had to promise the legislature that they would follow the law. Indeed, it was on those issues that mattered most to the public—those economic concerns New Yorkers expressed loudest—that Clinton feared they were least likely to accept the legislature's authority.

When the governor gave this speech in the summer of 1779, New York's legal system was in crisis. The state's economic troubles had become urgent concerns for New Yorkers. They believed that property redistribution would relieve economic distress and at the same time punish Loyalists whose support for an occupying army had caused those problems. But many New Yorkers became frustrated at their government's failure to enact confiscation, particularly when they saw similar laws in neighboring states. This popular anger eroded the legal authority of New York's new government and encouraged the revival of committees to address the issues that the state was not resolving. In this way, the war created challenges that many New Yorkers believed were beyond the reach of formal legal structures. And they began to reject those feeble institutions in favor of committees to develop price controls and, in at least one instance, begin considering redistribution. As committees grew, courts struggled to transact legal business, sometimes failing to hear any cases at all. The governor doubted whether the public would obey laws on crucial economic issues. Thus, New York's new legal system—already disrupted by military occupation—was losing the popular trust it had only just begun to earn.

Popular anger, however, soon became too intense for opponents of confiscation to hold out any longer. Through petitions, an energized committee system, and even the threat of insurrection, New Yorkers forced their leaders to change course, and a confiscation bill finally passed on October 22, 1779.[34] According to its title, the law was "An Act for the forfeiture and sale of the estates of persons who have adhered to the enemies of this State, and for declaring the sovereignty of the people of this State in respect to all property within the same." Its preamble described the underlying crime in more detail. The purpose of the law was to punish supporters of the British king for having "voluntarily been adherent to the said king his fleets and armies, enemies to this State and the said other United States, with the intent to subvert the government and liberties of this State and the said other United States, and to bring the same in subjection to the crown of Great Britain."[35] The statute itself attainted fifty-nine people for adhering to the enemies of the state and created a court procedure for convicting additional defendants of the same crime.[36] Those named in the statute were dispossessed of all property, real and personal, whether held as a present or a future interest, and banished. If after being banished they returned to New York, they would be guilty of a felony without benefit of clergy and subject to execution.[37] The defendants convicted in court received a different punishment. They were dispossessed of real and personal property, both present and future interests, but not formally banished.[38] Nevertheless, these court convictions still forced many Loyalists from their homes and severed their connections to the new state.

In addition to imposing severe punishment on enemies, the law offered favorable terms to tenants who had supported independence. Those tenants enjoyed preemptive rights under which they could buy the farms they rented, thereby preventing the land from ever going up for public sale. But however the forfeited land was transferred—whether sold through public auction or directly to a tenant—the law empowered Commissioners of Forfeitures to oversee all transactions, including issuing deeds to purchasers. Even though opponents of confiscation such as Livingston and Jay had lost the legislative fight, they succeeded in one aspect of redistribution. They managed to include a clause in the statute that delayed the start of sales until 1780.[39] After a year of demanding a forfeiture law, New Yorkers finally had one to relieve their economic distress and punish Loyalists.

The passage of this law in October 1779 marked an extraordinary change in New York's revolutionary history. Before its enactment, popular dissatisfaction and open war had degraded the authority of the province's legal structures. But, after enacting a forfeiture law, popular frustration and hostility became support for a legal system that finally offered economic relief and a chance to defeat Britain's allies. Local committees stopped their work just as quickly as they had begun it, and New Yorkers instead came forward to help prosecute hundreds of defendants for adhering to the enemies of the state. Through this enforcement—through the conviction of defendants and the redistribution of their land—New Yorkers rejuvenated the legal authority of their young state.

The enormous volume of prosecutions under the forfeiture act proved crucial in reviving New York's moribund legal system. An analysis of surviving minutes from both county and statewide courts reveals that, as measured by the number of convictions, adhering to the enemies of the state became the most commonly prosecuted crime in revolutionary New York.[40] From October 1779 until November 1783, when the British evacuated New York City, more defendants were convicted of that one crime (581) than all other crimes combined (346). No other offense even came close to the number of convictions for adhering to the enemies of the state: more than nine times as many defendants were convicted of that crime than for the second most commonly prosecuted offense (assault and battery, sixty-three convictions).[41] The crime of adhering to the enemies of the state did not even exist before October 1779. But, in a short time, it became a central priority of New York's legal system. Through that tremendous spike in convictions, New Yorkers rebuilt popular support for revolutionary legal institutions.

One such basis for that support was the material relief that redistribution offered. By the time the legislature passed the forfeiture law in October 1779, New Yorkers had been claiming for a year that redistribution would relieve their economic distress. In retrospect, we can see now that confiscation did not ultimately become the economic panacea that they thought it would be. Redistribution did not stabilize the currency; it did not ultimately provide the state with enough revenue to relieve the burden of public debt. But we see those failures only in hindsight. When the law was enacted, New Yorkers believed that redistribution would ameliorate their desperate economic condition. At a time when inflation made it hard to buy basic goods, redistribution would allow New Yorkers to grow their own subsistence, and thus purchasers came forward to buy forfeited land as soon as it became available.[42] Sales spread throughout the province as redistribution finally offered the material relief that New Yorkers had been demanding.

Redistribution also represented more than a short-term subsistence during the misery of war. It linked tenants to the young state and gave them good reasons to support the new legal system. It offered them the chance to buy the farms they had been leasing and thereby gain a freehold for the first time. Since the 1740s, tenants in the Hudson River valley had been trying unsuccessfully to secure stable land tenure. Their efforts had brought them into conflict with landlords who tried to control their property by ejecting tenants and modifying the terms of leases. These disputes sometimes exploded into riots and armed uprisings.[43] The last such tenant uprising of the colonial period occurred in 1766 in southern Dutchess County, where the revolt became so widespread that British troops had to put it down.[44] This animosity between landlords and tenants persisted into the Revolution, and many of the people involved in the 1766 uprising remained in the area when war broke out a decade later. For instance, Beverly Robinson, one of the Dutchess landlords whose tenants had revolted in 1766, became a Loyalist, and the forfeiture act attainted him for adhering to the enemies of the state. He lost his real property through the enforcement of the forfeiture law. Many tenants came forward and embraced the revolutionary state because, through the dispossession of landlords such as Robinson, it finally offered the stable land tenure they had been seeking for a generation.[45]

Once tenants bought land, they acquired a long-term stake in the new legal order. Sales to tenants created a constituency of new freeholders, people who could meet the property requirements for voting and serving on juries. In Dutchess County alone, redistribution of forfeited land increased the number freeholders there by approximately 22 percent.[46] New landowners could participate in public life, and they owed their political voice to the revolutionary state. Those new rights gave former tenants powerful reasons to support New York's independence. If the state survived, then purchasers would continue to enjoy both the material and the political benefits of redistribution; their land tenure and political influence would be secure. But a British victory would threaten those gains. Redistribution thus gave these new freeholders strong incentives to support the young state and resist any return to British rule.[47]

Some historians have argued that, by offering the chance to gain a freehold, redistribution alone cemented tenants' allegiance to the new state.[48] There is little doubt that the chance to buy farms linked purchasers to the new legal system by giving them political and material reasons to support its authority. But focusing exclusively on land sales, as these scholars have done, offers an incomplete view of the forfeiture act and its impact on the young state. As odd as it may sound, the actual forfeiture and sale of real property represented only a minor part of the law's implementation. In fact, the vast majority of prosecutions under New York's law did not lead to sales of real property: 984 people were either attainted in the statute or later indicted and convicted in court for adhering to the enemies of the state. Yet, of those defendants, only 235 had land confiscated and sold.[49] This discrepancy reveals that, for every one enemy of the state whose land was sold, there were roughly three other enemies who were prosecuted without making any land available for purchase.[50] Historians have analyzed the one defendant and ignored the many others whose prosecution did not create a single new freeholder. By examining only those who forfeited real property, scholars have assumed that the opportunity to buy land was the only basis of popular allegiance and that New Yorkers supported the revolutionary state because it offered stable land tenure. However, such an explanation leaves us to wonder how the statute generated support for the revolutionary regime even though most prosecutions did not result in land sales.

The statute built up support for the regime because, in addition to offering freeholds, it resonated with New Yorkers' deep desire to punish Loyalists. Watching British troops and their allies destroy towns, seize livestock, and turn families out of their homes convinced New Yorkers that they were being abused by a cruel and inhuman enemy. Moreover, the raids that bred such deep animosity toward Britain continued into the later years of the war. In the summer of 1778, a corps of Loyalist and Indian fighters led by John Butler and Joseph Brant raided the Wyoming Valley, along the Pennsylvania border. In November of that year, another group of Indians and Loyalists destroyed the settlement of Cherry Valley in Tryon County, killing some of its inhabitants, capturing others, and putting the rest to flight. The following summer, American troops led retaliatory strikes against Indian settlements in the Finger Lakes region. Then, in the fall of 1780, Sir John Johnson raided the area that he used to dominate. He returned from his exile in Canada and led a group of fighters who destroyed the region around Schoharie Creek, which lies south of the Mohawk River parallel to the Hudson.[51] This fighting decimated western New York and drove people from their homes while, at the same time, smaller-scale raids continued to plague other parts of the state. For instance, in November 1779, a party of Loyalists sailed from Canada down Lake Champlain. A newspaper reported: "They have carried off a number of men prisoners, and also have carried away some cattle." They also destroyed buildings along the way.[52] Even after the British invasions in 1776 and 1777, New Yorkers continued suffering the violence and destruction of war.

The ongoing occupation fed a powerful desire to win the war against the occupying army and its allies. Indeed, after years of constant raiding, New Yorkers had become convinced that Loyalists deserved tough treatment. As one anonymous newspaper correspondent put it in January 1779: "There is a certain degree of injury and abuse, beyond which human tolerance cannot go; and beyond which indeed it never ought to go." New Yorkers had reached that limit of injury and abuse. After Loyalists had guided the British in destroying Kingston and Danbury, Connecticut, after they had helped "desolate their country," New Yorkers could not even tolerate the sight of a Loyalist without striking out in revenge. "Let one of these *serpents*, I say, appear in the sight of a person, whose wife, child or brother had been butchered by them, and not all the patience of *Job*, nor the utmost meekness of the Christian temper, could restrain his hands from instantly killing him on the spot."[53] The same month, an anonymous letter to the printer echoed the view that New Yorkers' suffering demanded retribution. The Loyalists who passed intelligence to the British, provided them with supplies, or otherwise assisted them had "fill[ed] the land with violence and distress." Those "wretched miscreants" were "stained with the innocent blood that defiles the land, and cries to Heaven for vengeance."[54] New Yorkers heard those cries and wanted to defeat Britain and its Loyalist proxies.

The forfeiture law resonated with this intense desire to lash out at enemies. Over the summer of 1779, New Yorkers revived committees because they believed that formal structures could not address the Loyalist problem. But, once the forfeiture law offered an institutional means for punishing enemies, they stopped working through committees and enforced the statute so aggressively that adhering to the enemies of the state became the most commonly prosecuted crime in the state. The forfeiture law, therefore, rebuilt popular support for the new legal order because it put a powerful weapon in the hands of people who wanted revenge against British sympathizers. New Yorkers embraced that legal system and used it to punish the "serpents"—the "wretched miscreants"—who had supported Britain.

The forfeiture law created a legal environment that appealed to the great many New Yorkers who resented the occupation. The statute established certain procedures and evidentiary standards that made it easy to convict defendants of adhering to the enemies of the state. As a result, New Yorkers accepted the state's legal institutions because those structures helped defeat the enemies who had spread so much misery. By analyzing prosecutions under the statute, one can see how the actual implementation of the law helped New Yorkers punish their enemies.

Reconstructing the enforcement of the law begins with what constituted evidence of the crime. According to the statute, voluntarily moving to an area under British control any time after July 9, 1776, was evidence of adhering to the enemies of the state.[55] The law did not recognize a justification for seeking British protection, such as pleading military necessity.[56] Someone's flight was evidence of his guilt, and that evidentiary requirement explains why in these prosecutions grand jury testimony so often took the same form. A grand jury witness needed only to testify that the defendants had been in an area outside British control at some time after July 9, 1776 but had since moved behind enemy lines. For instance, in May 1780, Margaret Blauvelt appeared as a witness before a grand jury of the Orange County Court of General Sessions of the Peace. She testified that she had seen Joseph Dawers, once a saddler from Orangetown, now "living in frindship [*sic*] with the Citizens of New York [City]." Blauvelt did not have to explain what she herself was doing in British-occupied New York City. But, because Dawers had left his home in Orangetown to move to New York City, Blauvelt's testimony was sufficient to indict him.[57]

Witnesses offered similar testimony to grand juries throughout the state. In April 1781, Wilhelmus Lampman appeared before a grand jury of the Supreme Court of Judicature sitting in Albany. He testified that he had seen five of the defendants, once inhabitants of the independent state, living in New York City or on Long Island. They "all appeared to the Deponent to be there of their own voluntary free will and accord." They had chosen to live under British control, and that decision justified indicting them for adhering to the enemies of the state.[58] Witnesses from Westchester County described how defendants had once been in an area outside British control but had since moved behind the lines.[59] Other witnesses claimed that they had seen defendants fighting in Loyalist regiments.[60] The various courts then forwarded the indictments, along with transcripts of the witness testimony, to the Supreme Court of Judicature for final judgment.[61]

By targeting these absent defendants, the forfeiture law cleared the way for New Yorkers to secure the convictions they sought. During the colonial period in New York, criminal defendants did not present evidence to grand juries; only the prosecuting attorney or aggrieved parties did so.[62] If the grand jury indicted the defendant, then he would be asked to plead. If he pleaded not guilty, the case would move to the trial stage before a petty jury, and the defendant could present his own witnesses. Defendants had a right to present exculpatory evidence only at the later, trial stage and not to the grand jury. But the forfeiture law created a circumstance where few of those indicted would be present to answer the charges against them. After all, someone who had fled to seek British protection or left home to fight with a Loyalist regiment would not likely return to defend himself in a New York court. As a result, by singling out absentees, the statute set the defendants up for a prosecution in which it would be nearly impossible for them to present any evidence on their own behalf.[63] They did not have the right to do so at the grand jury stage. And, since they had gone off to the British, they would not have the opportunity at trial either. After hearing a one-sided presentation of the evidence, grand juries indicted defendants who had already fled and would never appear for trial. The statute, therefore, created an enforcement scheme that would appeal to New Yorkers. It made trials very unlikely and thereby paved the way for retribution.

Prosecuting absentees allowed highly dubious grand jury testimony to serve as the basis, not only of indictments, but of convictions as well. In April 1783, Nathan Daly appeared before a grand jury of the Supreme Court of Judicature in Albany. He recalled that, in August 1777, the British had captured him in Tryon County, in western New York. They then took him to Albany County, where he "was detained a prisoner near four Days" before he escaped. Yet, nearly six years later, he claimed before the grand jury that he remembered seeing all ninety-nine defendants organized in a Loyalist regiment at the British camp. And, though he spent barely four days as a prisoner, he also testified that he remembered the name, hometown, and occupation of every defendant. Moreover, Daly was a yeoman farmer from Albany County, yet he claimed to recognize defendants from Albany, Tryon, and Ulster Counties, people he was not likely to have known personally before the war. Just a few days after his testimony, the grand jury, in a single indictment, charged all the defendants with adhering to the enemies of the state.[64] But, because most of them had fled their homes, only five appeared to plead.[65] The remaining ninety-four defendants never appeared and were convicted by default judgment on November 1, 1783.[66] If all the defendants had still been in the state, they could have pleaded not guilty and presented their own witnesses at trial. A petty jury would then have had the opportunity to evaluate Daly's improbable testimony alongside contrary evidence. But, because most of the defendants had already fled, Daly's testimony, dubious though it was, went unchallenged and helped convict ninety-four people. By targeting absent defendants who could not answer charges, the forfeiture law gave New Yorkers the chance to strike back at their enemies and do so in a way that the defendants would not test witnesses' claims.

Other grand jury witnesses offered similarly thin evidence that supported convictions. In April 1781, Abraham Vollwyser appeared in Albany before a grand jury of the Supreme Court of Judicature. He testified that nearly four years earlier, in the fall of 1777, he had been in the British camp at Saratoga, where he had seen several defendants. He did not explain why he himself had been in a British camp. But he testified that one of the defendants told him that he was building boats for the British army. He also claimed that another defendant had been a wagoner there and that still another had been manning a raft. All were, he noted, doing those jobs "in the Service of the Brittish [*sic*] King." Two other defendants had not performed any particular act in the camp. They simply "appeared to the Deponent [Vollwyser] to be there of their own voluntary free will and accord." Vollwyser's testimony helped indict all five defendants.[67] Moreover, because the defendants had already fled from their homes, they never appeared to plead, and, in August 1782, the Supreme Court of Judicature entered default judgments against all of them.[68] Vollwyser never suggested what gave him the vague impression that two of the defendants were with the British voluntarily. And, since the case never went to trial, neither the wagoner nor the boatman had a chance to offer their own witnesses to establish what they were doing in the camp. Instead, a one-sided presentation of evidence served both to indict and to convict the defendants. The forfeiture law, therefore, provided an easy route to a conviction, one in which few adversaries would appear to contradict accusers' claims.

New Yorkers embraced the state's legal institutions because they were nearly assured of a conviction. With most defendants already gone, trials virtually disappeared, and there was little doubt about the outcome of these prosecutions. Between 1779 and 1783, 527 prosecutions for adhering to the enemies of the state reached final judgment in court.[69] Even though this was the most commonly prosecuted crime in the state during that time, only one of those judgments came after a trial, and that defendant was acquitted. In contrast to one trial, 517 defendants never appeared in court and were convicted by default judgment. In other words, 98 percent of all prosecutions under the forfeiture law that reached final judgment by 1783 ended in conviction by default (517 of 527).[70] With so few trials and so many convictions against absentees, the forfeiture law gave New Yorkers powerful reasons to accept the new legal order. As counterintuitive as it might sound, the statute resonated precisely because it did not provide a genuine opportunity to test accusations. One might assume that only a full trial would enjoy popular legitimacy, and perhaps that would be the case in a more peaceful time. But New Yorkers were seething with resentment after years of occupation, and they were not seeking a thoughtful examination of the evidence. They demanded punishment, and the legal system offered it through hundreds of default convictions for adhering to the enemies of the state.

These default judgments made it possible for New York's weak legal system to process as many defendants as it did. The war continued to disrupt courts and make it difficult to conduct legal business. But default judgments obviated the need for trials, relieving courts of the burden of empaneling petty juries, gathering witnesses, and performing many of the other procedural steps that were so difficult in an occupied society. As a result, not even the state's feeble court system prevented New Yorkers from processing defendants. A grand jury witness could offer vague or implausible testimony against defendants whom he knew to be absent and then just wait for the state's institutions to convict them.[71] Indicting suspects en masse—often ten or more in a single indictment—and convicting them by default saved courts the trouble of gathering people for trial. Thus, despite a struggling court system, the forfeiture law still provided New Yorkers with a legal infrastructure for their retribution, a set of procedures and institutions that helped them defeat their enemies.

New Yorkers' aggressive enforcement of the forfeiture law did more than satisfy an immediate desire to punish enemies. It also worked permanent changes that stabilized the new legal order over the long term. One such change was banishing the fifty-nine Loyalists attainted in the statute and driving countless others into exile. In doing so, the law removed a whole constituency of potential opponents, people who, if they had remained in the state, might have thwarted the new order or destabilized it. Many Loyalists became exiles in Britain, Canada, or the West Indies.[72] Indeed, throughout the 1780s, the legislature received many petitions from those who had fled or been banished requesting permission to return. But the legislature rejected the vast majority of them and allowed only about thirty exiles to reenter the state.[73] It was not until April 1792 that New York passed a law allowing everyone banished under the forfeiture act to return. But, even then, exiles could return only if they recognized the validity of the earlier property forfeitures.[74] Therefore, by driving out Loyalists, most of them permanently, New Yorkers removed enemies who might have continued to oppose the state after the war ended.

New Yorkers sensed that a connection existed between exile and stability. They suggested that, by removing Loyalists, they would protect the new state against enemies who wanted to destabilize it. In April 1783, "Publius" warned the people of New York that they must be vigilant against such insidious schemes to injure the state. He found "much reason to fear that those minions of tyranny who adhered to [the king] . . . will worm themselves into power if the deepest arts of dissimulation can possibly effect it."[75] Others echoed this fear that unreconstructed enemies might damage the fledgling state. In May, inhabitants of Poughkeepsie gathered to warn fellow New Yorkers of the danger they faced "if those who have wrapt our cities in flames, and covered our land with blood; and whose principles are utterly repugnant to our free government; are suffered to return." Rather than being granted such permission, exiles deserved nothing "from this country but detestation and chastizement [*sic*]."[76] Although this impulse was an aggressive one, it suggested how driving enemies from their homes helped stabilize the new order. Scattered by exile, Loyalists could not form a concerted counterrevolutionary movement after the war. Or, in Publius's evocative image, they could not destroy the state from within like an infestation of worms.

Not only did the forfeiture law help remove Loyalists; it also permanently severed the chain of title that connected them to New York. Hundreds of default judgments struck at these connections by declaring that the defendant had forfeited both present and future property interests. In fact, New Yorkers were convicting so many defendants for adhering to the enemies of the state that courts printed judgment forms so that all clerks would have to do would be fill in the personalized information, such as the defendant's name and the date of indictment. As a result, every judgment had preprinted on it the statement that the defendant did "forfeit all and singular the Estate, both real and personal, whether in Possession, Reversion or Remainder, held or claimed by [him/her] within this State, to the People of this State."[77] Convictions not only caused the forfeiture of present estates such as the house a defendant possessed or the tools that were in his shed. By seizing reversion and remainder interests, they prevented defendants from taking possession of property that had already been promised to them: land that the defendant would have received when a particular person died, tenant farms that would have reverted to a landlord at the expiration of a lease, or livestock that a Loyalist might have inherited. Convictions obliterated all such future interests in property, thereby permanently breaking the legal bonds that once linked Loyalists to the new state.

In addition to conviction forms, the documents that conveyed forfeited land also cut defendants off from the new order. When Commissioners of Forfeitures sold land, they wrote the defendants' attainder directly into both the sale agreements and the new deeds. In both documents, they set out the surveyed location of the property before concluding that the land was "deemed to have been forfeited by the attainder of" the defendant.[78] It is easy to overlook this boilerplate language; its constant repetition might make it appear unremarkable. But its ubiquity was precisely what helped continue purging the state of Loyalists. Many of them had already gone into exile. Every conviction under the forfeiture law severed the chain of title and permanently cut Loyalists off from their property. The conveyances then wrote the defendants' crime directly into the deeds, making it the basis of property ownership in the new state. In every subsequent sale of those lands, every time someone traced out the chain of title, he would find sale agreements and deeds reminding him why a previous owner had forfeited his rights to the property. Thus, even after Loyalists were physically absent from the state, all these documents, default judgments, sale agreements, and deeds methodically broke the legal links that once connected defendants to New York.[79]

Each document, moreover, attested to the state's willingness to cut enemies off from society. At a time when New Yorkers wanted to expel Loyalists, default judgments, sale agreements, and deeds all resonated with that desire and declared that the new legal order shared such priorities. The forfeiture law's aggressive partisanship thus helped rebuild popular support for the revolutionary legal system. New Yorkers could see in each of those documents a sign of trust, a statement that revolutionary legal institutions would help them permanently expel their enemies. And, as the war drew to a close in 1783, New Yorkers made it clear that driving out Loyalists was one of their chief public concerns.

In the spring of that year, one town after another announced in public meetings their refusal to allow Loyalists to resettle among them. In April, the people of Fredericksburgh, in Dutchess County, gathered in a "General Committee for preventing inimical persons returning." They recalled that, at the previous year's town meeting, they had resolved that "no person whatever that has joined or adhered to the enemies of the United States, should ever be suffered to abide in this precinct." The Fredericksburgh committee decided that the time had come to put that resolution into effect, thereby "ordering all such persons out of said precinct."[80]

In May, other New Yorkers followed suit. They gathered in Rhinebeck to decry the "many wretched men" who had left their homes to assist the occupying army. The meeting resolved that "these miscreants . . . shall not reside within this precinct," and, if any had come back, the resolution would serve as notice "that they must withdraw" by May 25. The meeting then appointed a subcommittee to enforce the resolutions.[81] That same month, "the good people" of Rombout, also in Dutchess County, met to declare that "the ambition, avarice, and perfidy of the tories have been the chief cause of all the blood that has been shed." Even though Britain and its supporters lost the fight, "yet the guilt of the tories has not been extenuated; because, from the beginning of the war to this day, they have been guilty of the most horrid and inhuman murders that ever disgraced the records of any country." It was resolved, therefore, that anyone who had left Rombout to join the British "shall never have our consent to live in this precinct." If any were "so hardy as to return," they would have seven days to leave after being warned, "on pain of experiencing the just punishment due to such infamous parricides."[82] After nearly seven years of war and occupation, New Yorkers wanted to purge Loyalists from their communities. That impulse found its legal counterpart in the forfeiture law. Every default judgment, every deed and sale agreement, told New Yorkers that they could trust revolutionary legal institutions to cut Loyalists off from the new state.

When Loyalists attempted to return, their former neighbors intimidated them and tried to drive them away. An anonymous correspondent from Goshen, in Orange County, wrote to a newspaper about what happened there when Loyalists returned to town. During elections in April 1783, many men reappeared and voted even though they had not done so during the war. Disputes broke out, and, when the polls opened for the second day of voting, a call to arms had been posted on the courthouse door. The announcement shouted at the town to "BE ASTONISHED" that Loyalists would come back and meddle in the independent state's politics. The anonymous author could not believe that they would have the audacity to do so "while the corps of our murdered brethren are not yet cold; and while the blood is yet smoaking [*sic*] on the hands and swords of their *murderers* the *Tories*." The broadside called on the people of Goshen to respond "by driving all those infernals from among us": "I say drive them into their lurking holes again, and teach them to bear the burdens, and wear the chains which they and the *devil* have taken so much pains to rivet on us."[83] Loyalists who tried to return, such as those in Goshen, faced neighbors who despised them and wanted to chase them from public life.

The desire to exclude Loyalists from the new state was so ubiquitous and so intensely felt that New Yorkers satirized those who wanted to let enemies return. In May 1783, "Ironicus" wrote "A Cautionary Card" warning against treating Loyalists too harshly. True to his pseudonym, Ironicus pretended to recommend patience in dealing with Loyalists: "The persevering *whigs* in the state of *New-York*, are desired to be very careful how they proceed against any of the *tories*, or persons who have been with the enemy during the war;—as they may depend on being *severely* handled if they take the least irregular step with these *worthy characters*." If the threat of retaliation did not urge caution in dealing with Tories, then their remarkable "*golden remedy*" would encourage New Yorkers to treat them carefully: "[When Tories applied the remedy] to the *palm* of your hand, and you *close* your *fingers* upon it, it electrifies you to such a degree, that all the gross particles of *prejudice* that have been collecting in your hearts during the course of the war, fly off in a *tangent*, and leave you in a state of perfect *amity* with them." Indeed, the remedy worked remarkably well: "You cannot recollect that there [*sic*, i.e., Tories'] hands were, directly, or indirectly *imbued* in the *blood* of your countrymen."[84]

These comments had their ironic implication in the fact that New Yorkers at the time knew that the exact opposite was true. They did not need to be cautious in dealing with Loyalists. There would be no consequences for taking revenge on those characters who, as Ironicus implied, were unworthy of forgiveness or gentle treatment. Even the explanation of "tory" was an ironic touch that suggests the issue of returning Loyalists was an urgent one that mattered deeply to New Yorkers. Ironicus defined "tory" as if his audience had never heard the word before and needed it explained. In fact, New Yorkers were all too familiar with the word since they wanted to punish those who had run off to support an occupying army. As Ironicus suggested, the only ones who would welcome such people back were either deluded or had been bribed. The mock caution of Ironicus reveals how deep anti-Loyalist sentiment ran and how New Yorkers believed that they could never forgive their enemies. For those who wanted to defeat Loyalists, convictions under the forfeiture law communicated a sense of shared aims. Every default judgment, every dispossession and new deed, signaled that they could trust New York's legal institutions to cut their enemies off from the new state.

The development of that trust between New Yorkers and the revolutionary state appears in the timing of convictions under the forfeiture law. There were a total of 522 convictions under the statute during the war and, as figure 4.1 demonstrates, the majority of those convictions occurred in the last year of the war.[85] Over the course of five court terms from October 1782 through October 1783, the last term of the Supreme Court of Judicature before the British evacuated New York City in November 1783, 282 defendants were convicted of adhering to the enemies of the state. To put that number in perspective, it represents an average of 56.4 convictions in each of the last five court terms of the war. By contrast, 240 defendants had been convicted over the preceding twelve court terms dating back to the enactment of the forfeiture law, which was an average of 20 convictions per term. Thus, every time the Supreme Court of Judicature met in the last year of the war, it convicted on average almost three times as many defendants of adhering to the enemies of the state as it had previously. Thus, the popular desire to cut Loyalists off from society found its legal expression in the increase in convictions. As one town after another vowed to drive out Tories, New Yorkers gave that revenge its legal effect by convicting and dispossessing political enemies in greater numbers than at any point during the war.

Driving out Loyalists and permanently dispossessing them was critical in consolidating the legal authority of New York's revolutionary state. Other

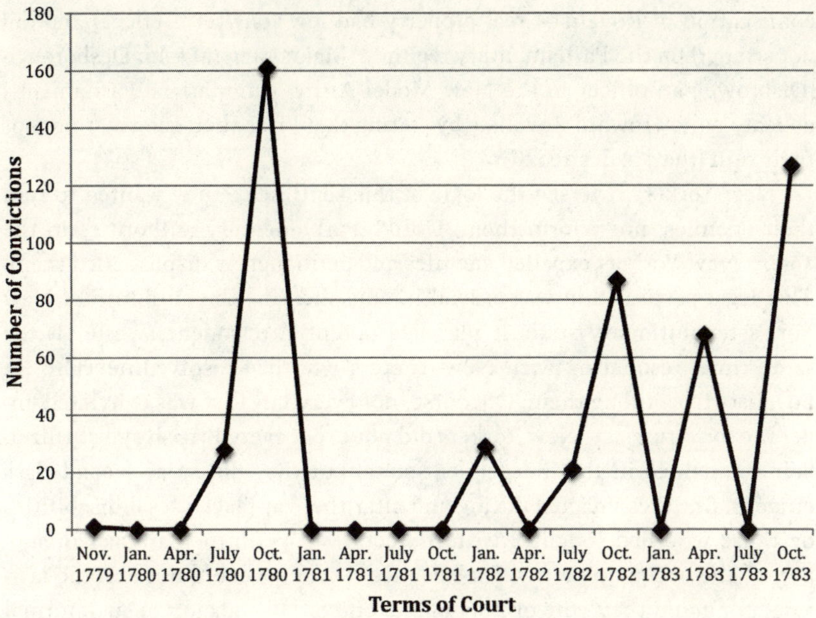

Fig. 4.1 Convictions for adhering to the enemies of the state, November 1779–October 1783
Sources: New York Supreme Court of the Judicature Minute Book, July 25, 1771–April 28, 1781 (Engrossed), and New York Supreme Court of the Judicature Minute Book, July 31, 1781–November 1, 1783 (Engrossed), NYCC. For the methods used in compiling these data, see the appendix.

moments of great upheaval remind us how failing to take such steps makes it hard to stabilize a new order and leaves that order vulnerable to ongoing attacks from enemies. After the English Civil War, Royalists remained in the country even after the fighting had ceased in England and the king had been executed. Moreover, when Parliament expropriated Royalists' land, it did not enforce a permanent change in ownership. Instead, the sales amounted to an elaborate shakedown in which Parliamentary officials confiscated Royalists' land and then immediately sold it back to the former owners at inflated prices.[86] Because so many Royalists remained in England and regained possession of their land, they were able to use Parliamentary legal institutions to thwart the effects of confiscation. In the 1650s, Royalists successfully sued tenants for back rent and, improbably enough, won favorable judgments from such institutions as the Committee for Indemnity, half of whose members were regicides.[87] Thus, Parliamentarians never expelled Royalists en masse, nor did they transfer Royalists' property to new owners. As a result, confiscation of Royalists' real property had few long-term effects and did not strengthen the Parliamentary regime.[88] Major General John Desborough [Disbrowe], an officer in the New Model Army, summarized Parliament's delicate policy toward Royalists by stating that "it is their reformation, not their ruin [that] is desired."[89]

New Yorkers reversed the logic of this sentiment; they wanted to ruin their enemies, not reform them. Unlike Parliamentary authorities in the 1650s, New Yorkers expelled enemies and permanently dispossessed them. This legal partisanship was crucial in consolidating the authority of New York's revolutionary state. It removed potential opponents while, at the same time, resonating with New Yorkers who had resolved never to let Loyalists live among them. Of course, not every Loyalist was convicted under the forfeiture act; New Yorkers did not expel every British sympathizer. Some remained in the independent state, but they did so as second-class citizens. Statutes enacted during and after the war placed legal disabilities on those who had sought British protection or performed any act in support of the occupying army. For instance, Loyalists could not become lawyers, nor could they vote or hold public office.[90] In addition to such formal restrictions, Loyalists faced the popular hatred that was so widespread and intense among New Yorkers. Thus, even though some returned at the end of the war, they did so as a beleaguered minority under harsh limitations that prevented them from actively opposing the new order.

These wide-ranging effects suggest why the forfeiture law and property redistribution were more influential than other legal issues taking place at the time. To be sure, New York's courts heard noncriminal matters such as assumpsit and trespass. Those civil matters occurred, and, if a court could empanel a jury and gather witnesses, then such a case might even reach final judgment. However, the forfeiture law and its enforcement had two characteristics that no other legal matter shared. First, property redistribution created new freeholders who had powerful reasons to support the state's authority. Second, conviction and dispossession cut enemies off from society in a way that spoke to New Yorker's urgent desire to win the war. Those who wanted land as well as those who wanted retribution against Loyalists could see that the forfeiture law offered both. No other legal matter had these broad effects. No debt obligation or lawsuit over wandering livestock drew in supporters and linked them to the new state while at the same time permanently dispossessing enemies. Only the forfeiture law accomplished both, which made it critical in consolidating revolutionary authority.

The forfeiture law caused major changes that stabilized society and strengthened the new legal system over the long term. Shortly before the law's passage, New Yorkers had believed that the state was incapable of resolving their basic needs. They re-created committees to address economic problems and punish Loyalists. But, when the forfeiture law finally passed in October 1779, they stopped working through committees and enforced the statute so aggressively that adhering to the enemies of the state became the most commonly prosecuted crime. This extraordinary spike in prosecutions created the processes through which New Yorkers consolidated the state's legal authority. The statute made it possible for people—particularly tenants—to buy farms and become freeholders, which gave them material reasons to support the new order and resist returning to British rule.

The forfeiture law did more than link new landowners to the state. It also created a legal environment that appealed more generally to the great numbers of New Yorkers who wanted revenge against Loyalists. The law created procedures that made it easy to secure convictions, thereby allowing New Yorkers to retaliate against their enemies without having to conduct trials or face contrary evidence. Hundreds of convictions helped drive out Loyalists and sever the legal bonds that once connected them to New York. Those who fled or were banished could no longer meddle in state politics from their exile in Barbados or Nova Scotia. Moreover, every default judgment—every sale agreement and new deed—attested to the new state's commitment to punishing Loyalists and cutting them off from society. At a time when New Yorkers burned with resentment, when one town after another promised to expel Loyalists, these documents signaled that formal authority would address popular desires and prevent those enemies from resettling in New York. By enforcing redistribution, New Yorkers developed a constituency of support for the new legal order while also exiling many potential opponents. That process drove a remarkable transformation that stabilized society and built the new legal system on a basis of popular support.

This process of revolutionary state building invites Americans to think about their war for independence in ways that might appear contradictory. On one hand, New Yorkers and other Americans managed to develop legal structures during a popular uprising. That was something many other movements never achieved, and it suggests that America's experience was unlike that of other countries, perhaps even exceptional because of it. On the other hand, Americans developed revolutionary authority through property redistribution, which would appear to many today as decidedly un-American and better suited to other revolutions than our own. America did in fact succeed where other uprisings have not. But that success grew out of processes that would be familiar to anyone who has considered popular uprisings in other times and places, especially to those familiar with the partisan legal practices such movements have enforced. In this way, America's experience links the country to revolutionary societies around the world. Rather than wondering what makes the American Revolution more legalistic than all others or how it was exceptional for some other reason, one might do better to ask why popular movements that are different in so many ways have all redistributed property.

CONCLUSION

As soon as the war ended, some of New York's leaders tried to convince ordinary people that their revolution had been more fair, more just and rule bound, than it actually had been. In January 1784, just two months after the British evacuated New York City, Alexander Hamilton wrote, under a pseudonym, *A Letter from Phocion to the Considerate Citizens of New-York*, criticizing those who wanted to disfranchise Loyalists, drive them from the state, and continue selling their property. He claimed that these actions constituted a breach of the treaty of peace that had ended the war.[1] Moreover, anti-Loyalist policies—particularly redistribution—"put in motion all of the furious and dark passions of the human mind" and did nothing but "inculcate revenge, cruelty, persecution, and perfidity." Hamilton believed that, by continuing such practices, New Yorkers violated not just the specific terms of the treaty but the very nature of their revolution. Rather than encourage such ugly passions, the "spirit of Whiggism cherishes legal liberty, holds the rights of every individual sacred, condemns or punishes no man without regular trial and conviction of some crime declared by antecedent laws."[2] According to Hamilton, fairness and respect for due process had characterized the Revolution, and he scolded those who would tarnish its legacy with revenge and persecution.

Other polemicists also found it useful to portray the American Revolution as a legalistic movement to protect property and other ancient rights. Authors who praised the Revolution in such terms usually have done so to persuade their contemporaries that some other movement occurring at the time was dangerous. For instance, in the 1790s, Federalists rejected the French Revolution and feared that its influence would corrupt American society. To prevent such a possibility, authors such as John Quincy Adams sought to convince Americans that, unlike the anarchic violence of the

French Revolution happening at the time, the American Revolution had been a principled effort to defend long-standing rights. While serving as American minister in Berlin, Adams read Friedrich von Gentz's comparison of the two revolutions and believed that it would help his father, John Adams, in his reelection campaign against Thomas Jefferson, whose sympathies with the French Revolution were well known. Quincy Adams translated Gentz's work into English and had it published in Philadelphia in 1800.[3]

Gentz praised the American Revolution as a conservative movement to protect colonists' laws and institutions against the mother country's unprecedented changes. The French, however, did not even attempt to establish the legality of their movement, relying instead on "the chimerical principle of the sovereignty of the people" to justify all their abuses.[4] Quincy Adams, writing as "an American gentleman," explained that Americans needed to hear such views to rescue their revolution "from the disgraceful imputation of having proceeded from the same principles as that of France."[5] Many other American authors, translators, and newspaper printers had a similar purpose when they published works decrying the French Revolution.[6] Gentz's work has shown a great deal of longevity among those seeking to distinguish America's experience from other, supposedly less noble revolutions. The conservative author Russell Kirk wrote the introduction to a paperback edition of Gentz's pamphlet that was published in 1955, during the Cold War.[7]

Such works reveal more about the authors' contemporary political concerns—whether Jacobinism in the eighteenth century or communism in the twentieth—than they do about the nature of the American Revolution. In particular, claims that the Revolution was an orderly affair or that it had little in common with other popular movements obscure the ubiquity of redistribution during America's struggle for independence. Every state enforced property forfeiture, and, despite hectoring from people like Adams and Hamilton, strong popular support persisted for the policy in New York and elsewhere. Not even the federal Constitution, which prohibited bills of attainder such as the 1779 forfeiture law, stopped New Yorkers from selling Loyalist lands.[8] In fact, in the summer of 1787, at the same moment that delegates were in Philadelphia writing the Constitution, Commissioners of Forfeitures were enforcing just such a law throughout New York.[9] While the volume of sales diminished in the 1790s, New Yorkers continued implementing a bill of attainder and selling Loyalist land for decades. Sales of forfeited land were recorded as late as 1843.[10]

After the war, other Americans showed similar enthusiasm for redistribution by enforcing property rules that made redistribution permanent.

Purchasers of confiscated movable goods retained the property and thus legal protections against theft, conversion, and other loss. Moreover, every time a piece of confiscated land was sold, partitioned, bequeathed, or transferred some other way, the state extended the chain of title that stretched back to revolutionary redistribution. But the legal benefits of redistribution were not the only ones that Americans experienced; they also enjoyed material gains. In fact, the effects of redistribution were so widespread that those gains went far beyond the purchasers. For instance, in Pennsylvania, the statute that confiscated real property required that enough estates be transferred to the College of Philadelphia—later renamed the University of Pennsylvania—to provide the institution with an income of £1,500 per year. It also required that the purchasers of certain confiscated estates pay, with interest, a portion of the sale price directly to the college. These direct payments added up to a significant amount of revenue.[11] Effects such as these, along with the ongoing sale of confiscated property, extended revolutionary property rules and their consequences far into the nineteenth century.

We can see these practices only if we look to the actual implementation of law on the ground rather than relying on abstract constitutional provisions that banned bills of attainder or the counterrevolutionary hopes of authors like Hamilton and Quincy Adams. Such polemicists might advance their own political goals by explaining how America's founding was unlike the French or Russian Revolutions. Other authors in our own time make a similar point when they insist on the primacy of property rights in America's legal tradition. Whatever these views might achieve, they mischaracterize the American Revolution and get a basic fact of chronology wrong. Not only was property redistribution in America widespread, but it also happened before other modern movements that we are told are so different from our own. That is, America was first in this line of supposedly un-American revolutions. In that regard, America's founding was indeed exceptional. It radically altered property rights in the name of the people and did so before other revolutions also built a new order on confiscated property.

APPENDIX

Crimes Prosecuted in New York, October 1779–November 1783

Crimes	Indictments/ Informations	Convictions	Acquittals	Other Dispositions
Adhering to the enemies of the state	1,048	581	1	4
Assault and battery	146	63	7	33
Riot	104	59	9	16
Assault (without battery)	90	57	1	23
Rescue	40	36	3	4
Grand larceny	58	24	8	5
Misdemeanor (no specific crime named)	48	16	0	12
Nuisance in exercising a private lottery	11	10	0	0
Receiving stolen goods scienter	10	8	1	2
Seditious words or speeches (misdemeanor)	15	8	0	3
Taking and carrying away goods of another	10	7	0	0
Robbery	26	6	0	0

(continued)

Crimes Prosecuted in New York, October 1779–November 1783 (*continued*)

Crimes	Indictments/ Informations	Convictions	Acquittals	Other Dispositions
Aiding an escape to the enemy (offering provisions, escape routes, etc.)	4	6	0	0
Murder	11	5	3	0
False imprisonment	18	4	0	2
Sabbath breaking	4	4	0	0
Accessory to felony	20	3	1	0
Harboring fugitives	4	3	0	1
Refusing to accept New York money as payment	3	3	0	0
Theft (without value of goods declared)	3	2	0	0
Purchasing goods with intent to resell them	5	2	0	0
Horse stealing	5	2	1	0
Refusing to assist constable or other officer	8	2	1	1
Extortion in public office	7	2	0	2
Knowingly passing counterfeit notes or dollars	9	2	1	0
Encouraging others to follow enemies or to submit to king (misdemeanor)	12	2	1	0
Burglary	6	1	0	0
Petty larceny	2	1	0	0
Assault with intent to murder	4	1	1	0
Assault with intent to commit a rape	0	1	0	0
Rescuing goods from tax collector	2	1	0	0

Crimes Prosecuted in New York, October 1779–November 1783 (*continued*)

Crimes	Indictments/ Informations	Convictions	Acquittals	Other Dispositions
Engrossing	1	1	0	0
Obstructing a court-martial	8	1	0	7
Neglect of official duty	3	1	0	1
Escape from jail or furthering an escape	10	1	1	1
Bigamy	1	1	0	0
Corresponding or trading with the enemy	6	0	3	1
Obstructing the highway	1	0	0	0
Attempt to bribe an official	1	0	0	0
Perjury	2	0	0	1
Petty felony	2	0	0	0
Trespass	19	0	1	2
Arson	1	0	1	0
Declaring allegiance to king of Great Britain (felony)	1	0	0	1
Dissuading people from their allegiance to New York (felony)	5	0	2	0
Buggery	4	0	3	0
"Divers [*sic*] frauds and Deceipts [*sic*]"	3	0	0	0
Leaving a jury before it brought in a verdict	2	0	0	0
Forgery	1	0	0	0
Treason	109	0	1	0
Totals	1,913	927	51	118

SOURCES

New York Supreme Court of Judicature Minute Book, July 25, 1775–April 28, 1781 (Engrossed), and New York Supreme Court of the Judicature Minute Book, July 31, 1781–November 1, 1783 (Engrossed), NYCC.

BV McKesson—Engrossed Minutes for the Court of Oyer and Terminer for Albany, New York, Suffolk, and Ulster Counties, NYHS.

Minutes of the Court of General Sessions and of Common Pleas, Liber E-1771–1774; Liber F-1775–1781; Liber G-1782–1785, microfilm reel 127, DCCO.

Minutes of Court of Sessions, 1685–1689, 1717–1723, 1763–1782, Canvass of Voters 1820, ACHR.

Court of Sessions Minutes, Ser. 43, A-0048 (1)L, WCARC.

ADHERING TO THE ENEMIES OF THE STATE

The data on convictions for adhering to the enemies of the state have been compiled from the minutes of the Supreme Court of Judicature. The procedure for prosecutions has made the records of that particular court an invaluable source because it was the only one empowered both to indict and to try defendants for the crime. According to the forfeiture law, two county-level courts and one statewide court had the power to indict defendants for adhering to the enemies of the state. The county-level courts were the Court of Oyer and Terminer and General Gaol Delivery and the Court of General Sessions of the Peace. The statewide venue was the Supreme Court of Judicature, which, despite its name, had general civil and criminal jurisdiction.[1] New Yorkers indicted defendants in many different counties outside British control, such as the Westchester County Court of General Sessions of the Peace or the Ulster County Court of Oyer and Terminer. Once these courts indicted a defendant, the clerks would send a copy of the indictment along with examination(s) of witness(es) to the Supreme Court in Albany for trial. The clerk of the Supreme Court then entered those indictments in the Supreme Court's minutes, along with the court's own indictments for the same crime. This jurisdictional arrangement has resulted in the indictments, where they survived, being funneled from different courts throughout the state into the Supreme Court's minutes. All the indictments and convictions for adhering to the enemies of the state appear there. As a result, although there are redundant entries for indictments in both county courts and the Supreme Court, the procedural requirements for prosecutions were such that the minutes of the Supreme Court are the only record with both indictments and convictions for adhering to the enemies of the state.

The total number of convictions for adhering to the enemies of the state includes two categories of defendant: the 59 people attainted in the statute as well as the 522 defendants convicted in the Supreme Court. Of those 522 convictions, 517 were entered by default (i.e., the defendants never appeared to plead to the charges), and 5 were guilty pleas. The category of "Other Dispositions" for this crime includes the defendants who availed themselves of section 5 of the forfeiture law. They appeared in court to plead that they had taken an oath of allegiance to the state, thereby barring the indictment found against them.

ALL OTHER CRIMES

The data on convictions for other crimes have been compiled from the surviving minutes of county and statewide courts in those parts of the province not occupied by the British. As the list of sources given above suggests, these records include minutes from county-level courts in Dutchess, Albany, Ulster, and Westchester Counties as well the statewide Supreme Court of Judicature. However, it would be misleading to suggest that these numbers were the product of simply finding widely scattered court minutes and tabulating their contents. In fact, arranging these data required a great deal of interpretation to impose order on a convoluted collection of records. One area that required interpretation was the names of offenses. Modern legal experts might assume that what counted as assault during the American Revolution was self-evident; or, at least, they might assume that courts always applied consistent names to their prosecutions for assault. But, like other Americans at the time, late eighteenth-century New Yorkers did not often share modern lawyers' concern for exact legal terminology. As a result, the court minutes might change the names of offenses over the course of a prosecution: someone indicted for assault, without more, could be arraigned for aiding an assault, before being convicted of aiding and encouraging an assault and wounding. The data in the table have accommodated such variation by arranging the offenses into categories that captured the common element in all the different names. In the example of changing names for assault, the variations were placed under one heading: *assault (without battery)*.

However, even if New Yorkers employed consistent terminology throughout proceedings, they might describe the same crime in different ways. As a result, it is often difficult to determine whether different defendants were being prosecuted for the same offense. For instance, a defendant might be indicted for receiving stolen goods scienter (i.e., knowingly receiving stolen goods), or he might be indicted as an accessory to felony. The first crime was a subcategory of the second, insofar as that someone who had knowingly received stolen goods had been an accessory to felony, just as one who aided the escape of a fugitive was also an accessory to felony. Thus, New Yorkers sometimes employed consistent but broad terminology, such as choosing to prosecute someone for "accessory to felony" rather than naming the particular type of accessory. To accommodate this vagueness, the data are arranged under the most specific headings that the records allow. If a defendant was convicted for receiving stolen goods, then it was added to the total for that offense. But, if he was convicted only for the vaguer crime of accessory to felony, then the indictment was added to that total, even though it describes only a broad category of offense.

In addition to the challenge of categorizing each offense, it was also necessary to determine how to account for each of them. After all, a defendant might be prosecuted for more than one crime. He might also be prosecuted for multiple instances of the same offense. Since the purpose of this analysis is comparing the frequency of prosecutions during the Revolution, the data account for each offense separately. For instance, someone indicted for both robbery and assault counted in two categories, once for robbery and once for assault. Similarly, one defendant convicted of two counts of the same crime would be counted twice in that crime.

It is also worth noting why the numbers do not always add up for particular crimes. The number of indictments does not always equal the number of convictions, acquittals, and other dispositions. Indeed, for some of the crimes listed above, there are more convictions and acquittals than there are indictments, which might seem to defy sense. But the totals do not add up in part because the data—taken from October 1779 through November 1783—pick up many prosecutions in the middle of their history. Someone might have been indicted in July 1779—before the period under study—before being convicted in January 1780. In such instances, a conviction but no indictment would appear in the data. Moreover, many defendants were indicted, were released on their own recognizance, and fled before trial, leaving the records with an indictment but no final judgment. In addition, particular phases of some prosecutions do not appear in the records. For instance, a conviction might appear for which no indictment was recorded. These issues have all contributed to making the totals appear as they do. The only exceptions are the indictments for treason. Ninety-eight people were indicted for treason in the Supreme Court of Judicature in May 1783. Most of the same defendants were also indicted for adhering to the enemies of the state during the same term of court. However, those indicted for both crimes were convicted of adhering to the enemies of the state, not for treason.[2] As a result, the appendix table shows a large number of indictments for treason but no convictions.

A final word on "other dispositions" of all crimes other than adhering to the enemies of the state. Most of the prosecutions that fell under this heading were no-contest pleas. However, courts did occasionally quash indictments for insufficiency, which also added to the total.

NOTES

INTRODUCTION

1. "The Property of Beverly Robinson Sold at Vendue," November 24, 1777, box labeled "Dutchess County, N.Y./May 20, 1773–June 1887," Dutchess County Collection, 1696–ca. 1910, NYHS.

2. Book of Deeds, "Abstract of Forfeiture & Sales Act of 1779," vols. 2 and 8, various dates, DCCO. Summaries of the sales of lots are arranged in rough chronological order, and sales of parcels once owned by Beverly Robinson appear in both volumes.

3. New York [State], *Minutes of the Committee*, 1:148–50.

4. For a brief outline of the Checka and its powers, see Juviler, *Revolutionary Law and Order*, 22–24.

5. Kim, *Landlord and Tenant*, chap. 8.

6. New York [State], *Minutes of the Committee*, 1:150 n. 6; "The Property of Beverly Robinson Sold at Vendue," November 24, 1777, box labeled "Dutchess County, N.Y./May 20, 1773–June 1887," Dutchess County Collection, 1696–ca. 1910, NYHS.

7. Thomas Jefferson to Benjamin Franklin, August 3, 1777, Boyd, ed., *Papers of Thomas Jefferson*, 2:26.

8. For an analysis of the committee system throughout the colonies and its impact on popular mobilization, see Breen, *American Insurgents*. See also Ammerman, *Common Cause*. For a discussion of New York's committees, see Countryman, *People in Revolution*, pt. 2.

9. Wood, *Creation of the American Republic*. (Wood even titles a section "The Easy Transition to Republicanism." See ibid., 92.) See also Wood, *Radicalism*; and Bailyn, *Ideological Origins*.

10. Hulsebosch, *Constituting Empire*; Nelson, *Americanization of the Common Law*; Horwitz, *Transformation of American Law*; Kramer, *The People Themselves*; Fritz, *American Sovereigns*; Reid, *Constitutional History*. The debate over how many constitutions existed in the British Atlantic, their sources, and how they interacted is the subject of Desan, Hulsebosch, Konig, and Mann, "Constitutions on Edge."

11. Bradburn, *Citizenship Revolution*; Griffin, *America's Revolution*; Brooke, *Columbia Rising*.

12. Forbath, Hartog, and Minow, "Legal Histories from Below," 759.

13. The work of Stephen Holmes is particularly insightful on the volatile nature of societies that lack settled states. In examining liberal political thought, Holmes has argued that rights cannot exist in such circumstances. When governments become weak or fail entirely, "rights can be imagined but not experienced." Without legal structures such as courts, abstract rights to personal security or property vanish because there is no institutional framework for guaranteeing them. Holmes, *Passions and Constraint*, 19.

14. The literature on the social history of the Revolution—particularly the literature exploring the influence of those traditionally overlooked in stories of American independence—is vast and growing. An insightful analysis of how Americans mobilized support for the uprising on the eve of the war appears in Breen, *American Insurgents*. Other prominent examples of this approach to the period include Nash, *Unknown American Revolution*, and *Forgotten Fifth*; Young, Nash, and Rafael, eds., *Revolutionary Founders*; Young and Nobles, *Whose American Revolution Was It?*; Young, ed., *The American Revolution*; and Holton, *Forced Founders*.

15. For a thoughtful examination of how social reality predisposed people to embrace particular ideas during the Revolution, see Breen, *Tobacco Culture*, 3–15.

16. Guinea-Bissau's fight for independence from Portugal offers an illuminating comparison to New York's experience of revolutionary state building. Amílcar Cabral, a leader in Guinea-Bissau's national liberation movement, explained how abstractions alone did not win popular support for insurgent legal authority. Few people would accept revolutionary legal authority unless the guerrillas provided the public with the basic necessities of life. If the guerrillas failed to do so, no amount of idealism or soaring language could win popular support. In a message to leaders of the governing party, Cabral urged them: "Remember always that the people do not fight for ideas, for things that only exist in the heads of individuals. . . . National liberation, the struggle against colonialism, working for peace and progress, independence—all these will be empty words without significance for the people, unless they are translated into real improvements in the conditions of life. It is useless to liberate a region, if the people of the region are then left without the elementary necessities of life." Quoted in Rudebeck, "Political Mobilisation in Guinea-Bissau," 433–34. Historians have identified this process in other revolutions as well. See also Brown, *Ending the French Revolution*, 25; Wickham-Crowley, *Exploring Revolution*, 39–40; Tone, *The Fatal Knot*, 6; and Kedward, *In Search of the Maquis*, 96–97.

17. One of the defining features of law, and particularly criminal justice, during periods of political transition is that it drives the change from the old order to the new. Public trials, clemency, and various forms of punishment disavow past abuses and announce a new beginning for the successor state. Teitel, *Transitional Justice*, chap. 2. As one historian demonstrated for the French Revolution, the National Convention's failure to come to terms with the gruesome legacy of the Terror undermined the legitimacy of the successor government, the Directory, and deepened divisions in the country. Brown, *Ending the French Revolution*, 26–37.

18. For an analysis of how British abuse and incompetence turned neutral New Yorkers in one occupied county against Britain, see Tiedemann, "Patriots by Default."

19. For analyses of the ways that property holding and disputes surrounding property shaped New York from the earliest European settlement through the early republic, see

Kim, *Landlord and Tenant*; Mark, *Agrarian Conflicts in Colonial New York*; Countryman, *People in Revolution*, 46–54; Lynd, *Anti-Federalism in Dutchess County, New York*; Bonomi, *A Factious People*; and Humphrey, *Land and Liberty*. Property and conflict over it had powerful effects in other provinces as well. See Taylor, *Liberty Men and Great Proprietors*; McConville, *These Daring Disturbers*; and Richter, *Trade, Land, Power*. In stressing the centrality of property—particularly land—in both Native and European conceptions of America, Richter explains how "a matrix of trade, land, and power defined [Native] relations with European colonizers. The colonizers' failure to understand the cultural significance of exchange and their single-minded focus on real estate lay at the heart of the struggle for control of eastern North America." Richter, *Trade, Land, Power*, 5. Taylor identifies "a national pattern of backcountry resistance" from the mid-eighteenth century to the mid-nineteenth century. During that time, property disputes erupted in Maine, New York, Pennsylvania, New Jersey, North Carolina, and elsewhere as yeoman farmers sought land and fell into conflict with the great proprietors who claimed to own huge swaths of the continent. Taylor, *Liberty Men and Great Proprietors*, 4–5. For the extensive literature examining all the ways that property shaped early America, see ibid., 4 n. 6.

20. One scholar has described this phenomenon in terms of the cost of revolutionary participation. A successful insurgency will lower the cost of supporting the movement by making it possible for unaligned people to take some small action on its behalf. At the same time, insurgents will increase the cost, or danger, of opposition through reprisals against those who refuse to help. In this way, insurgencies intimidate people into acquiescing to their authority. See Petersen, *Resistance and Rebellion*.

21. For a discussion of Loyalists returning after the war, see MacKinnon, *This Unfriendly Soil*; and Maas, *Return of the Massachusetts Loyalists*. More recent scholarship has demonstrated that reliable numbers of Loyalists who fled the United States are hard to come by. See Ranlet, "How Many American Loyalists Left the United States?" Consequently, it is hard to know how many might have returned. But it is clear that those who returned to places like New York did so without getting their property back and without enjoying the same rights to practice certain professions and hold office that supporters of independence enjoyed. Chapter 4 below examines this issue in greater detail.

CHAPTER ONE

1. Prior to serving in New York, Tryon had been the governor of North Carolina, where he personally led troops against the Regulators. One of his last acts as North Carolina's governor was attending the executions of the uprising's leaders in June 1771. Two weeks later he sailed for New York. Kars, *Breaking Loose Together*.

2. Frey, ed., *Minute Book*, 105–6.

3. He never married Molly Brant, but he acknowledged being the father of her eight children.

4. Richter, "Sir William Johnson."

5. Bailyn, *Voyagers to the West*, 576–82; Richter, "Sir William Johnson."

6. Campbell, *Annals of Tryon County*, 113–14.

7. In the summer of 1774, popular committees started to emerge throughout the colonies to coordinate a response to the deepening conflict with Britain. The First Continental

Congress met in September of that year and encouraged the spread of these extralegal groups. For an analysis of the committees and the ways in which they mobilized opposition to royal government, see Breen, *American Insurgents*.

8. Frey, ed., *Minute Book*, 1–3.

9. Campbell, *Annals of Tryon County*, 37–41.

10. Frey, ed., *Minute Book*, 7 n. 20.

11. Ibid., 55–56.

12. Jacob Seeber was a captain in the New York militia and later fought in the battle at Oriskany in August 1777. Ibid., 57 n. 20, 61–62.

13. Sir John informed the committee that he would relinquish ownership if he were reimbursed the £700 that he, or more likely his father, spent in building the county court-house and jail. But, even if the committee did not buy the buildings from him, he would allow anyone into them "for the Use . . . these houses have been built for." However, he told the committee that, if it made "any Unlawful use of the Goal [*sic*], he would oppose it." Ibid., 84. One suspects that anything the committee did with the buildings would appear to Sir John as an "Unlawful use." The Provincial Congress, which was the extralegal body that tried to coordinate the actions of New York's local committees, disagreed with Sir John's claims. Congress informed the committee in Tryon that Sir John's father, Sir William, had conveyed the buildings to two people for them to hold in trust for the use of the county. As a result, Sir John "can claim no title to the court-house and jail in your county." New York [State], *Journals of the Provincial Congress*, 1:212.

14. Frey, ed., *Minute Book*, 1–10.

15. Ibid., 7–8.

16. Ibid., 12.

17. Ibid., 49–51.

18. Albany Committee, *Minutes of the Albany Committee*, 1:165–66.

19. Ibid., 167, 172.

20. Ibid., 199. Jailing White began a period of years in which committees monitored his behavior. The Albany committee put him in close confinement, then released him on parole under the condition that he not oppose any congresses or committees. But it soon arrested him again and required him to post a £500 bond for his good behavior, before moving him to Kingston in August 1777, two years after the confrontation at Johnson Hall. See ibid., 206, 292, 643, 836.

21. Ibid., 313, 357, 366, 372, 409–10; Campbell, *Annals of Tryon County*, 61–62. Johnson returned a few years later to lead a series of devastating raids in the Mohawk Valley. Ibid., chap. 9.

22. Roberts, comp., *New York in the Revolution*, 2:250.

23. Sales of various Johnson lots appear in a folder labeled "A4032 Account Book, Commissioners of Forfeitures for the Western District, 1784–1785," Lists of Sales of and Accounts of Payments for Confiscated Lands, 1784–1788, A4032, NYSA.

24. Quoted in Kim, *Landlord and Tenant*, 14.

25. For an examination of how governors expected such grants to consolidate the colony's central government, see ibid., 14–16.

26. Although landownership and allegiance were linked as early as 1664, the nature of these connections changed during the Revolution. See chapter 4 below.

27. Bonomi, *A Factious People*, 182.

28. For the different types of patents, their sizes, and which governors made them, see Kim, *Landlord and Tenant*, chap. 1. The legal conditions of these grants appear in Bonomi, *A Factious People*, 60–75, 179–88.

29. Bonomi, *A Factious People*, 6.

30. For the factors that destroyed feudal privileges in New York, see Kim, *Landlord and Tenant*, chap. 3.

31. Kulikoff, *From British Peasants*, 134.

32. Bonomi, *A Factious People*, 193–95.

33. Such competition proved so intense that New York's political culture became highly divisive as different families fought for advantage over rivals. Ibid.

34. Countryman, *People in Revolution*, 27; Humphrey, *Land and Liberty*, 30–31.

35. Descriptions of this wedding appear in Humphrey, *Land and Liberty*, 12–13; Countryman, *People in Revolution*, 27; and Lynd, "Who Should Rule at Home?" 332.

36. One early but influential example of this approach came when a historian cited the sum of £3.3 million that the British government paid to indemnify Loyalists for their property losses. This figure was a "quantitative and objective" measure of the revolutionary nature of the American Revolution. Palmer, *Age of the Democratic Revolution*, 1:188. Similarly, Alexander C. Flick was one of the few historians to mention the confiscation of personal property. But he did so only by providing numbers of Loyalists dispossessed, the value of their confiscated property, and the challenges involved in determining precise values in a period of severe currency fluctuation. Flick, *Loyalism in New York*, chap. 7. Flick's appendix lists information about sales of real property: Loyalist owners, new purchasers, number of acres, sale price, and surveyed locations of some but not all confiscated lots. Flick has one paragraph stating how confiscation and sale of real estate weakened "the feudal element in the social system of New York." Ibid., 159. The claim here is not that such figures are irrelevant or that the value of confiscated property does not at least suggest the importance of revolutionary confiscation. Rather, these rough estimates only hint at the centrality of redistribution and do not go far enough in analyzing its radical effects.

37. New York was not alone in facing enforcement problems. New Jersey also suffered from violence against colonial officials and institutions, particularly in the 1740s and 1750s, which often made it impossible to maintain basic order. McConville, *These Daring Disturbers*, esp. pt. 2. Other colonies such as Pennsylvania failed to enforce the law because their populations grew so quickly and spread so far from established towns that parts of the colony were beyond the authority of government. Marietta and Rowe, *Troubled Experiment*, chap. 5.

38. The records do not reveal what happened to Mariners. Catharine Van Alstyne to William Kempe, January 31, 1757, Kempe Papers, box 4, William Kempe Letters, "v-Yeamans," NYHS, cited in Greenberg, *Crime and Law Enforcement*, 159.

39. The percentage of contempt of authority crimes appears with the totals for other categories of crime in ibid., 54. The percentage of those crimes involving attacks on law enforcement appears in ibid., 158.

40. Jacob Van Schajck [*sic*] to Cadwallader Colden, December 21, 1760, in Colden, *Letters and Papers*, 5:383–84. In the same letter, Van Schaack described an incident in which three army officers were arrested but "rescued themselves and used the Subsheriff ill."

41. O'Callaghan, *Calendar of Historical Manuscripts*, 2:809. Many of the documents listed in this calendar burned in a fire at the capitol building in Albany in 1911, leaving only O'Callaghan's brief summaries.

42. Greenberg, *Crime and Law Enforcement*, 162–63.

43. O'Callaghan, *Documentary History*, 3:575. The petition is addressed to "George Clarke, Esq., Commander in Chief of the Province of New York." The colony's governor was also commander in chief of the militia, and Clarke was governor 1736–43, which suggests that the petition dates from those years.

44. *King v. Thomas Jarvis*, April 24, 1767, "Minute Books of the Supreme Court of Judicature of the Colony of New York," 1704–1740 and 1750–1781 in the Queens College Historical Documents Collection, cited in Greenberg, *Crime and Law Enforcement*, 114.

45. Greenberg, *Crime and Law Enforcement*, 165–66 n. 24.

46. Act of March 8, 1773, ch. 1605, in New York [Colony], *Colonial Laws*, 5:527.

47. Both quotations appear in O'Callaghan, *Documentary History*, 3:125. Whitehead was not the only doubting justice in Queens County. A few months earlier, John Talman had declared that the scriptures were not a rule to walk by because men wrote them and men were inherently sinful. Ibid., 124.

48. A list that suggests the variety of official crime appears in Greenberg, *Crime and Law Enforcement*, 165 n. 23.

49. Ibid., 71, 87–88.

50. Rosen, "Supreme Court of Judicature."

51. The percentage of contempt of authority crimes in Massachusetts varied by time and county, but it never dropped below 11.1 percent. Hindus, *Prison and Plantation*, 64. Hindus confines himself to the years 1767–1878, but data for criminal prosecutions in Massachusetts stretch back to the seventeenth century. Similar statistics do not appear for South Carolina.

52. For officers such as justices and sheriffs to do their jobs, ordinary people had to assist them, or at least acquiesce in their authority. As one historian has demonstrated, officials "had no choice but to depend on the willingness of local citizens to accede to their positions as representatives of legitimate governmental authority." Greenberg, *Crime and Law Enforcement*, 176.

53. Goebel and Naughton, *Law Enforcement in Colonial New York*, 710–12.

54. Greenberg, *Crime and Law Enforcement*, 130.

55. Goebel and Naughton, *Law Enforcement in Colonial New York*, 715–16. Instead of sentencing defendants to execution and forfeiture, courts imposed a variety of punishments such as fines, the lash, the pillory, imprisonment, and public shaming by wearing a sign announcing the offense, being drawn around town in a cart, or wearing a halter. For a quantitative summary of the numbers of each type of punishment and the crimes for which they were imposed, see ibid., 702 n. 139.

56. For this example and other similar ones, see ibid., 713.

57. Hulsebosch, *Constituting Empire*, 120–22; Goebel and Naughton, *Law Enforcement in Colonial New York*, 300–302, 235–38.

58. Using that phrase to describe takings in the colonial period, as many historians have done, is misleading. One historian has found that *eminent domain* did not appear

in American law in its current sense until cases were argued in Pennsylvania and South Carolina in 1796. Reynolds, *Before Eminent Domain*, 82.

59. Some historians have suggested that forfeiture for public use was almost always uncompensated in colonial America. However, this view has a narrow evidentiary base and relies on statutes, overlooking other administrative mechanisms of forfeiture. See, e.g., Horwitz, *Transformation of American Law*, 63; and Treanor, "Origins and Original Significance," and "Original Understanding." For an explanation of the shortcomings of the no-compensation argument, see Reynolds, *Before Eminent Domain*, 78.

60. Hart, "Takings and Compensation," 260–61.

61. Ely, "'That Due Satisfaction Be Made,'" 6.

62. Becker, *History of Political Parties*, chap. 5.

63. Tiedemann, *Reluctant Revolutionaries*, chaps. 8–11; Mason, *Road to Independence*, 1–40. For an analysis of how the Association helped to organize resistance to Britain and to give it coherence throughout the colonies, not just in New York, see Breen, *American Insurgents*, chap. 6.

64. Becker, *History of Political Parties*, 137–41.

65. The Committee of Sixty sent a circular letter to other counties asking inhabitants to participate in the selection of delegates, which added to the complexity of this political maneuvering. The responses among different counties were as varied as they had been the previous year during the debate over elections to the First Continental Congress. Mason, *Road to Independence*, chap. 4; Becker, *History of Political Parties*, chap. 8.

66. New York [State], *Journals of the Provincial Congress*, 1:1–5.

67. Of course, not every county supported the Provincial Congress with equal fervor, and turnout for the elections to Congress varied. But nowhere did opponents prevent elections as they had in the past, and the fact that every county sent delegates suggests how Lexington and Concord deepened opposition to Britain. Becker, *History of Political Parties*, 201.

68. For the Committee of Sixty's circular letter calling for elections to a provincial congress, and for the first meeting of the Congress, see New York [State], *Journals of the Provincial Congress*, 1:5–7.

69. Countryman, *People in Revolution*, 138, 141.

70. For a powerful story demonstrating how the battles galvanized ordinary people, see Breen, *American Insurgents*, 21–24.

71. Dawson and Tomlinson, eds., *New York City during the American Revolution*, 54; Force, comp., *American Archives*, 4th ser., 2:364.

72. Force, comp., *American Archives*, 4th ser., 2:364.

73. Colden to Capt. Vandeput, and Colden to Maj. Hamilton, both May 27, 1775, Colden, *Colden Letter Books*, 2:413–14; Maj. Hamilton to Colden, June 5, 1775, Colden, *Letters and Papers*, 7:299–300.

74. New York [State], *Journals of the Provincial Congress*, 1:28.

75. Dawson and Tomlinson, eds., *New York City during the American Revolution*, 57–58.

76. Ibid., 58.

77. Maj. Hamilton to Cadwallader Colden, June 8, 1775, Colden, *Letters and Papers*, 7:300–301; Dawson and Tomlinson, eds., *New York City during the American Revolution*, 59.

78. Dawson and Tomlinson, eds., *New York City during the American Revolution*, 63–64.

79. Ibid., 65; Maj. Hamilton to Colden, June 8, 1775, Colden, *Letters and Papers*, 7:301.

80. Colden to Maj. Hamilton, June 9, 1775, Colden, *Letter Books*, 2:426.

81. Force, comp., *American Archives*, 4th ser., 3:1707–8. Sears was not the only such insurgent who in late 1775 believed that New Yorkers needed to adopt much harsher measures against British sympathizers. See Champagne, *Alexander McDougall*, 95–98; and Ranlet, *New York Loyalists*, 56–58.

82. *Constitutional Gazette*, November 25, 1775.

83. Force, comp., *American Archives*, 4th ser., 3:1708. Episodes such as these where violence frightened British sympathizers into public admissions of wrongdoing characterized a great deal of revolutionary activity throughout the colonies. See Breen, *American Insurgents*, chap. 6.

84. Governor William Tryon was in England at the time, and he did not return to New York until June. Colden served as governor in his absence.

85. New York's Septennial Act, which the colony enacted in 1743, did not permit the same assembly to sit for more than seven years. By December 1775, the Assembly was about to reach that time limit, so the governor called for new elections. The Septennial Act appears in New York [Colony], *Colonial Laws*, 3:295–96.

86. For an excellent outline of every colonial assembly in New York, including when they convened, when governors prorogued them, and who the representatives were, see Bonomi, *A Factious People*, app. C. For a discussion of the governor's decision not to allow the Assembly to sit during a time of intense popular anger, see Becker, *History of Political Parties*, 199–200.

87. The Provincial Congress, and later the Provincial Convention, would continue to rely on this procedure in the following years, appointing the Committee (later Council) of Safety to sit when the main body could not do so.

88. For a description of the Congress's difficulties in gathering a quorum, see Becker, *History of Political Parties*, 234–36.

89. For a discussion of how revolutionary mobilization varied throughout New York, see Countryman, *People in Revolution*, 148–54.

90. Ibid., 160.

91. For courts' schedules, including their last colonial terms, see Minutes of the Court of General Sessions and of Common Pleas, Liber E 1771–1774, Liber F 1775–1781, Liber G 1782–1785, microfilm reel 127, DCCO; Westchester County Minutes of the Court of Common Pleas, ser. 9, A-0010 (1)L, volume labeled "1774–1793," WCARC; Albany Court of Common Pleas, 1763–1799, ser. 87-09085, Minutes of Court of Sessions, 1685–1689, 1717–1723, 1763–1782, and Canvass of Voters 1820, ACHR; and New York Supreme Court of Judicature Minute Book, July 25, 1775–April 28, 1781 (Engrossed), NYCC.

CHAPTER TWO

1. The first court to reconvene was the Supreme Court of Judicature, New York's statewide trial court of general civil and criminal jurisdiction, in September 1777. However, it soon fled a British raiding party and did not reconvene until the following year.

There are no minutes for any session between September 1777 and October 1778. See New York Supreme Court of Judicature Minute Book, July 25, 1775–April 28, 1781 (Engrossed), NYCC. However, *The New-York Journal and the General Advertiser* from August 10, 1778, refers to a July session of court that met in Albany. And the minutes from April 23, 1779, refer to a session that met in April 1778. Neither of these sessions appears in the engrossed minutes. County-level courts—Common Pleas and General Sessions of the Peace—started to reconvene at different times throughout 1778. Even when courts finally reconvened, they had very short dockets. For instance, when the Dutchess County Court of Common Pleas reconvened for the first time in May 1778, it received the return of a single writ, then adjourned until October. For the courts' schedules and their short dockets, see Minutes of the Court of General Sessions and of Common Pleas, Liber E 1771–1774, Liber F 1775–1781, Liber G 1782–1785, microfilm reel 127, DCCO; Westchester County Minutes of the Court of Common Pleas, ser. 9, A-0010 (1)L, volume labeled "1774–1793," WCARC.

2. For an analysis of the committee system throughout the colonies and its impact on popular mobilization, see Breen, *American Insurgents*. For a discussion of New York's committees, see Countryman, *People in Revolution*.

3. In May 1776, the Provincial Congress acknowledged what had already occurred in actual practice: royal government no longer existed in New York. The Congress resolved: "By the voluntary abdication of the late Governour, *Tryon*, the dissolution of our Assembly for want of due prorogation, and the open and unwarrantable hostilities committed against the persons and properties of the inhabitants of all the United Colonies in *North-America* by the *British* Fleets and Armies, under the authority, and by the express direction and appointment of, the King, Lords, and Commons of *Great Britain*, the said old form of Government is become, *ipso facto*, dissolved." Force, comp., *American Archives*, 4th ser., 6:1338. Of course, the presence of the Royal Navy in the harbor suggested one form of British authority. But traditional institutions such as a legislature, courts, and a governor had failed. Moreover, even military authority did not exert much influence onshore since Washington continued building up the city's defenses against a British invasion directly under the ships' guns and the navy did not stop him.

4. When British troops evacuated Boston in March 1776, they retreated by ship to Halifax, where they resupplied. As Washington correctly predicted, the troops then sailed from Halifax in June to launch their invasion of New York.

5. Force, comp., *American Archives*, 4th ser., 6:790.

6. Ibid., 993.

7. Ibid., 1160.

8. Ibid., 1385–86.

9. Ibid., 1056.

10. Ibid., 5th ser., 1:1408.

11. Bangs, ed., *Journal of Lieutenant Bangs*, 138–39.

12. Peter Elting to Capt. Richard Varick, June 13, 1776, Dawson and Tomlinson, eds., *New York City during the American Revolution*, 97.

13. New York [State], *Journals of the Provincial Congress*, 1:491.

14. Referring to Westchester County, one historian has described how its inhabitants had never seen "a concatenation of forces so violent and menacing as the revolutionary war." Kim, "Limits of Politicization," 881. Another historian has described New York

more generally as being "thoroughly shattered" by the war. Countryman, *People in Revolution*, 160.

15. One of the most rigorous studies puts the 1771 population of New York County, which included all of Manhattan Island, at 21,863 people. Greene and Harrington, *American Population*, 102–3. A demographer estimated that 20,000 people fled New York City. But that figure is based on a single source that put the city's prewar population at 25,000. Rosenwaike, *Population History*, 14–15. Another scholar, relying on the estimates of British officers, believed that the city had only 400 inhabitants left at the time of the invasion. Ranlet, *New York Loyalists*, 70. If one goes by these estimates and includes refugees from areas around the city such as Richmond County (Staten Island) and Queens County, the number of refugees may have exceeded 20,000.

16. An undated census of British-occupied New York City found that enough people moved back into the city to create a population of 12,408 civilians. Ranlet, *New York Loyalists*, 70.

17. *The New-York Journal and the General Advertiser*, July 7, 1777.

18. New York [State], *Journals of the Provincial Congress*, 1:638.

19. Ibid. John Shy has demonstrated that militias throughout the states, and not just New York, helped coerce political obedience to the Revolution. He argued that, rather than fighting the British, the "chief purpose [of the militias] was to engineer consent, by force if necessary." In that regard, one should think of them as police forces that monitored political belief rather than battlefield units that fought the British. Shy, *People Numerous and Armed*, 176.

20. New York [State], *Journals of the Provincial Congress*, 1:638.

21. The Committee on Conspiracies was not the provisional government's first attempt to confront Loyalists. On June 5, 1776, the Provincial Congress created a committee that called itself a group for "hearing and trying disaffected persons and those of equivocal characters." The committee, however, accomplished little. It did not convene for almost two weeks after June 5 and then met only intermittently before the British invasion forced its members to flee. The surviving minutes from the June 5 committee meeting appear in Force, comp., *American Archives*, 4th ser., 6:1152–83. The Provincial Convention dissolved the committee on August 7. New York [State], *Journals of the Provincial Congress*, 1:560.

22. New York [State], *Minutes of the Committee*, 1:2.

23. Ibid., 1.

24. Ibid., 2. The Committee chose New Hampshire after John Jay asked a militia officer from that state, Lieutenant-Colonel Joseph Welch, whether he thought New Hampshire would accept prisoners. Welch, stationed along the Hudson River, said he believed it would, and it appears that the Committee did not seek permission from any higher authority. Force, comp., *American Archives*, 5th ser., 2:1313–14.

25. The short-lived committee created on June 5 sent thirteen prisoners to Litchfield, Connecticut. New York [State], *Journals of the Provincial Congress*, 1:530, 541. On October 11, the Committee on Conspiracies deported thirty-three prisoners to Pennsylvania. New York [State], *Minutes of the Committee*, 2:413. Unfortunately, a fire in Albany in 1911 destroyed many of the Committee's earliest records, including the details of this earlier deportation. Some local committees also removed Loyalists before the Committee on

Conspiracies existed. See, e.g., the Albany committee's removal of Loyalists to Hartford, Connecticut, in June 1776, in Force, comp., *American Archives*, 4th ser., 6:1072–73.

26. New York [State], *Minutes of the Committee*, 1:2.

27. Ibid.

28. New York [State], *Journals of the Provincial Congress*, 2:344.

29. The Convention referred the letter to Major General Philip Schuyler. New York [State], *Journals of the Provincial Congress*, 1:688. While the Albany committee sent the letter to the Convention, it sent the prisoners directly to the Committee on Conspiracies. For the Albany committee's resolution sending the prisoners to the Committee, see Albany Committee, *Minutes of the Albany Committee*, 1:587. For the Committee's receipt of the prisoners and the resolutions deporting them, see New York [State], *Minutes of the Committee*, 1:7–9.

30. These removals were part of a broader effort to confront the British invasion and the Loyalists who were aiding it in Albany County. On October 19, 1776, the province-wide Committee of Safety created a subcommittee to go to Albany to stop British and Loyalist infiltration on the northern frontier, especially around Lake Champlain. For the resolution creating the subcommittee, see New York [State], *Journals of the Provincial Congress*, 1:684. The subcommittee operated for several weeks, and, though it spent most of its time coordinating the movement of materiel and troops, it uncovered a plot to raise a Loyalist regiment. The records of this subcommittee appear in Force, comp., *American Archives*, 5th ser., 3:561–91.

31. This number is based on the removals mentioned in New York [State], *Minutes of the Committee*, 1:1–13, 2:413. However, the Committee's records for these weeks are highly fragmentary. Other sources suggest that the Committee continued deporting prisoners throughout November, which would increase the number of those removed. For instance, on November 26 the Albany County committee sent to the Committee twenty-four prisoners who would likely have been deported along with the others. But the Committee's records do not mention this group. Albany Committee, *Minutes of the Albany Committee*, 1:622.

32. New York [State], *Minutes of the Committee*, 1:7.

33. Ibid., 10.

34. Ibid., 7.

35. Ibid., 52.

36. Ibid., 38, 40, 43.

37. Ibid., 52. The records do not indicate what the Committee concluded in the case. However, local militia officers had already imprisoned Maloyd before Noxon's testimony, which suggests that, even if the Committee reached no immediate decision, Maloyd would remain in jail until it did.

38. Ibid., 130. The Committee soon arrested Carman but later released him on parole. Ibid., 299, 318.

39. In February 1777, the Convention dissolved the Committee to allow its members more time to draft the state constitution. But it immediately re-created the group as the Commission on Conspiracies with exactly the same powers as the previous Committee had. The new members were Melancton Smith, Egbert Benson, and Jacobus Swartwout. New Yorkers regularly mixed their terminology, calling the group variously a *committee*,

a *commission*, or a *board*. Moreover, there were at least three lieutenants named Lawrence in the New York militia, and it is unclear which one made this denunciation. For the Committee's name change, see New York [State], *Journals of the Provincial Congress*, 1:803; and New York [State], *Minutes of the Committee*, 1:128. For the preponderance of lieutenants named Lawrence, see Roberts, comp., *New York in the Revolution*, 1:41, 68, 74, 82, 161, 207.

40. New York [State], *Minutes of the Committee*, 1:3.

41. Ibid., 209–10.

42. Ibid., 28.

43. Kim, *Landlord and Tenant*, chap. 8; Countryman, *People in Revolution*, 20–21; Bonomi, *A Factious People*, 218–24; Mark and Handlin, "Land Cases in Colonial New York."

44. New York [State], *Minutes of the Committee*, 1:40.

45. For his interrogation, see ibid., 1:43. For the preparations regarding his expropriation, see Theodorus Van Wyck to Henry Livingston Jr., September 5, 1779, Dutchess County Collection, box labeled "Dutchess County, N.Y./May 20, 1773–June 1887," NYHS.

46. Act of October 22, 1779, ch. 25, 1779 N.Y. Laws 173 (punishing those who have "voluntarily been adherent to the said king his fleets and armies, enemies to this State and the said other United States, with intent to subvert the government and liberties of this state and the said other United States, and to bring the same in subjection of the crown of Great Britain").

47. Kane also told the Committee that he burned the protection because his wife and daughter feared what would happen to him if it was discovered. New York [State], *Minutes of the Committee*, 1:40.

48. In this regard, New York resembled other revolutionary societies in which denunciations served private goals such as revenge. Russians used denunciations in this way during Stalin's Great Purges, a time when the "practice of denunciation served many private purposes in the Soviet Union: if you denounced a personal enemy or an unwelcome neighbor as a hidden Trotskyite or a former noble concealing his class identity, there was a good chance that the state would step in to settle your scores for you." Fitzpatrick, *Everyday Stalinism*, 116.

49. The implied demand for a government response is part of the nature of denunciations, which Sheila Fitzpatrick and Robert Gellately have defined as "spontaneous communications from individual citizens to the state (or to another authority such as the church) containing accusations of wrongdoing by other citizens or officials and implicitly or explicitly calling for punishment." Fitzpatrick and Gellately, eds., *Accusatory Practices*, 1.

50. Kalyvas, *Logic of Violence*, 218–19. This effort to build new institutions represents the definitive element of an insurgency: the desire among supporters to build permanent institutions that replace the old order and assume the responsibilities of governing. Unlike mere banditry or mafia behavior, insurgencies are an effort at competitive state building. They attempt to build a legal infrastructure that competes with and ultimately takes over the position of the state. Vega, *Guerrillas in Latin America*.

51. Substantial evidence suggests that violence—especially indiscriminate violence—provokes a counterrevolution by emboldening rather than terrifying the population. Kalyvas, *Logic of Violence*, 152. Even brutal insurgencies earned public acceptance in part by creating institutions that addressed popular concerns. For instance, the Shining

Path in Peru oversaw teachers, punished livestock thieves, and resolved marital disputes. Manrique, "War for the Central Sierra," 203–5.

52. One scholar has characterized the growth of insurgent institutions as an exchange. In Latin American revolutions, when central authority was in disarray, guerrillas resolved public concerns that governments had traditionally addressed, concerns such as providing security as well as legal and administrative functions. In exchange, people obeyed those revolutionary structures and came to rely on them as they would rely on a state. Wickham-Crowley, *Exploring Revolution*, esp. chap. 2. Wickham-Crowley refers to this as a *macro-social exchange process* through which insurgents establish their institutions as the new governing authority.

53. Remember that, in February 1777, the Convention reorganized the Committee as a commission.

54. New York [State], *Minutes of the Committee*, 1:268–69, 291, 315.

55. Ibid., 102–3.

56. Ibid., 84.

57. This began years of trouble for Dusenbury, who was later released only to be arrested and jailed again. Ibid., 1:133, 2:327, 361, 364.

58. In this regard, the Committee helped create an atmosphere that resembled Stalin's Great Purges, when Russians hid their backgrounds and beliefs to avoid denunciation or to escape the stigma of being connected to someone who had already been sent to the gulag. Russians lied about themselves and their backgrounds to avoid denunciation or ostracism. According to one historian, "the most important consequence" of being denounced as a class enemy and the stigmatization that it caused was the "large-scale concealment of social origin and misrepresentation of identity." Fitzpatrick, *Everyday Stalinism*, 137.

59. New York [State], *Minutes of the Committee*, 2:343.

60. *The New-York Packet and the American Advertiser*, July 31, 1777.

61. New York [State], *Minutes of the Committee*, 2:343, 354.

62. Crosby first joined the movement for independence in 1775 when he enlisted in a militia company in Danbury, Connecticut. After joining the failed expedition to Canada, his company retreated through New York just as his Connecticut enlistment expired. He then enlisted in a Dutchess County, New York, regiment in August 1776. While he was traveling to join his company, he helped uncover a plot to raise Loyalist troops. After that success, the Westchester County committee removed him from his regiment and brought him to the attention of the Committee on Conspiracies. Pickering, "Enoch Crosby, Secret Agent," 62–65. In 1821, James Fenimore Cooper wrote a best-selling novel whose main character some have claimed was based on Crosby. See Cooper's *The Spy*. The first person to identify Crosby as the model for the novel's protagonist was Barnum, *The Spy Unmasked*. Cooper, however, always claimed that he based the character of Harvey Birch on stories that his friend John Jay told him and that he never knew the person Jay was describing.

63. Pickering, "Enoch Crosby, Secret Agent," 66.

64. Ibid. The Committee later released some prisoners because they took the oath of allegiance and others because of illness. The order to confine the prisoners appears in New York [State], *Minutes of the Committee*, 1:25. For the prisoners' release, see ibid., 80.

65. Pickering, "Enoch Crosby, Secret Agent," 66–67. Crosby spent about nine months in late 1776 and early 1777 performing what the Committee called *secret services*. On one such mission in late 1776, the Committee ordered him to travel to a particular region under the name Levi Foster "and use his utmost Art to discover the designs, places of Resort, and Route, of certain disaffected Persons in that Quarter." New York [State], *Minutes of the Committee*, 1:47–48. But, after these operations, he had become "somewhat apprehensive that a longer continuance in that employment would be dangerous." He then enlisted in New York's militia twice more over the course of the war, serving most of his time in Westchester County and New Jersey. Pickering, "Enoch Crosby, Secret Agent," 69.

66. New York [State], *Minutes of the Committee*, 2:418.

67. Ibid., 1:114.

68. New York had sent very few supplies and little money to feed and clothe the prisoners, which only angered people in New Hampshire more. Ibid., 2:426–27.

69. Albany Committee, *Minutes of the Albany Committee*, 1:668.

70. New York [State], *Minutes of the Committee*, 2:431.

71. New York [State], *Journals of the Provincial Congress*, 1:827.

72. New York [State], *Minutes of the Committee*, 1:215.

73. Ibid., 218.

74. Ibid., 2:436, 437. The Convention relieved some of the overcrowding on May 2 when it commissioned two prison ships to be anchored in the Hudson River. It ordered the Committee to send all those "whose characters are suspicious" on board the ships. New York [State], *Journals of the Provincial Congress*, 1:908.

75. Although courts-martial convened when other courts ceased meeting, military trials had a limited jurisdiction. They heard cases arising only within the militia or the Continental army, such as fights between soldiers. See, e.g., *Constitutional Gazette*, June 26, 1776.

76. While the April 1 resolution is mentioned in the *Journals of the Provincial Congress*, it does not appear in that volume. It was printed as a broadside at the time of passage, and the full text is available in New York [State], *In Convention of the Representatives of the State of New-York*.

77. New York [State], *Journals of the Provincial Congress*, 1:883, 884.

78. Ibid., 889, 908–9, 969–72.

79. Ibid., 921–27.

80. Ibid., 904.

81. See, e.g., ibid., 969–72.

82. The April 1 resolution initially empowered courts-martial to try defendants for specific crimes: supplying the British, enlisting soldiers for them, spying, or passing intelligence. New York [State], *In Convention of the Representatives of the State of New-York*. On April 17, the Convention allowed courts-martial to prosecute "all such persons as shall be taken in going off privately to the enemy." Then, on April 21, it added treason prosecutions to their jurisdiction. New York [State], *Journals of the Provincial Congress*, 1:885, 898. It had defined treason as far back as July 16, 1776, and ordered that all traitors be executed. Ibid., 527. But this resolution, like so many others, had remained unenforceable without formal legal institutions.

83. New York [State], *Minutes of the Committee*, 2:325. The Council of Safety convened when the Convention was not in session or could not gather a quorum.

84. For a summary of the laws governing these county-level committees, see Paltsits, ed., *Minutes of the Commissioners for Detecting and Defeating Conspiracies*, app. 1. Although the new Committees met in various counties, these published Albany County minutes are the only such records that survive.

85. One indication of the diminished influence of county-level boards was that their members did not spend much time detecting conspiracies. For instance, three of the Commissioners for the Albany board rarely did any work in their posts. Rynier Mynderse submitted financial accounts for only eighty days spent as a Commissioner from 1780 through 1782. Hugh Mitchell sought his salary for ninety-five days and Henry Oothout for only eighty-six days over those same three years. Paltsits, ed., *Minutes of the Commissioners for Detecting and Defeating Conspiracies*, 2:809.

86. The Albany committee suggested exchanging Loyalist prisoners for French sailors who had just arrived in American ports. Such an exchange would supply America with experienced sailors while at the same time removing enemies to a place—the French navy—that was so awful it would scare other Loyalists into abandoning their support for Britain. The committee hoped that "such an exile would perhaps be looked upon as more terrible than a New-England one." New York [State], *Journals of the Provincial Congress*, 1:875–76.

CHAPTER THREE

1. Reynolds, "Bartholomew Crannell," 39. Reynolds erroneously calls Bartholomew's wife Catherine. However, she also quotes his application for compensation from the British government after the war as declaring that Bartholomew "married Sarah, Daughter of Peter Van Cleek." Ibid., 74.

2. Ibid., 46; Platt, *Eagle's History of Poughkeepsie*, 38.

3. Reynolds, "Bartholomew Crannell," 46. One branch was the Livingstons of Clermont, which included Judge Robert Livingston, a leading jurist and politician in late colonial New York, the judge's wife, Margaret Beekman Livingston, and their son, Robert R. Livingston. Robert R. became the famous Federalist leader and chancellor of New York. A second branch grew out of Livingston Manor in Albany County. The Gilbert Livingston who became Crannell's son-in-law belonged to a less prominent part of the family that included successful lawyers and local officeholders. Lynd, "Who Should Rule at Home?" 330 n. 2.

4. Poucher, "Dutchess County," 38.

5. Reynolds, "Bartholomew Crannell," 66–70.

6. Platt, *Eagle's History of Poughkeepsie*, 30.

7. Quoted in Reynolds, "Bartholomew Crannell," 78.

8. Ibid., 70–73.

9. Clark, "Problem of Allegiance," 288–89.

10. Reynolds, "Bartholomew Crannell," 73–74.

11. Ibid., 70.

12. Quoted in ibid., 76.

13. Memorandum of Tory Goods, n.d., Dutchess County Collection 1696–ca. 1910, box labeled "Dutchess County, N.Y./May 20, 1773–June 1887," NYHS.

14. Inventory of the Personal Estate of Mr. Bartholomew Crannel [*sic*] taken May 31, 1777, Dutchess County Collection 1696–ca. 1910, box labeled "Dutchess County, N.Y./ May 20, 1773–June 1887," NYHS.

15. The Council of Safety was a part of the provisional government that sat when the Provincial Convention was not in session. The resolution expelling Beardsley and others appears in New York [State], *Journals of the Provincial Congress*, 1:1093.

16. Andrew Billings and Peter Tappen to Henry Livingston Jr., letter received December 12, 1777, Dutchess County Collection 1696–ca. 1910, box labeled "Dutchess County, N.Y./May 20, 1773–June 1887," NYHS.

17. Platt, *Eagle's History of Poughkeepsie*, 38.

18. Quoted in Reynolds, "Bartholomew Crannell," 65.

19. Ibid., 64.

20. Poucher, "Dutchess County," 38, 40.

21. Quoted in Reynolds, "Bartholomew Crannell," 76.

22. Quoted in ibid., 74.

23. Quoted in ibid., 61.

24. Mason, *Road to Independence*, 78–79.

25. New York [State], *Journals of the Provincial Congress*, 1:671.

26. Ibid., 979.

27. Ibid., 879.

28. Ibid., 721, 769, 804.

29. Ibid., 730, 760.

30. When the Convention adjourned, it appointed a group of delegates to convene as the Committee of Safety while the Convention was not meeting. Very often the Committee, and not the Convention, received these inquiries about Loyalist property.

31. New York [State], *Journals of the Provincial Congress*, 1:721 (see also 769).

32. Ibid., 826.

33. The Provincial Convention did not outline the Commissioners' duties exclusively in terms of confiscation. As their title suggests, Commissioners technically sequestered property. They sold it and handed the proceeds over to the regime, which, in turn, could pay to former owners all the money received at sale. As the resolution put it, after the Commissioners deposited money into the regime's treasury, those proceeds would "be hereafter paid to the respective owners . . . or otherwise disposed of at the discretion of the Legislature of this State." Ibid. Although the resolution held out the possibility that Loyalists could receive the value of their goods, they never did. It was the second clause that was given full effect, and, as a result, a policy termed sequestration was confiscation in actual practice.

34. Ibid.

35. Ketchum, *Saratoga*; Furneaux, *Saratoga*.

36. *The New-York Journal and the General Advertiser*, July 7, 1777.

37. New York Supreme Court of Judicature Minute Book, July 25, 1775–April 28, 1781 (Engrossed), NYCC.

38. For courts' schedules and their short dockets, see Minutes of the Court of General Sessions and of Common Pleas, Liber E 1771–1774, Liber F 1775–1781, Liber G 1782–1785, microfilm reel 127, DCCO; Westchester County Minutes of the Court of Common Pleas, ser. 9, A-0010 (1)L, volume labeled "1774–1793," WCARC; and Albany Court of Common Pleas, 1763–1799, ser. 87-09085, Minutes of Court of Sessions, 1685–1689, 1717–1723, 1763–1782, and Canvass of Voters 1820, ACHR.

39. New York [State], *Journals of the Provincial Congress*, 2:460.

40. Ibid., 1:1077–78.

41. Ibid., 845.

42. While Livingston proved an active Commissioner during the war, his interests afterward led him in a very different direction. He became fond of writing music and light verse with such titles as "To My Niece, Sally Livingston, on the Death of a Little Serenading Wren She Admired" and "Careless Philosopher's Soliloquy." He also very likely wrote the poem "A Visit from Old St. Nicholas," which was published anonymously in the *Troy Sentinel* in 1823 and became known as "The Night before Christmas." The Bible scholar Clement Clark Moore claimed to have written it, but Livingston's descendants have long believed that he wrote it since his children recalled hearing him recite the poem before it was published. Thomas, "Henry Livingston," 32–45. For a more recent and rigorous analysis of "The Night before Christmas" that argues persuasively in favor of Livingston's authorship, see Foster, *Author Unknown*, chap. 6.

43. *The New-York Packet and the American Advertiser*, May 8, 1777.

44. There were three Benjamin Birdsalls in New York at that time. Two of the three were officers in the militia, while the third was an enlisted man in the Sixth Regiment of the Dutchess County militia. The author of this inventory was most likely the enlisted Birdsall because no officer rank appears in the document. See Roberts, comp., *New York in the Revolution*, 1:145.

45. Five people named French had their personal property confiscated. However, this document probably refers to Jeremiah French, who appears on the tax lists in Pawling's Precinct, in Dutchess County, until 1778, the same year that Birdsall took this inventory. Before then, he appeared on the tax rolls of Beekman Precinct. Buck, "Tax Lists of Beekman and Pawling's Precincts."

46. "Benjamin Birdsalls [*sic*] Account of Confiscated Goods," December 7, 1778, Dutchess County Collection 1696–ca. 1910, box labeled "Dutchess County, N.Y./May 20, 1773–June 1887," NYHS.

47. "Benjamin Birdsalls [*sic*] Account of Confiscated Goods," December 7, 1778, Dutchess County Collection 1696–ca. 1910, box labeled "Dutchess County, N.Y./May 20, 1773–June 1887," NYHS.

48. Similar looting occurred in Massachusetts in 1775–76. After Lexington and Concord, many Massachusetts Loyalists fled their homes to seek the protection of the British army that was occupying Boston at the time. Just as happened in New York, neighbors then plundered their estates. See Maas, "Honest Graft." Maas gives a fuller account of that plundering and private enrichment in *Return of the Massachusetts Loyalists*, chap. 6.

49. "An Account of Effects Taken from People at Old and Little Hosick," September 1777. This document is bound with various others, the first one of which is "An Account

of Cash Received for Different Articles since Settlement," various dates, Revolutionary War Box 5, New York State Revolutionary Committees and Commissions, NYHS.

50. [Thomas?] Storms, Information, August 8, 1778, Dutchess County Collection 1696–ca. 1910, box labeled "Dutchess County, N.Y./May 20, 1773–June 1887," NYHS.

51. Capt. Bernardus Swartwout to Commissioners of Sequestration, List of People to Examine, n.d., Dutchess County Collection 1696–ca. 1910, box labeled "Dutchess County, N.Y./May 20, 1773–June 1887," NYHS.

52. Copy of Warrant Given by Commissioners of Sequestration, August 30, 1779, Dutchess County Collection 1696–ca. 1910, box labeled "Dutchess County, N.Y./May 20, 1773–June 1887," NYHS.

53. Militias throughout the colonies enforced adherence to the Revolution among their neighbors more often than they fought the British on the battlefield. Shy, *People Numerous and Armed*, 176.

54. Alexander Lamb, Voucher to Theodorus Van Wyck, September 18, 1779, Revolutionary War Box 5, New York State Revolutionary Committees and Commissions, NYHS.

55. John Haines, Voucher to James Hunt, September 5, 1777, Revolutionary War Box 5, New York State Revolutionary Committees and Commissions, NYHS.

56. Account Book for George Palmer, various dates, Revolutionary War Miscellaneous Manuscripts, box 2, NYHS. Although Palmer and his helpers began gathering these particular goods in May 1777, Burgoyne's invasion delayed the auction until September. Albany Committee, *Minutes of the Albany Committee*, 1:769–70, 846–47.

57. Account Book for George Palmer, various dates, Revolutionary War Miscellaneous Manuscripts, box 2, NYHS.

58. "The State of New-York Their Account Current with Elihu Marvin & Isaac Nicolls Commissioners of Sequestration Orange County," various dates, Revolutionary War Box 5, New York State Revolutionary Committees and Commissions, NYHS.

59. "An Account of Disbursments [*sic*] since Settlement," various dates, bound with "An Account of Cash Received for Different Articles since Settlement," Revolutionary War Box 5, New York State Revolutionary Committees and Commissions, NYHS.

60. "Account of Contingent Expences Paid by Peter S. Dygart Esq., One of the Commissioners of Sequestration for Tryon County," various dates, Revolutionary War Box 5, New York State Revolutionary Committees and Commissions, NYHS. Dygart listed the voucher numbers corresponding with each expense. Unfortunately, those vouchers have not survived.

61. Rea's occupation appears on the town's tax lists through 1779. See Buck, "Northeast Tax Lists," 12.

62. Hugh Rea to Isaac Sheldon, December 10, 1777, Dutchess County Collection 1696–ca. 1910, box labeled "Dutchess County, N.Y./May 20, 1773–June 1887," NYHS.

63. Account Book for George Palmer, various dates, Revolutionary War Miscellaneous Manuscripts, box 2, NYHS; "An Account of Cash Received for Different Articles since Settlement," various dates, Revolutionary War Box 5, New York State Revolutionary Committees and Commissions, NYHS.

64. "Persons Indebted to the Commissioners of Sequestration from Dutchess County," various dates, Dutchess County Collection 1696–ca. 1910, box labeled "Dutchess County, N.Y./May 20, 1773–June 1887," and "An Account of Outstanding

Debts due to the State of New-York for Sequestrd [*sic*] Property Sold by Samuel Drake Israel Honeywell & James Hunt Commissioners of Sequestration for Westchester County," various dates, Revolutionary War Box 5, New York State Revolutionary Committees and Commissions, NYHS.

65. For itemized lists, see "Persons Indebted to the Commissioners of Sequestration from Dutchess County," various dates, and "Lists of Property Sold at Auction," various dates, Dutchess County Collection 1696–ca. 1910, box labeled "Dutchess County, N.Y./May 20, 1773–June 1887." See also "An Account of Cash Received for Different Articles since Settlement," various dates, Revolutionary War Box 5, New York State Revolutionary Committees and Commissions, and Account Book for George Palmer, various dates, Revolutionary War, Miscellaneous Manuscripts Box 2, NYHS.

66. Theodorus Van Wyck to Henry Livingston Jr., December 13, 1777, Dutchess County Collection 1696–ca. 1910, box labeled "Dutchess County, N.Y./May 20, 1773–June 1887," NYHS.

67. Commissioners even listed themselves among the bad debts when they filed accounts with the state. Samuel Drake acknowledged that he still owed the state for wheat in "An Account of Outstanding Debts Due to the State of New York for Sequestrd [*sic*] Property Sold by Samuel Drake Israel Honeywell & James Hunt, Commissioners of Sequestration for Westchester County," various dates, Revolutionary War Box 5, New York State Revolutionary Committees and Commissions, NYHS.

68. "Messrs. John Coe and Gilbert Cooper Commissioners of Sequestration for Orange County in Account Current with the State of New-York," various dates, Revolutionary War Box 5, New York State Revolutionary Committees and Commissions, NYHS. For other examples of Commissioners buying goods at their own auctions, see "An Account of Cash Received for Different Articles since Settlement," various dates, Revolutionary War Box 5, New York State Revolutionary Committees and Commissions, and Account Book for George Palmer, various dates, Revolutionary War, Miscellaneous Manuscripts Box 2, NYHS.

69. "An Account of Cash Received for Different Articles since Settlement," various dates, Revolutionary War Box 5, New York State Revolutionary Committees and Commissions, NYHS.

70. The fire destroyed many of New York's revolutionary era records. But, before these sale books burned, the state comptroller mentioned them in a compilation of manuscripts. See Roberts, comp., *New York in the Revolution*, 2:250.

71. Ibid., 253–58.

72. New York [State], *Journals of the Provincial Congress*, 1:930–31.

73. *The New-York Packet and the American Advertiser*, June 19, 1777. The Commissioners did not quote the resolutions accurately in the announcement. The resolution, as quoted in the newspaper, specifically gave the leasing power to the Dutchess Commissioners. However, the resolution refers only generally to "the commissioners for sequestering the personal estates of persons gone over to the enemy." New York [State], *Journals of the Provincial Congress*, 1:930.

74. Theodorus Van Wyck to Henry Livingston Jr., December 8, 1777, Dutchess County Collection 1696–ca. 1910, box labeled "Dutchess County, N.Y./May 20, 1773–June 1887," NYHS.

75. Hugh Rea to Isaac Sheldon, December 10, 1777, Dutchess County Collection 1696–ca. 1910, box labeled "Dutchess County, N.Y./May 20, 1773–June 1887," NYHS.

76. Herman Hoffman to Theodorus Van Wyck and Henry Livingston Jr., October 28, 1778, Dutchess County Collection 1696–ca. 1910, box labeled "Dutchess County, N.Y./ May 20, 1773–June 1887," NYHS.

77. Peter Heermans to Henry Livingston Jr. and Theodorus Van Wyck, March 10, 1778, Dutchess County Collection 1696–ca. 1910, box labeled "Dutchess County, N.Y./ May 20, 1773–June 1887," NYHS.

78. John Campbell to Henry Livingston Jr., January 31, 1780 [1779], Dutchess County Collection 1696–ca. 1910, box labeled "Dutchess County, N.Y./May 20, 1773–June 1887," NYHS. The year written on the letter is 1780. However, various references in it suggest that the year is almost certainly a mistake and that the correct one is 1779.

79. It seems that Van Wyck had already begun preparing for Campbell to take possession before Campbell ever sent the letter to Livingston. Campbell and the other families thus could have moved onto the farm without writing to Livingston. Theodorus Van Wyck to James Cox, January 26, 1779, Dutchess County Collection 1696–ca. 1910, box labeled "Dutchess County, N.Y./May 20, 1773–June 1887," NYHS.

80. Jonathan Sloss Hobart to Messrs. Theodorus Van Wyck, Henry Livingston Jr., and Isaac Sheldon, July 14, 1777, Dutchess County Collection 1696–ca. 1910, box labeled "Dutchess County, N.Y./May 20, 1773–June 1887," NYHS.

81. Isaac Sheldon to [Henry Livingston], November 13, 1777, Dutchess County Collection 1696–ca. 1910, box labeled "Dutchess County, N.Y./May 20, 1773–June 1887," NYHS.

82. Theodorus Van Wyck to Henry Livingston Jr., February 16, 1779, Dutchess County Collection 1696–ca. 1910, box labeled "Dutchess County, N.Y./May 20, 1773–June 1887," NYHS.

83. Act of October 21, 1779, ch. 23, 1779 N.Y. Laws 168 (granting "certain powers to the joint committees of both houses of the legislature appointed to enquire into the conduct of the commissioners of sequestration"). For the legislative resolutions leading up to the creation of the joint committee of inquiry, see New York [State], *Votes and Proceedings of the Assembly of the State of New-York; at Their Third Session*, 19–20, 40.

84. The objections to farm leases resembled another minor complaint. When the Commissioners hurried to auction goods off, they sometimes sold property claimed by people who had not fled to the British. In May 1777, the Convention passed a resolution that would supposedly address this problem. See New York [State], *Journals of the Provincial Congress*, 1:930. However, the resolution remained unenforceable because it relied on seeking remedies in courts that did not yet exist. Moreover, the objections to selling certain goods, just like the objections to particular leases, had no effect on the Commissioners' ability to redistribute property. They continued selling the goods, paying assistants, and leasing farms with undiminished enthusiasm.

85. Jonathan Pearsee, Indemnification, April 2, 1779, Jonathan G. Thompkins, Indemnification, April 21, 1779, and Jonathan P. Waldron, Indemnification, on Behalf of the Widow Mrs. Catherine Waldron, May 1, 1780, Dutchess County Collection 1696–ca. 1910, box labeled "Dutchess County, N.Y./May 20, 1773–June 1887," NYHS.

86. "An Account of Monies Received for House Rent &c," various dates, bound with a document headed "An Account of Cash Received for Different Articles since

Settlement," and "An Account of Outstanding Debts Due to the State of New York for Sequestrd [*sic*] Property Sold by Samuel Drake Israel Honeywell & James Hunt, Commissioners of Sequestration for Westchester County," Revolutionary War Box 5, New York State Revolutionary Committees and Commissions, NYHS.

87. A similar process occurred in one of the most chaotic periods of early modern English history. During the English Reformation, many people helped strip religious institutions bare, taking everything from floorboards to beehives. Looting on such a large scale implicated many people in acts of desecration. Shagan, *Popular Politics*, chap. 5.

88. *The New-York Packet and the American Advertiser*, November 27, 1777.

89. *The New-York Packet*, December 11, 1777. This newspaper was the same as *The New-York Packet and the American Advertiser*. However, the war made it difficult for the printer to find paper, and he was forced to reduce the size of some issues. As a result, only the shorter title would fit across the top of the page.

90. *The New-York Packet and the American Advertiser*, November 27, 1777.

91. *The New-York Packet*, October 23, 1777.

92. Ibid., December 11, 1777.

93. New York [State], *Journals of the Provincial Congress*, 2:454.

94. Gen. [Horatio] Gates to Maj. Gen. John Vaughan, October 20, 1777, *The New-York Packet and the American Advertiser*, November 27, 1777.

95. New York [State], *Journals of the Provincial Congress*, 1:910.

96. Clinton, *Public Papers of George Clinton*, 2:854.

97. For an analysis of these Loyalist plots and their effects, see chapter 2 above.

98. New York [State], *Journals of the Provincial Congress*, 1:1030–31.

99. Ibid., 2:440–41.

100. "Inventory of the Personal Estate of Mr. Bartholomew Crannel [*sic*] Taken May 31, 1777," Dutchess County Collection 1696–ca. 1910, box labeled "Dutchess County, N.Y./May 20, 1773–June 1887," NYHS.

101. Countryman, *People in Revolution*, 20–21; Bonomi, *A Factious People*, 218–24; Mark and Handlin, "Land Cases in Colonial New York."

102. New York [State], *Minutes of the Committee*, 1:40–41.

103. For the preparations regarding his expropriation, see Theodorus Van Wyck to Henry Livingston Jr., September 5, 1779, Dutchess County Collection, box labeled "Dutchess County, N.Y./May 20, 1773–June 1887," NYHS.

104. Roberts, comp., *New York in the Revolution*, 2:250.

105. For an analysis of Crosby's work with the Committee and an example of one of his missions, see chapter 2 above.

106. Pickering, "Enoch Crosby, Secret Agent," 69.

107. Shagan, *Popular Politics*, chap. 5.

CHAPTER FOUR

1. Brown, *The King's Friends*, and *The Good Americans*; Calhoon, *Loyalists in Revolutionary America*. These books also consider the geographic distribution of Loyalists, possible reasons for supporting the king, and which social groups were likeliest to be Loyalists.

2. Loyalists from throughout the provinces left their homes during the war to seek British protection in New York City, where they tried to end the conflict and reunite the colonies with Britain. For an analysis of these refugees and their efforts, see Chopra, *Unnatural Rebellion*. For studies of how Loyalist exiles struggled to develop communities in unfamiliar places and shape British imperial policy, see Norton, *British-Americans*; and Jasanoff, *Liberty's Exiles*.

3. *The New-York Packet and the American Advertiser*, May 15, 1783.

4. Although Tappen employed the symbol for pounds sterling (£), he referred to the sums of money as "Continentals." He then converted that amount to pounds sterling, which offers a guide to both the rising price of flour and the falling value of Continental currency.

5. State of New York, D[ebtor] to Teunis Tappen, various dates 1779–81, in folder labeled "2nd Commissioners for Detecting Conspiracies [*sic*] in N.Y., 1778—Boards of Charlotte Co./Dutchess Co./Orange Co./Ulster Co./Albany Co.," box Revolutionary War, box 5, New York State Revolutionary Committees and Commissions, NYHS.

6. Ebenezer Russell to George Clinton, August 17, 1778, Clinton, *Public Papers of George Clinton*, 3:688–89.

7. See chapter 3 above.

8. Quoted in Johnson, *Colonel Henry Ludington*, 154–55.

9. Ibid.

10. Ibid., 155–56.

11. Residents of Dutchess County knew that they would benefit from the redistribution of real property. The county's largest landlords, including people such as Beverly Robinson, had become Loyalists. If the state confiscated Loyalist property, then the tenants of those Dutchess landlords would have the chance to buy the farms where they lived. Moreover, by the fall of 1778, the county had been receiving refugees from other parts of the state for over two years. Those refugees had struggled to find housing and a subsistence, which heightened the sense in Dutchess that they were bearing the war's heaviest burdens. It is little surprise, therefore, that some of the earliest organized demands for redistribution came from a part of the state that had absorbed many refugees and where many farms would go up for sale. The petitioners saw redistribution as a way to take revenge on Loyalists while at the same time providing economic stability during a period of great disruption.

12. New York [State], *Votes and Proceedings of the Senate of the State of New-York, at Their First Session*, 159.

13. New York [State], *Votes and Proceedings of the Assembly of the State of New-York, at Their Second Session*, 54.

14. Like the one from Dutchess County, the petitions from Philips Manor and Skenesboro came from parts of the state with high rates of tenancy and where the landlords had become Loyalists. The petitioners no doubt understood that, if the state confiscated Loyalist land, they would as the tenants of Loyalists have the chance to buy their farms.

15. Scott, "Price Control in New England"; Bezanson, "Inflation and Controls"; Handlin and Handlin, *Commonwealth*, chap. 1.

16. The Council's resolution appears in Pennsylvania [State], *Colonial Records of Pennsylvania*, 11:745–47. Pennsylvania went on to confiscate the real property of 490

people. For a description of Pennsylvania's confiscation, see Ousterhout, "Pennsylvania Land Confiscations," 328–43.

17. Both laws were enacted on April 30, 1779. One dispossessed former colonial officials, whom the law referred to as "notorious conspirators," for having "wickedly conspired to overthrow and destroy the constitution of government of the late province of Massachusetts Bay . . . and also to reduce the said inhabitants [of Massachusetts] under the absolute power and domination of the present king, and of the parliament of Great Britain." The other created a court procedure for expropriating "absentees," those who had fled their homes to seek British protection or who had otherwise "adhered to the said king of Great Britain." The laws appear in Massachusetts [State], *Acts and Resolves*, 5:966–71. For an analysis of how officials applied these laws in a way that enriched themselves and their friends, see Maas, *Return of the Massachusetts Loyalists*, chap. 6.

18. The Council of Revision was a body composed of the governor, the judges of the Supreme Court of Judicature, and the Chancellor. The Council reviewed all legislation passed by the Assembly and the Senate. It suggested revisions to laws that, as the Constitution of 1777 put it, violated the state constitution, were contrary to the public good, or had been "hastily and unadvisedly passed." The legislature could override the Council's revisions by a two-thirds vote of both the Assembly and the Senate. But, without that supermajority, the Council's objections prevented a bill from becoming law. N.Y. Const. of 1777, art. III. The first confiscation bill lacked the votes to override the Council's objections. For the legislative wrangling over the first failed effort to pass a confiscation bill, see Countryman, *People in Revolution*, 186, 207.

19. *The New-York Journal and the General Advertiser*, May 17, 1779.

20. "W.D. in Orange County," *The New-York Packet and the American Advertiser*, August 12, 1779. For the reemergence of committees in Philadelphia in 1779 and their spread to other places, see Buel, "The Committee Movement of 1779"; Alexander, "Fort Wilson Incident of 1779," 589–612; and Morris, *Government and Labor*, 110–14.

21. *The New-York Journal and the General Advertiser*, July 19, 26, 1779.

22. *The New-York Packet and the American Advertiser*, July 22, 1779.

23. Ibid., August 12, 1779.

24. *The New-York Journal and the General Advertiser*, August 9, 1779.

25. November 1778 Term of Court, "Records of the Court of Sessions," ser. 43, A-0048 (1)L, WCARC.

26. October 1778 and January 1779 Terms of Court, microfilm labeled "Minutes of Court of Sessions 1685–1689, 1717–1723, 1763–1782, Canvass of Voters 1820," ACHR.

27. After transacting legal business only one-quarter of the session days in 1779, the January 1780 term was canceled and all matters continued until May because of "an exceeding deep Snow falling the day before Court was to be held." January, May, and October Terms of Court, "Minutes of the Court of General Sessions and of Common Pleas, Liber E-1771–1774; Liber F-1775–1781; Liber G-1782–1785," microfilm reel 127, DCCO. The quotation about the snowfall appears at the end of the minutes for the October 1779 term.

28. November 1779 Term of Court, New York Supreme Court of Judicature Minute Book, July 25, 1775–April 28, 1781 (Engrossed), NYCC.

29. *The New-York Packet and the American Advertiser*, September 16, 1779.

30. November 1779 Term of Court, New York Supreme Court of Judicature Minute Book, July 25, 1775–April 28, 1781 (Engrossed), NYCC.

31. Fighting in the western part of New York—particularly Tryon County—was especially fierce over this time. In the summer of 1778, British and Indian forces destroyed settlements in Pennsylvania's Wyoming Valley, near the border with New York. The following summer, the Americans Major General John Sullivan and General James Clinton led retaliatory raids against Indian settlements in the Finger Lakes region of New York. This Sullivan-Clinton campaign in the summer of 1779 involved New York militia regiments, drawing people, attention, and resources away from legal institutions in the rest of the state. Additional troops, of course, had to remain in the southern Hudson Valley to prevent, or at least discourage, British raids from New York City. For a summary of the 1779 expedition and its failure to prevent future Indian raids, see Fischer, *Well-Executed Failure.*

32. Historians have examined how, after the adoption of the federal Constitution in 1787, Americans claimed the right as the nation's sovereign authority to enforce their own notion of constitutional order. Some Americans claimed that popular sovereignty gave people the right to use force or violence outside of formal institutions to implement what they believed to be correct law. Others, however, claimed that once the sovereign people created a constitutional system and elected representatives, everyone had to act through formal channels. For analyses of these different views of how popular sovereignty operated under the federal Constitution, see Fritz, *American Sovereigns*; and Kramer, *The People Themselves.* These later debates were a conversation about the correct application of law under an established constitution. Revolutionary New York, however, had no settled constitutional system. As a society under military occupation, New York's legal order remained fragile, its institutions weak, and committees represented New Yorkers' doubts about whether the state was capable of resolving even their most basic problems, such as gaining a subsistence.

33. *The New-York Packet and the American Advertiser*, September 16, 1779.

34. For a discussion of how opponents of confiscation in the legislature tried, and ultimately failed, to prevent the law from passing, see Countryman, *People in Revolution*, chap. 6. Countryman argues that the 1779 forfeiture law represented a radical shift in the state's policy toward Loyalists. Before this statute, according to Countryman, New York's leaders had been unwilling to take the kind of aggressive action against Loyalists that ordinary people demanded. For years elites had aimed simply to keep Loyalists under loose control and perhaps convince a few to give up their support for the king. But the enactment of confiscation marked a shift to a punitive approach that ordinary New Yorkers and their committees favored. As Countryman claims: "Men in power turned to a policy of punishment only in 1779, after four years of trying to do no more to the Tories than control and convert them." Ibid., 175. However, New York's leaders had been punishing Loyalists for years before the confiscation act. Those leaders, with the help of local committees, had arrested Loyalists, sent them to neighboring provinces without trial, stripped them of their personal property, resettled refugees in their homes, and left their families hungry. Rather than a shift toward punishment, the forfeiture law of 1779 was part of this ongoing legal assault on Loyalists that revolutionary leaders had begun in the earliest years of the war.

35. Act of October 22, 1779, ch. 25, 1779 N.Y. Laws 173.

36. Ibid., sec. 1. The statutory language might seem imprecise to modern legal scholars, who expect that a bill of attainder always meant a legislative conviction of treason. However, the confiscation law did not convict defendants of treason. It declared the fifty-nine defendants attainted of the crime of having adhered to the enemies of the state. Moreover, all the indictments and convictions taken in court under this law named the crime as having adhered to the enemies of the state. Thus, contrary to what some historians have assumed, an attainder was not always synonymous with a conviction for treason; it could have other meanings as well. See Hulsebosch, "Discrete and Cosmopolitan Minority," 836–37. At least one English legal scholar of the late eighteenth century believed that, as a type of statute, bills of attainder covered a broad range of offenses and that the charge of treason, if such was the accusation, would have to appear in clear language in the bill itself. See Wooddeson, *Systematical View*, 2:621–47. Wooddeson described bills of attainder as instances when the legislative authority takes on the duties of the magistrate and enacts a law "adapted to exigencies unprovided for in the criminal code." Ibid., 621.

37. Act of October 22, 1779, ch. 25, 1779 N.Y. Laws 173, sec. 2.

38. Ibid., sec. 5.

39. The forfeiture law prohibited sales from taking place before October 1, 1780. Act of October 22, 1779, ch. 25, 1779 N.Y. Laws 173, sec. 15, par. 3. However, owing to worsening inflation and continued popular pressure to redistribute property, the legislature did not wait that long and instead began sales in March 1780. For an analysis of the legislature's decision to begin sales then, see Reilly, "Confiscation and Sale," chap. 2. The first sale law appears in Act of March 10, 1780, ch. 51, N.Y. Laws 230 (authorizing "the immediate sale of part of the forfeited estates"). A discussion of how opponents of confiscation tried to delay sales as long as possible appears in Countryman, *People in Revolution*, 208.

40. According to the forfeiture law, three different courts had the power to indict defendants: county-level Courts of General Sessions of the Peace, Courts of Oyer and Terminer and General Gaol Delivery, and the Supreme Court of Judicature, which had statewide jurisdiction. However, only the Supreme Court had the power to try cases. If the grand jury for General Sessions or Oyer and Terminer indicted a defendant, the judges in those courts then referred the case to the Supreme Court for final judgment. This jurisdictional distinction between indictment and trial appears in Act of October 22, 1779, ch. 25, 1779 N.Y. Laws 173, secs. 3 and 6. The numbers given here are the result of an analysis of all three courts. For a discussion of which court minutes have survived and the methodology employed in analyzing them, see the appendix.

41. For a table listing all the crimes prosecuted in New York from October 1779 through November 1783, see the appendix.

42. For the sales in Dutchess County, see Book of Deeds, "Abstract of Forfeiture & Sales Act of 1779," vols. 2 and 8, various dates, DCCO. These are original documents prepared by the Commissioners of Forfeitures that summarize all the sales in Dutchess County under the forfeiture act. They list the surveyed location of each lot, the former owner, the purchaser, the date of conveyance, and the sale price.

43. Humphrey, *Land and Liberty*, chaps. 1–3. See also Mark, *Agrarian Land Conflicts in Colonial New York*.

44. Kim, *Landlord and Tenant*, chap. 8.

45. Humphrey, *Land and Liberty*, chap. 4. The rate of tenant purchasers was uneven throughout the state. Nevertheless, many tenants availed themselves of their preemptive rights under the forfeiture act and bought the farms they occupied. On the whole, therefore, the law proved successful. Moreover, tenants remained in possession of the land and did not lose their purchases through unpaid mortgages. For an analysis of tenant participation in redistribution and the law's overall success in making it possible for tenants to buy their farms, see Reilly, "Confiscation and Sale."

46. This percentage is based on the data compiled in Lynd, *Anti-Federalism in Dutchess County, New York*, chap. 4.

47. Land redistribution during the English Reformation also created powerful reasons for purchasers to resist a reversion to the old order. When Queen Mary wanted to return England to papal jurisdiction, many members of Parliament resisted her efforts. They, or their families, had purchased monastic lands, and they feared that the pope would nullify the sales and reconstitute the monasteries. They had a stake in protecting religious reforms; their wealth and political influence depended on it. Mary ultimately overcame this opposition only when she guaranteed the sales of monastic land. The statute that repealed nineteen Henrician and Edwardian reforms explicitly confirmed the sales. For a discussion of parliamentary opposition to Mary's efforts to restore Catholicism, see Loach, *Parliament and the Crown*, chap. 6. For the statute that repealed nineteen previous laws and confirmed sales of monastic lands, see 1&2 Philip and Mary, c. 8.

48. As one historian has put it: "Tenants and other farmers wanted to own their land, and they wanted to reap the full harvest of their labor. These men and women based their support for one side or the other, or neither, on their perception of which side was more likely to satisfy their hunger for land." Humphrey, *Land and Liberty*, 10. For a similar argument that redistribution was the key element in convincing tenants to support the new state, see Lynd, "Who Should Rule at Home?" Other historians who have also examined redistribution exclusively in terms of the transfer of land include Yoshpe, *Disposition of Loyalist Estates*; Crary, "Forfeited Loyalist Lands"; and Reubens, "Pre-Emptive Rights."

49. For the number of Loyalists who had real property confiscated and sold, see Reilly, "Confiscation and Sale," 264–65. Reilly also lists everyone attainted in the statute or convicted in court, whether or not they had property to forfeit. See ibid., app. 2. His numbers represent everyone convicted under the law, including those convicted after the war. By contrast, the appendix to this book contains data on convictions for all crimes between October 1779 and November 1783.

50. The enforcement of Pennsylvania's confiscation laws reveals a similar disparity. In that state, 490 defendants were convicted of treason. But, of those 490 traitors, only 121 forfeited any land, a figure that constituted about 25 percent of all those convicted. For a summary of land sales in Pennsylvania, including how many acres were sold and how many different purchasers participated, see Ousterhout, "Pennsylvania Land Confiscations," 333.

51. Campbell, *Annals of Tryon County*, 96–150.

52. *The New-York Journal and the General Advertiser*, January 4, 1779.

53. Ibid.

54. Ibid., January 11, 1779.

55. July 9, 1776, was the day that New York's Provincial Congress ratified the Declaration of Independence. The forfeiture law's definition of what constituted evidence of adhering to the enemies of the state appears in Act of October 22, 1779, ch. 25, 1779 N.Y. Laws 173, sec. 9. The same section of the statute also stated that anything that would be evidence of treason under English law would constitute evidence of adhering to the enemies of the state. However, as discussed below, there were so few trials under the statute that the court records offer little insight into how, in practice, New Yorkers incorporated English rules of evidence.

56. Although the statute did not recognize any circumstances that would excuse seeking British protection, it did create one affirmative defense against the charge of adhering to the enemies of the state. Someone who had gone to an area under British control but had returned and been pardoned or returned and taken an oath of allegiance to the state could plead such facts to bar the indictment. Act of October 22, 1779, ch. 25, 1779 N.Y. Laws 173, sec. 5.

57. Examination of Margaret Blauvelt and Indictment of Joseph Dawers, May 11, 1780, ser. "Pleadings, 1754–1837," microfilm reel 80, document PL-1754-1837 P1717, NYCC. The indictment of Dawers contains a note stating that judgment was entered against him on October 28, 1780.

58. Examination of Wilhelmus Lampman, April 23, 1781, ser. "Pleadings, 1754–1837," microfilm reel 78, document PL-1754-1837 P1131, NYCC.

59. See, e.g., Examination of Benjamin Devoe, August 20, 1783, ser. "Pleadings, 1754–1837," microfilm reel 78, document PL-1754-1837 P1322, NYCC.

60. See, e.g., Examination of Isaac Austin, April 26, 1781, ser. "Pleadings, 1754–1837," microfilm reel 80, document PL-1754-1837 P1821, NYCC.

61. The section of the forfeiture law that granted the Supreme Court of Judicature exclusive jurisdiction over trials appears in Act of October 22, 1779, ch. 25, 1779 N.Y. Laws 173, sec. 6. For the jurisdictions that different courts had to indict or convict defendants under the forfeiture act, see n. 40 above. Such jurisdictional distinctions represent more than a procedural point; they have affected where these records can be found. After county-level courts such as General Sessions of the Peace indicted defendants for adhering to the enemies of the state, the clerks of those courts then sent copies of the testimony to the Supreme Court. As a result, even though the testimony was taken in county courts all over the province, copies of the full depositions are housed in the same archive as the records for the Supreme Court. These depositions appear in NYCC in the series titled "Pleadings, 1754–1837." Of course, not all the depositions have survived, occasionally leaving just the indictment without the supporting testimony on which it was found. But, where the testimony does exist, it appears in the "Pleadings, 1754–1837" series organized alphabetically by the name of the person who appears first in the case caption.

62. In colonial New York, the grand jury phase of a prosecution could proceed in a number of different ways. A grand jury witness might submit an affidavit or deposition to a grand jury, and that written document would constitute his testimony. Other witnesses would appear in person before the judge and jury to testify against the defendant. Still others offered both forms of testimony, submitting a written document and appearing in person. Procedures in the colonial period were so variable and surviving records so vague that historians trying to summarize the process had to admit: "We are badly informed as

to how the work of the grand jury was managed when there were cases pending." Goebel and Naughton, *Law Enforcement in Colonial New York*, 347. But, whatever the grand jury procedure might have been, nothing in the records suggests that grand juries in colonial New York regularly heard exculpatory evidence from defendants.

63. The structure of the law suggests that its drafters anticipated that few defendants would appear for trial. The statute created a procedure by which courts could process defendants who did not plead to their indictments. According to the law, sheriffs had to publish notice of the indictments. If the defendants did not appear after the printed notice, then the sheriff would submit the names of the defendants and copies of the notice to the Supreme Court, which would then enter default judgment. Act of October 22, 1779, ch. 25, 1779 N.Y. Laws 173, secs. 4–5.

64. Examination of Nathan Daly, April 25, 1783, ser. "Pleadings, 1754–1837," microfilm reel 78, document PL-1754-1837 P1123, NYCC. A copy of the indictment does not survive. However, the indictments were entered in the minutes of the Supreme Court in Minutes for May 3, 1783, New York Supreme Court of Judicature Minute Book, July 31, 1781–November 1, 1783 (Engrossed), NYCC.

65. All five pleaded not guilty—Michael Gates on July 29, 1783, Jacob Shafer and Jacob Myers on October 24, 1783, and George Rightmyer and George Snider on October 25, 1783. Those pleas appear under each of those dates in New York Supreme Court of Judicature Minute Book, July 31, 1781–November 1, 1783 (Engrossed), NYCC. Unfortunately, their cases did not conclude by the end of 1783, and the Supreme Court minutes for 1784 do not exist, which makes it impossible to follow these prosecutions.

66. Minutes for November 1, 1783, New York Supreme Court of Judicature Minute Book, July 31, 1781–November 1, 1783 (Engrossed), NYCC. Although the Supreme Court entered the convictions in the minutes in one long list, it wrote an individual default judgment for each defendant. And, because the state was convicting so many defendants, the judges did not sign the convictions until the following month. As a result, while the default judgments were entered in the court minutes on November 1, 1783, the judges did not get around to signing the judgments until December. For some of those individual default judgments, see Conviction of Matthew Dies, December 29, 1783, and Conviction of Jacob Dies, December 29, 1783, ser. "Parchments," document folder P-220-B4, NYCC.

67. Examination of Abraham Vollwyser, April 24, 1781, and indictment of Andreas Tollhamer, John Morril, Daniel Frazier, John Lattimore, and Jacob Deetswort, April 28, 1781, ser. "Pleadings, 1754–1837," microfilm reel 78, document PL-1754-1837 P1134, NYCC. The defendants were charged in a single indictment that appears under the same document number as Vollwyser's examination.

68. Although the minutes of the Supreme Court of Judicature do not record the convictions, the indictment of Tollhamer, Morril, Frazier, Lattimore, and Deetswort has a notation stating that judgment was entered on August 3, 1782. Moreover, some of the individual default judgments have survived and demonstrate that the defendants were ultimately convicted. They appear in Conviction of Jacob Deetswort, July 14, 1783, ser. "Parchments," document folder P-220-B4, and Conviction of Andreas Tollhamer, July 14, 1783, ser. "Parchments," document folder P-219-B2, NYCC.

69. This number represents only those defendants prosecuted in court. It does not include the fifty-nine people attainted in the forfeiture law itself.

70. The breakdown of the 527 cases that reached final judgment is as follows: 517 ended in conviction by default judgment; five defendants pleaded guilty; four were released because they pleaded and proved, under sec. 5 of the forfeiture law, that they had taken an oath of allegiance to New York; and one was acquitted. These numbers are based on an analysis of the minutes of the Supreme Court of Judicature, which was the only court empowered to enter judgment in prosecutions for adhering to the enemies of the state. The minutes appear in New York Supreme Court of Judicature Minute Book, July 25, 1775–April 28, 1781 (Engrossed), and New York Supreme Court of Judicature Minute Book, July 31, 1781–November 1, 1783 (Engrossed), NYCC. For a full discussion of the methods employed in compiling these data, see the appendix.

71. To be sure, not every indictment for adhering to the enemies of the state went unanswered. Defendants sometimes appeared to plead, but they did so only rarely. Between 1779 and 1783, 106 defendants appeared to answer the indictments: ninety-seven pleaded not guilty, five pleaded guilty, and four pleaded that they had taken an oath of allegiance to the state. By way of comparison, 517 defendants never appeared to enter a plea and were convicted by default. Thus, nearly five times more absentees were convicted by default (517) than were defendants who showed up in court to plead (106). These numbers are based on the indictments and convictions as recorded in the Supreme Court of Judicature. New York Supreme Court of Judicature Minute Book, July 25, 1775–April 28, 1781 (Engrossed), and New York Supreme Court of Judicature Minute Book, July 31, 1781–November 1, 1783 (Engrossed), NYCC. For a full discussion of the methods employed in compiling these data, see the appendix.

72. Jasanoff, *Liberty's Exiles*; Norton, *British-Americans*; and Brown, *The Good Americans*, chaps. 5–6. Not everyone who left was a strong supporter of Britain. As with other moments of great upheaval, New Yorkers undoubtedly used the chaos of war to settle scores against personal enemies. Fitzpatrick, *Everyday Stalinism*, 116. However, an accuser in New York or Russia with a personal score to settle concealed his true motives to denounce an enemy, couching his personal feuds in political terms. As a result, it is impossible to tell how many of those Loyalists driven into exile actually supported Britain and how many were victims of private retribution.

73. Zeichner, "Loyalist Problem in New York," 297–98.

74. Act of April 11, 1792, ch. 68, N.Y. Laws 375 (permitting "certain persons, to return to and reside within this State").

75. *The New-York Packet and the American Advertiser*, April 17, 1783.

76. Ibid., May 29, 1783. It is worth noting that this view was not unanimous among New Yorkers. A small group of elite leaders—people such as John Jay, Alexander Hamilton, and Gouverneur Morris—wanted a conciliatory approach to Loyalists. Zeichner, "Loyalist Problem in New York," 288–89. However, most New Yorkers did not share that view.

77. This is one of the few instances where legal terms such as *reversion* and *remainder* carried the same meaning in the late eighteenth century as they do today. The forfeiture law prescribed the form of these default judgments. Act of October 22, 1779, ch. 25, 1779 N.Y. Laws 173, sec. 25. For examples of default judgments, see Conviction of John Rice, July 15, 1783, ser. "Parchments," document folder P-36-A1, Conviction of John Dop, July 14, 1783, Conviction of Peter Doran, July 15, 1783, and Conviction of Abraham

Defoot, July 14, 1783, ser. "Parchments," document folder P-220-B4, Conviction of Stephen Tuttle, July 14, 1783, Conviction of Walter Trumbull, December 29, 1783, and Conviction of Archibald Thompson, December 29, 1783, ser. "Parchments," document folder P-219-B2, NYCC.

78. For examples of deeds with the attainder written into the documents, see Records of Surveys and Maps of State Lands, ser. A4016-77, vol. 8. For examples of sale agreements that include the attainder, see Records of Surveys and Maps of State Lands, ser. A4016-77, vol. 17, pp. 51–100. Both collections are available at NYSA. In 1787, the legislature eliminated the Commissioners of Forfeitures and transferred their responsibilities to the Surveyor General's office. As a result, deeds to forfeited land sold after 1787 were issued in the name of the Surveyor General, not the Commissioners of Forfeitures. Moreover, many documents related to the surveying, appraisal, and sale of forfeited land appear with the records of the Surveyor General's Office at the state archives.

79. Years after the war ended, New Yorkers severed the property connections of Loyalists' widows as well. Ancient common law practice recognized dower rights, which were a widow's interest in one-third of her deceased husband's property. Sometimes called *widow's thirds* or *a widow's share,* dower rights were a life estate in a third of the deceased husband's estate. But, in 1796, New York enacted a private bill that offered cash payments to eight widows of dispossessed Loyalists, but on the condition that they release their claim to dower rights. In this way, the state obliterated rival property claims and settled the title of those who had purchased confiscated land. One presumes that many of the purchasers were married. If the state had not extinguished the claims of Loyalist widows, then it could have occurred that two widows would claim dower rights in the same property: the widow of the Loyalist from whom the land was confiscated and the widow of the purchaser to whom it was sold. See Act of April 11, 1796, ch. 59, 1796 N.Y. Laws 717 (ordering the treasurer to pay various sums to eight named widows once they sign "a release of their dower and right of dower" in the forfeited estates of their deceased husbands).

80. *The New-York Packet and the American Advertiser*, April 17, 1783.

81. Ibid., May 15, 1783.

82. Ibid., May 29, 1783.

83. Ibid., May 15, 1783.

84. Ibid., May 29, 1783.

85. Note that this number represents only convictions in court and excludes the fifty-nine people attainted in the statute.

86. Thirsk, "Sales of Royalist Land," 188–207. Royalists' land was not the only real property confiscated at that time. Parliamentary authorities also seized Crown and Bishops' lands. Some controversy remains over whether the sale of these other enemies' property had leveling effects by redistributing land among New Model Army soldiers. See Gentles, "Sales of Crown Lands," 614–35. For a response to Gentles, see Kishlansky, "Sales of Crown Lands," 125–30.

87. Shedd, "Parliamentary Committee."

88. Thirsk, "Restoration Land Settlement," 315–28. Thirsk demonstrates how, among other reasons, the Royalists' repurchase of their confiscated land helped ease the

restoration of Charles II. Since Parliament had sold confiscated Royalist land back to its former owners, there was no group of new purchasers who felt a strong attachment to the parliamentary government; there was no constituency of new landowners to oppose restoration out of fear that they would lose their new gains.

89. Quoted in Thirsk, "Sales of Royalist Land," 193 n. 1.

90. For the statute prohibiting Loyalists from voting or holding office, see Act of March 27, 1778, ch. 16, 1778 N.Y. Laws 28 (regulating "elections in this State"). The list of crimes that disqualified Loyalists from voting or holding office was expanded in Act of May 24, 1784, ch. 66, 1784 N.Y. Laws 772 (attempting "to preserve the freedom and independence of this State, and for other purposes therein mentioned"). See also Act of October 9, 1779, ch. 12, 1779 N.Y. Laws 155 (requiring "attornies, solicitors and counsellors at law . . . to produce certificates of their attachment to the liberties and independence of America"). For a more comprehensive list of anti-Loyalist statutes, see [Anonymous], *Laws of the Legislature of the State of New York.*

CONCLUSION

1. Hamilton claimed that passing additional anti-Loyalist statutes violated several sections of the treaty. However, Hamilton believed that continuing to punish Loyalists and sell their land, as New Yorkers were doing, most clearly violated the sixth article. That article declared: "There shall be no future Confiscations made nor any Prosecutions commenced against any Person or persons for, or by Reason of, the Part which he or they may have taken in the present War, and that no Person shall on that Account suffer any future Loss or Damage either in his Person, Liberty or Property." Treaty of Peace between the United States of America and His Britannic Majesty, U.S.–Gr. Brit., art. 6, September 3, 1783, 8 Stat. 80.

2. [Hamilton], *Letter from Phocion*, 484.

3. Palmer, *Age of the Democratic Revolution*, 2:542.

4. Gentz, *Origin and Principles*, 39.

5. Ibid., n.p. (Quincy Adams preface).

6. Palmer, *Age of the Democratic Revolution*, 2:541–43.

7. See Gentz, *The French and American Revolutions.*

8. U.S. Const. art 1, sec. 9, clause 3 (prohibiting Congress from passing bills of attainder), and sec. 10, clause 1 (prohibiting states from passing bills of attainder).

9. Report of Sales by Commissioners of Forfeitures of the Eastern District, various dates, folder labeled "A4032 Report of Sales-Commissioners of Forfeitures for the Eastern District 1784–1788," Commissioners of Forfeitures, Western District, various dates, folder labeled "A4032-83, Record of Sales, Commissioners of Forfeitures for the Western District 1784–1787," and "Sales of the Commissioners of Forfeitures of the Western District from June 27, 1787–August 27, 1788," various dates, folder labeled "A4032-83, Record of Sales, Commissioners of Forfeitures for the Western District 1781–1788," Lists of Sales and Accounts of Payments for Confiscated Lands, 1784–1788, ser. A4032, NYSA.

10. Reilly, "Confiscation and Sale," app. 1.

11. Ousterhout, "Pennsylvania Land Confiscations," 334–35.

APPENDIX

1. Act of October 22, 1779, ch. 25, 1779 N.Y. Laws 173.

2. The indictments for treason appear in May 1783 Term of Court, New York Supreme Court of Judicature Minute Book, July 31, 1781–November 1, 1783 (Engrossed), NYCC. The indictments for adhering to the enemies of the state appear with Examination of Nathan Daly, April 25, 1783, ser. "Pleadings, 1754–1837," microfilm reel 78, document PL-1754-1837 P1123, NYCC.

BIBLIOGRAPHY

ARCHIVAL AND MANUSCRIPT SOURCES

Albany Court of Common Pleas, 1763–1799. Series 87-09085. Minutes of Court of Sessions, 1685–89, 1717–23, 1763–82, and Canvass of Voters, 1820. Albany County Hall of Records. Albany, NY.

Buck, Clifford M., comp. "Northeast Tax Lists," p. 12. Available in the Local History Section of the Adriance Memorial Library, Poughkeepsie, NY.

———. "Tax Lists of Beekman and Pawling's Precincts." Available in the Local History Section of the Adriance Memorial Library, Poughkeepsie, NY.

Dutchess County Collection, 1696–ca. 1910. Manuscripts Department, New-York Historical Society, New York.

Lists of Sales of and Accounts of Payments for Confiscated Lands, 1784–1788. A4032. New York State Archives. Albany, NY.

Minutes of the Court of General Sessions and of Common Pleas. Liber E 1771–1774, Liber F 1775–1781, Liber G 1782–1785, microfilm reel 127. Dutchess County Clerk's Office, Poughkeepsie, NY.

New York Supreme Court of Judicature Minute Book, July 25, 1775–April 28, 1781 (Engrossed). New York County Clerk Hall of Records, New York.

New York Supreme Court of Judicature Minute Book, July 31, 1781–November 1, 1783 (Engrossed). New York County Clerk Hall of Records, New York.

Parchments. New York County Clerk Hall of Records, New York.

Pleadings, 1754–1837. New York County Clerk Hall of Records, New York.

Records of Surveys and Maps of State Lands. Ser. A4016-77. New York State Archives, Albany, NY.

Records of the Court of Sessions. Ser. 43, A-0048 (1)L. Westchester County Archives and Records Center, Elmsford, NY.

Revolutionary War Box 5. New York State Revolutionary Committees and Commissions. Manuscripts Department, New-York Historical Society, New York.

Revolutionary War Miscellaneous Manuscripts. Box 2. Manuscripts Department, New-York Historical Society, New York.

Westchester County Minutes of the Court of Common Pleas. Ser. 9, A-0010 (1)L, vol. 1774–93. Westchester County Archives and Records Center, Elmsford, NY.

PUBLISHED PRIMARY SOURCES

Albany [NY] Committee of Correspondence. *Minutes of the Albany Committee of Correspondence, 1775–1778*. 2 vols. Albany: University of the State of New York, 1923–25.

[Anonymous]. *Laws of the Legislature of the State of New York, in Force against the Loyalists*. London, 1786.

Bangs, Edward, ed. *Journal of Lieutenant Bangs, April 1 to July 29, 1776*. New York: New York Times/Arno Press, 1968.

Boyd, Julian P., ed. *The Papers of Thomas Jefferson*. 39 vols. Princeton, NJ: Princeton University Press, 1950–.

Clinton, George. *Public Papers of George Clinton, First Governor of New York, 1771–1795—1801–1804*. 10 vols. Albany, NY: Wynkoop Hallenbeck, 1899–1914.

Colden, Cadwallader. *The Colden Letter Books*. 2 vols. New York: Printed for the New-York Historical Society, 1876–77.

———. *The Letters and Papers of Cadwallader Colden*. 9 vols. New York: Published for the New-York Historical Society, 1918–37.

Dawson, Henry B., and Abraham Tomlinson, eds. *New York City during the American Revolution: Being a Collection of Original Papers (Now First Published) from Manuscripts in the Possession of the Mercantile Library Association of New York City*. New York: Printed for the Association, 1861.

Force, Peter, comp. *American Archives: Consisting of a Collection of Authentick Records, State Papers, and Letters and Other Notices of Publick Affairs*. 9 vols. Washington, DC, 1837–53.

Frey, Samuel Ludlow, ed. *The Minute Book of the Committee of Safety of Tryon County, the Old New York Frontier, Now Printed Verbatim for the First Time*. New York: Dodd, Mead & Co., 1905.

[Hamilton, Alexander]. *A Letter from Phocion to the Considerate Citizens of New-York on the Politics of the Day*. In *The Papers of Alexander Hamilton*, ed. Harold C. Syrett and Jacob E. Cooke (27 vols.), 3:484–97. New York: Columbia University Press, 1961–87.

Massachusetts [State]. *The Acts and Resolves, Public and Private, of the Province of the Massachusetts Bay*. 21 vols. Boston: Wright & Potter, 1869–1922.

New York [Colony]. *The Colonial Laws of New York from the Year 1664 to the Revolution*. 5 vols. Albany, NY: J. B. Lyon, 1894.

New York [State]. *In Convention of the Representatives of the State of New-York*. Kingston, NY, April 1, 1777.

———. *Journals of the Provincial Congress, Provincial Convention, Committee of Safety and Council of Safety of the State of New-York: 1775–1776–1777*. 2 vols. Albany: Thurlow Weed, 1842.

———. *Minutes of the Committee and of the First Commission for Detecting and Defeating Conspiracies in the State of New York, December 11, 1776–September 23 1778*. 2 vols. New York: Printed for the New-York Historical Society, 1924.

———. *The Votes and Proceedings of the Assembly of the State of New-York, at Their Second Session, Begun and Holden in the Assembly Chamber at Poughkeepsie, in Dutchess County, on Thursday, First Day of October 1778*. Poughkeepsie, NY: John Holt, 1779.

———. *The Votes and Proceedings of the Assembly of the State of New-York, at Their Third Session, Begun and Holden in the Assembly-Chamber, at Kingston, in Ulster County*. Fishkill, NY: Samuel Loudon, 1779.

———. *The Votes and Proceedings of the Senate of the State of New-York, at Their First Session, Held at Kingston, in Ulster County*. Kingston, NY: John Holt, 1777. Despite the publication year printed on the title page, this document contains the Senate Journal for both the first and the second sessions, September 1777–March 1779.

O'Callaghan, E. B. *Documentary History of the State of New-York*. 4 vols. Albany, NY: Weed, Parsons & Co., 1850–51.

O'Callaghan, Edmund B. *Calendar of Historical Manuscripts in the Office of the Secretary of State, Albany, N.Y.* 2 vols. Albany, NY: Weed, Parsons & Co., 1865–66.

Ousterhout, Anne M. "Pennsylvania Land Confiscations during the Revolution." *Pennsylvania Magazine of History and Biography* 102 (1978): 328–43.

Paltsits, Victor Hugo, ed. *Minutes of the Commissioners for Detecting and Defeating Conspiracies in the State of New York: Albany County Sessions, 1778–1781*. 3 vols. Albany, NY: Published by the State, 1909.

Pennsylvania [State]. *Colonial Records of Pennsylvania*. 16 vols. Harrisburg, PA: T. Fenn, 1838–53.

———. *The Documentary History of the State of New-York; Arranged under the Direction of the Hon. Christopher Morgan, Secretary of State*. 4 vols. Albany, NY: Weed, Parsons & Co., 1849–51.

Pickering, James H. "Enoch Crosby, Secret Agent of the Neutral Ground: His Own Story." *New York History* 47, no. 1 (1966): 61–73.

Reinke, A. A. "Occupation of New York City by the British, 1776." *Pennsylvania Magazine of History and Biography* 1 (1877): 133–48.

Roberts, James A., comp. *New York in the Revolution as Colony and State: A Compilation of Documents and Records from the Office of the State Comptroller*. 2 vols. Albany, NY: J. B. Lyon Co., 1904.

SECONDARY SOURCES

Alexander, John K. "The Fort Wilson Incident of 1779: A Case Study of the Revolutionary Crowd." *William and Mary Quarterly*, 3rd ser., 31 (1974): 589–612.

Ammerman, David. *In the Common Cause: American Response to the Coercive Acts of 1774*. Charlottesville: University of Virginia Press, 1974.

Bailyn, Bernard. *The Ideological Origins of the American Revolution*. Enlarged ed. Cambridge MA: Belknap Press of Harvard University Press, 1992.

———. *Voyagers to the West: A Passage in the Peopling of America on the Eve of Revolution*. New York: Alfred A. Knopf, 1986.

Barnum, H. L. *The Spy Unmasked; or, Memoirs of Enoch Crosby, alias Harvey Birch, the Hero of Mr. Cooper's Tale of the Neutral Ground*. New York: J. & J. Harper, 1828.

Becker, Carl Lotus. *The History of Political Parties in the Province of New York, 1760–1776*. Madison: University of Wisconsin Press, 1909.

Bezanson, Anne. "Inflation and Controls, Pennsylvania, 1774–1779." *Journal of Economic History* 8 (1948): 1–20.

Bonomi, Patricia U. *A Factious People: Politics and Society in Colonial New York*. New York: Columbia University Press, 1971.

Bradburn, Douglas. *The Citizenship Revolution: Politics and the Creation of the American Union, 1774–1804*. Charlottesville: University of Virginia Press, 2009.

Breen, T. H. *American Insurgents, American Patriots: The Revolution of the People*. New York: Hill & Wang, 2010.

———. *Tobacco Culture: The Mentality of the Great Tidewater Planters on the Eve of Revolution*. Princeton, NJ: Princeton University Press, 1985.

Brooke, John L. *Columbia Rising: Civil Life on the Upper Hudson from the Revolution to the Age of Jackson*. Chapel Hill: University of North Carolina Press, 2010.

Brown, Howard G. *Ending the French Revolution: Violence, Justice, and Repression from the Terror to Napoleon*. Charlottesville: University of Virginia Press, 2006.

Brown, Wallace. *The Good Americans: The Loyalists in the American Revolution*. New York: William Morrow, 1969.

———. *The King's Friends: The Composition and Motives of the American Loyalist Claimants*. Providence, RI: Brown University Press, 1965.

Buel, Richard, Jr. "The Committee Movement of 1779 and the Formation of Public Authority in Revolutionary America." In *The Transformation of Early American History: Society, Authority, and Ideology*, ed. James A. Henretta, Michael Kammen, and Stanley N. Katz, 151–69. New York: Alfred A. Knopf, 1991.

Calhoon, Robert C. *The Loyalists in Revolutionary America, 1760–1781*. New York: Harcourt Brace Jovanovich, 1965.

Campbell, William W. *Annals of Tryon County; or, The Border Warfare of New-York during the Revolution*. New York: J. & J. Harper, 1831.

Champagne, Roger J. *Alexander McDougall and the American Revolution in New York*. Schenectady, NY: Union College Press, 1975.

Chopra, Ruma. *Unnatural Rebellion: Loyalists in New York City during the Revolution*. Charlottesville: University of Virginia Press, 2011.

Clark, Jonathan. "The Problem of Allegiance in Revolutionary Poughkeepsie." In *Saints and Revolutionaries: Essays on Early American History*, ed. David D. Hall, John W. Murrin, and Thad W. Tate. New York: W. W. Norton, 1984.

Cooper, James Fenimore. *The Spy: A Tale of the Neutral Ground*. New York: AMS Press, 2002.

Countryman, Edward. *A People in Revolution: The American Revolution and Political Society in New York, 1760–1790*. New York: W. W. Norton, 1981.

Crary, Catherine Snell. "Forfeited Loyalist Lands in the Western District of New York—Albany and Tryon Counties." *New York History* 35 (1954): 239–56.

Desan, Christine A., Daniel J. Hulsebosch, David Thomas Konig, and Bruce H. Mann. "Forum: Constitutions on Edge: Empire, State, and Legal Culture in Eighteenth-Century New York." *Law and History Review* 16 (1998): 257–401.

Ely, James W., Jr. "'That Due Satisfaction Be Made': The Fifth Amendment and the Origins of the Compensation Principle." *American Journal of Legal History* 36, no. 1 (1992): 1–18.

Fischer, Joseph R. *A Well-Executed Failure: The Sullivan Campaign against the Iroquois, July–September 1779*. Columbia: University of South Carolina Press, 1997.

Fitzpatrick, Sheila. *Everyday Stalinism: Ordinary Life in Extraordinary Times: Soviet Russia in the 1930s*. New York: Oxford University Press, 2000.

Fitzpatrick, Sheila, and Robert Gellately, eds. *Accusatory Practices: Denunciation in Modern European History, 1789–1989*. Chicago: University of Chicago Press, 1997.

Flick, Alexander C. *Loyalism in New York during the American Revolution*. New York: Columbia University Press, 1901.

Forbath, William E., Hendrick Hartog, and Martha Minow. "Introduction: Legal Histories from Below." *Wisconsin Law Review* 4 (1985): 759–766.

Foster, Don. *Author Unknown: On the Trail of Anonymous*. New York: Henry Holt, 2000.

Fritz, Christian G. *American Sovereigns: The People and America's Constitutional Tradition before the Civil War* Cambridge: Cambridge University Press, 2008.

Furneaux, Rupert. *Saratoga: The Decisive Battle*. London: George Allen & Unwin, 1971.

Gentles, Ian. "The Sales of Crown Lands during the English Revolution." *Economic History Review* 26 (1973): 614–35.

Gentz, Friedrich von. *The French and American Revolutions Compared*. Chicago: Henry Regnery, 1955.

———. *The Origin and Principles of the American Revolution, Compared with the Origin and Principles of the French Revolution*. Philadelphia, 1800.

Goebel, Julius, Jr., and T. Raymond Naughton. *Law Enforcement in Colonial New York: A Study in Criminal Procedure, 1664–1776*. Montclair, NJ: Patterson Smith, 1944.

Greenberg, Douglas. *Crime and Law Enforcement in Colonial New York*. Ithaca, NY: Cornell University Press, 1974.

Greene, Evarts B., and Virginia D. Harrington. *American Population before the Federal Census of 1790*. New York: Columbia University Press, 1932.

Griffin, Patrick. *America's Revolution*. New York: Oxford University Press, 2012.

Handlin, Oscar, and Mary Flug Handlin. *Commonwealth: A Study of the Role of Government in the American Economy, Massachusetts, 1774–1861*. Rev. ed. Cambridge, MA: Belknap Press of Harvard University Press, 1969.

Hart, John F. "Takings and Compensation in Early America: The Colonial Highway Acts in Social Context." *American Journal of Legal History* 40, no. 3 (1996): 253–306.

Hindus, Michael S. *Prison and Plantation: Crime, Justice, and Authority in Massachusetts and South Carolina, 1767–1878*. Chapel Hill: University of North Carolina Press, 1980.

Holmes, Stephen. *Passions and Constraint: On the Theory of Liberal Democracy*. Chicago: University of Chicago Press, 1995.

Holton, Woody. *Forced Founders: Indians, Debtors, Slaves, and the Making of the American Revolution in Virginia*. Chapel Hill: University of North Carolina Press, 1999.

Horwitz, Morton J. *The Transformation of American Law, 1780–1860*. Cambridge, MA: Harvard University Press, 1977.

Hulsebosch, Daniel J. *Constituting Empire: New York and the Transformation of Constitutionalism in the Atlantic World, 1664–1830*. Chapel Hill: University of North Carolina Press, 2005.

———. "A Discrete and Cosmopolitan Minority: The Loyalists, the Atlantic World, and the Origins of Judicial Review." *Chicago-Kent Law Review* 81 (2006): 825–67.

Humphrey, Thomas J. *Land and Liberty: Hudson Valley Riots in the Age of Revolution*. DeKalb: Northern Illinois University Press, 2004.

Jasanoff, Maya. *Liberty's Exiles: American Loyalists in the Revolutionary World*. New York: Alfred A. Knopf, 2011.

Johnson, Willis Fletcher. *Colonel Henry Ludington: A Memoir*. New York: privately printed, 1907.

Juviler, Peter H. *Revolutionary Law and Order: Politics and Social Change in the USSR*. New York: Free Press, 1976.

Kalyvas, Stathis N. *The Logic of Violence in Civil War*. Cambridge: Cambridge University Press, 2006.

Kars, Marjoleine. *Breaking Loose Together: The Regulator Rebellion in Pre-Revolutionary North Carolina*. Chapel Hill: University of North Carolina Press, 2002.

Kedward, H. R. *In Search of the Maquis: Rural Resistance in Southern France, 1942–1944*. Oxford: Clarendon Press, 1993.

Ketchum, Richard M. *Saratoga: Turning Point of America's Revolutionary War*. New York: Henry Holt, 1997.

Kim, Sung Bok. *Landlord and Tenant in Colonial New York: Manorial Society, 1664–1775*. Chapel Hill: University of North Carolina Press, 1978.

———. "The Limits of Politicization in the American Revolution: The Experience of Westchester County, New York." *Journal of American History* 80 (1993): 868–89.

Kishlansky, Mark. "The Sales of Crown Lands and the Spirit of the Revolution." *Economic History Review* 29 (1976): 125–30.

Kramer, Larry. *The People Themselves: Popular Constitutionalism and Judicial Review*. New York: Oxford University Press, 2004.

Kulikoff, Allan. *From British Peasants to Colonial American Farmers*. Chapel Hill: University of North Carolina Press, 2000.

Loach, Jennifer. *Parliament and the Crown in the Reign of Mary Tudor*. Oxford: Clarendon Press, 1986.

Lynd, Staughton. *Anti-Federalism in Dutchess County, New York: A Study of Democracy and Class Conflict in the Revolutionary Era*. Chicago: Loyola University Press, 1962.

———. "Who Should Rule at Home? Dutchess County, New York in the American Revolution." *William and Mary Quarterly*, 3rd ser., 18, no. 3 (1961): 330–59.

Maas, David E. "Honest Graft in Revolutionary Massachusetts." *Boston Bar Journal* 23 (1979): 7–15.

———. *The Return of the Massachusetts Loyalists*. New York: Garland Publishing, 1989.

MacKinnon, Neil. *This Unfriendly Soil: The Loyalist Experience in Nova Scotia, 1783–1791*. Kingston, ON: McGill-Queen's University Press, 1986.

Manrique, Nelson. "The War for the Central Sierra." In *Shining and Other Paths: War and Society in Peru, 1980–1995*, ed. Steve J. Stern, 193–223. Durham, NC: Duke University Press, 1998.

Marietta, Jack D., and G. S. Rowe. *Troubled Experiment: Crime and Justice in Pennsylvania, 1682–1800*. Philadelphia: University of Pennsylvania Press, 2006.

Mark, Irving. *Agrarian Conflicts in Colonial New York, 1711–1775*. New York: Columbia University Press, 1940.

Mark, Irving, and Oscar Handlin. "Land Cases in Colonial New York, 1765–1767: The King v. William Prendergast." *New York University Law Quarterly Review* 19 (1942): 165–94.

Mason, Bernard. *The Road to Independence: The Revolutionary Movement in New York, 1773–1777*. Lexington: University of Kentucky Press, 1966.

McConville, Brendan. *These Daring Disturbers of the Public Peace: The Struggle for Property and Power in Early New Jersey*. Ithaca, NJ: Cornell University Press, 1999.

Morris, Richard B. *Government and Labor in Early America*. New York: Columbia University Press, 1946.

Nash, Gary B. *The Forgotten Fifth: African Americans in the Age of Revolution*. Cambridge, MA: Harvard University Press, 2006.

———. *The Unknown American Revolution: The Unruly Birth of Democracy and the Struggle to Create America*. New York: Viking, 2005.

Nelson, William E. *The Americanization of the Common Law: The Impact of Legal Change on Massachusetts Society, 1760–1830*. Cambridge, MA: Harvard University Press, 1994.

Norton, Mary Beth. *The British-Americans: The Loyalist Exiles in England, 1774–1789*. Boston: Little, Brown, 1972.

Palmer, R. R. *The Age of the Democratic Revolution: A Political History of Europe and America, 1760–1800*. 2 vols. Princeton, NJ: Princeton University Press, 1959–61.

Petersen, Roger D. *Resistance and Rebellion: Lessons from Eastern Europe*. Cambridge: Cambridge University Press, 2001.

Platt, Edmund. *The Eagle's History of Poughkeepsie: From the Earliest Settlements, 1683 to 1905*. Poughkeepsie, NY: Platt & Platt, 1905.

Poucher, J. Wilson. "Dutchess County Men of the Revolutionary Period: Dr. Peter Tappen." *Year Book of the Dutchess County Historical Society* 19 (1934): 38–44.

Ranlet, Philip. "How Many American Loyalists Left the United States?" *Historian* 76, no. 2 (Summer 2014): 278–307.

———. *The New York Loyalists*. 2nd ed. New York: University Press of America, 2002.

Reid, John Phillip. *Constitutional History of the American Revolution*. 4 vols. Madison: University of Wisconsin Press, 1986–93.

Reilly, John Thomas. "The Confiscation and Sale of the Loyalist Estates and Its Effect upon the Democratization of Landholding in New York State: 1799 [*sic* (for 1779)]–1800." Ph.D. diss., Fordham University, 1974.

Reubens, Beatrice G. "Pre-Emptive Rights in the Disposition of a Confiscated Estate, Philipsburgh Manor, New York." *William and Mary Quarterly*, 3rd ser., 22 (1965): 435–56.

Reynolds, Helen Wilkinson. "Bartholomew Crannell: A Twentieth Century Plea for Anglo-American Good Will." *Year Book of the Dutchess County Historical Society* 8 (1922): 37–79.

Reynolds, Susan. *Before Eminent Domain: Toward a History of Expropriation of Land for Common Good*. Chapel Hill: University of North Carolina Press, 2010.

Richter, Daniel K. "Sir William Johnson." *Oxford Dictionary of National Biography*. 2008.

———. *Trade, Land, Power: The Struggle for Eastern North America*. Philadelphia: University of Pennsylvania Press, 2013.

Rosen, Deborah A. "The Supreme Court of Judicature of Colonial New York: Civil Practice in Transition, 1691–1760." *Law and History Review* 5, no. 1 (1987): 213–47.

Rosenwaike, Ira. *Population History of New York City*. Syracuse, NY: Syracuse University Press, 1972.

Rudebeck, Lars. "Political Mobilisation in Guinea-Bissau." In *Revolutionary Guerrilla Warfare*, ed. Sam C. Sarkesian, 431–51. Chicago: Precedent Publishing, 1975.

Scott, Kenneth. "Price Control in New England during the Revolution." *New England Quarterly* 19 (1946): 453–73.

Shagan, Ethan H. *Popular Politics and the English Reformation*. Cambridge: Cambridge University Press.

Shedd, John A. "The Parliamentary Committee for Indemnity and Property Confiscation Disputes, 1647–1655." *Historical Journal* 43 (2000): 1093–1107.

Shy, John W. *A People Numerous and Armed: Reflections on the Military Struggle for American Independence*. New York: Oxford University Press, 1976.

Taylor, Alan. *Liberty Men and Great Proprietors: The Revolutionary Settlement on the Maine Frontier, 1760–1820*. Chapel Hill: University of North Carolina Press, 1990.

Teitel, Ruti G. *Transitional Justice*. New York: Oxford University Press, 2000.

Thirsk, Joan. "The Restoration Land Settlement." *Journal of Modern History* 26 (1954): 315–28.

———. "The Sales of Royalist Land during the Interregnum." *Economic History Review* 5 (1952): 188–207.

Thomas, William S. "Henry Livingston." *Year Book of the Dutchess County Historical Society* 5 (1919): 32–45.

Tiedemann, Joseph S. "Patriots by Default: Queens County, New York, and the British Army, 1776–1783." *William and Mary Quarterly*, 3rd ser., 43, no. 1 (1986): 35–63.

———. *Reluctant Revolutionaries: New York City and the Road to Independence, 1763–1776*. Ithaca, NY: Cornell University Press, 1997.

Tone, John Lawrence. *The Fatal Knot: The Guerrilla War in Navarre and the Defeat of Napoleon in Spain*. Chapel Hill: University of North Carolina Press, 1994.

Treanor, William M. "The Original Understanding of the Takings Clause and the Political Process." *Columbia Law Review* 95 (1995): 782–887.

———. "The Origins and Original Significance of the Just Compensation Clause of the Fifth Amendment." *Yale Law Journal* 94 (1985): 694–716.

Vega, Luis Mercier. *Guerrillas in Latin America: The Technique of the Counter-State*. Translated by Daniel Weissbort. New York: Praeger, 1969.

Wickham-Crowley, Timothy P. *Exploring Revolution: Essays on Latin American Insurgency and Revolutionary Theory*. Armonk, NY: M. E. Sharpe, 1991.

Wood, Gordon S. *The Creation of the American Republic, 1776–1787*. Chapel Hill: University of North Carolina Press, 1998.

———. *The Radicalism of the American Revolution*. New York: Alfred A. Knopf, 1992.

Wooddeson, Richard. *A Systematical View of the Laws of England*. 3 vols. London, 1792–93.

Yoshpe, Harry B. *The Disposition of Loyalist Estates in the Southern District of the State of New York*. New York: Columbia University Press, 1939.

Young, Alfred F., ed. *The American Revolution*. DeKalb: Northern Illinois University Press, 1976.

Young, Alfred F., Gary B. Nash, and Ray Raphael, eds. *Revolutionary Founders: Rebels, Radicals, and Reformers in the Making of the Nation*. New York: Alfred A. Knopf, 2011.

Young, Alfred F., and Gregory H. Nobles. *Whose American Revolution Was It? Historians Interpret the Founding*. New York: New York University Press, 2011.

Zeichner, Oscar. "The Loyalist Problem in New York after the Revolution." *New York History* 21 (1940): 284–302.

INDEX

Page numbers in italics indicate figures.